ECO-THOUGHTS

What if the pollution of the world did not only concern the environment in which we live, but also the flow of our thoughts in every moment of everyday life? What if those thoughts, invasive like locusts, could transform and become "eco-thoughts" that make us and others feel good? Ecology concerns us from the inside, passes through us, and literally shapes us: "what is inside is outside". This book offers "eco-words" and "eco-thoughts" as it sheds light on the traps that our minds construct for ourselves, that we so often fall into whether we mean to or not. It examines the erroneous paths that we sometimes meander down while we are thinking in our everyday lives in order to help us to identify and avoid them.

The thoughts we formulate are not really ours, as if our mind prefers to flow in what has already been thought, lived, and felt. The author offers her reflections and insights to those who wish to direct their minds towards streams of thought that really do belong to us, that make us feel good. In order to do this, we must learn how to disable the "traps" and free ourselves of what is "contaminating" before they take hold and harm us.

An original and thought-provoking examination of how our own internal lives can become toxic, and how to prevent this, that will be of particular value to students and scholars of sociology, philosophy, communication studies, memory studies, and social psychology.

Anna Lisa Tota is Vice-Rector of the University Roma Tre in Rome, Italy, and Full Professor of Sociology of Communication and Culture at the Department of Philosophy, Communication, and Performing Arts in the same university. Among her publications are the *Routledge International Handbook of Memory Studies* (edited with Trever Hagen, 2016) and *Eco-Words: The Ecology of Conversation* (2024).

ECO-THOUGHTS

ECO-THOUGHTS

Conversations with a Polluted Mind

Anna Lisa Tota

LONDON AND NEW YORK

Designed cover image: Freepik

First published 2025
by Routledge
4 Park Square, Milton Park, Abingdon, Oxon OX14 4RN

and by Routledge
605 Third Avenue, New York, NY 10158

Routledge is an imprint of the Taylor & Francis Group, an informa business

© 2025 Anna Lisa Tota

The right of Anna Lisa Tota to be identified as author of this work has been asserted in accordance with sections 77 and 78 of the Copyright, Designs and Patents Act 1988.

All rights reserved. No part of this book may be reprinted or reproduced or utilised in any form or by any electronic, mechanical, or other means, now known or hereafter invented, including photocopying and recording, or in any information storage or retrieval system, without permission in writing from the publishers.

Trademark notice: Product or corporate names may be trademarks or registered trademarks, and are used only for identification and explanation without intent to infringe.

British Library Cataloguing-in-Publication Data
A catalogue record for this book is available from the British Library

Library of Congress Cataloging-in-Publication Data
Names: Tota, Anna Lisa, 1965– author.
Title: Eco-thoughts: conversations with a polluted mind / Anna Lisa Tota.
Description: Abingdon, Oxon; New York, NY: Routledge, 2024. |
Includes bibliographical references and index.
Identifiers: LCCN 2024026944 (print) | LCCN 2024026945 (ebook) |
ISBN 9781032777474 (hbk) | ISBN 9781032777375 (pbk) |
ISBN 9781003484592 (ebk)
Subjects: LCSH: Thought and thinking. | Social psychology.
Classification: LCC BF441 .T64 2024 (print) | LCC BF441 (ebook) |
DDC 153.4/2—dc23/eng/20240709
LC record available at https://lccn.loc.gov/2024026944
LC ebook record available at https://lccn.loc.gov/2024026945

ISBN: 978-1-032-77747-4 (hbk)
ISBN: 978-1-032-77737-5 (pbk)
ISBN: 978-1-003-48459-2 (ebk)

DOI: 10.4324/9781003484592

Typeset in Sabon
by codeMantra

To Mattia

Quite empty, quite at rest,
The Robin locks her Nest, and tries her Wings.
She does not know a Route
But puts her Craft about
For rumored Springs –
She does not ask for Noon –
She does not ask for Boon,
Crumbless and homeless, of but one request –
The Birds she lost –

EMILY ELIZABETH DICKINSON

CONTENTS

Foreword	*x*
Preface to the English edition	*xv*
Acknowledgements	*xviii*

1 Architectures of the mind and mindscapes   3
   1. *Natural landscapes and mindscapes 5*
   2. *"Everyday scripts": the arcane order of our ideas 7*
   3. *Flats, villas, and other dwellings: where the self resides 10*
   4. *The school of thoughts: brief notes on school violence 17*

2 Forms of symbolic pollution   25
   1. *Speech pollution 25*
      1.1 Daily conversations and strategies of manipulation 27
      1.2 Techniques for constructing unreality and verbal microaggressions 39
      1.3 Ethnography of a polluting mind: the "enemy within" 41
   2. *Pathological forms of time perception 42*
      2.1 When the past is present 45
      2.2 The time machine: what if the future floods the present? 47

viii Contents

    2.3 Domesticating the wild future: black swans
       and other unresolved issues *50*
    2.4 A brief digression on the concept of control:
       from design to growth *55*
  3. *Pathological forms of domestic space*
    organisation 58
  4. *From skin-ego to Self-Home 61*
  5. *The market as a "solution" in everyday life 64*

3 Visual pollution   71
  1. *From words to images 71*
    1.1 We are not the images we see, but rather
       the images we think *72*
    1.2 The war of dreams or the power of images *75*
    1.3 The imaginary at stake in social conflicts *77*
  2. *Thoughts and images in television series 80*
    2.1 *La Casa de Papel* and the aesthetics
       of money *82*
    2.2 *The Good Wife, The Queen's Gambit,*
       and the other female characters: neoliberal
       feminism *84*
    2.3 *Extraordinary Attorney Woo:* genius and
       Asperger's syndrome *88*
    2.4 *Downton Abbey* and the nostalgia for lost
       dwellings *90*
  3. *The hero's journey: Harry Potter's fantasy world 92*
  4. *Sexism, racism, and other mental pathologies: toxic*
    cultures 94
    4.1 Brief theoretical digression on
       intersectionality *94*

4 Soundscapes and the ecology of sounds   99
  1. *Soundtracks of everyday life: reflections on noise*
    pollution 101
  2. *The musical self and the metaphor of the wax*
    candle 106
  3. *Sounds/music and memory: the "acoustic past" 109*

5 The ecological mind   117
  1. *Itinerary for an ecological mind 118*
  2. *Ecology of public discourse 128*
  3. *Reflections on impermanence 130*

Contents **ix**

6   Inter-speciesism, anti-speciesism, and other beliefs   137
    1. The idea of home as a partition between nature
       and culture 137
    2. "Reconnecting our thoughts with the flesh of the
       world": on the relationship between sustainable
       thinking and responsible action 142
       2.1 The birth of environmental humanities and
           the concept of the Anthropocene 145
    3. "How forests think": the dialogue of plants 148
       3.1 If plant neurobiology were to meet
           anthropology 151
       3.2 The memories of woods and seas: the oblivion
           of the living 152
    4. How other animals think 154
       4.1 The ecology of animal bodies 158
       4.2 The song of the cicadas 159
    5. What about cyborgs? A conversation between Siri
       and my washing machine 162

    Postscript: En route. Diary of everyday happiness   169
       Notes for the future 170

   Bibliography   *180*
   Index   *191*

FOREWORD

I began writing this book during lockdown. Confined to my home, I walk back and forth on the balcony, scanning the rooftops of the city as if I were searching for a way out. We are all in quarantine. All waiting to live, while COVID-19 dictates its own rules. Everything seems to be extreme, bare, and direct. No half-truths are possible, no hypocritical kindness, detestable people, toxic words, junk thoughts. COVID-19 forces us to remember that we are not immortal, that we are still here only by chance. It dispels the illusion that things are destined to last; there is no more time. There is no time to be different from what we are. No matter what we are.

Everything and the opposite of everything happens: large NGO ships carrying shipwrecked migrants sail from one port to another in the Mediterranean in search of a landing place, while majestic cruise ships are forced to stay at sea because COVID-19 has transformed them into luxury leprosariums filled with sick and infected people who are struggling to return home. All novel Ulysses they cannot find peace or shelter. Safe harbour, the possibility to return home or to be welcomed in a new one, is denied to both without distinction of class, ethnicity, or nationality.

In suffering and death, we rediscover sisterhood and brotherhood. Gifted with it at birth, we have disowned it.

Coronavirus does not care about the intricate borders of the Schengen area or the bans on expatriation; it travels from one continent to another, sparing no one. These pages are dedicated to all those who, unfortunately, encountered COVID-19.

Rome, 20 April 2020

Let's imagine that all the conversations that shape our daily life contribute to weaving a sort of invisible web around us – a thickly woven fabric wrapped around our body like a cloak, however unwanted. Let's also imagine that this cloak, once formed, tends to become thicker, increasingly opaque, dense, and impenetrable, like the bramble bush that in the fairy tales we listened to in childhood kept the brave prince out of the castle where his beloved and usually endangered princess was. So, imagine this cloak really exists, would you allow someone to start weaving one – a thick, black cloak – around a person you love? In other words, would you let someone "speak badly" to your child, your elderly mother, your partner, your friend, or yourself? Certainly not. Yet, metaphors aside, this is what happens every day. We are the targets of an uninterrupted flow of words and conversations, which are often toxic, poisonous, and indigestible for our subjectivity. These flows of words wrap themselves around our identities like bramble bushes, around our self-perception, and, slowly, like invisible vampires, they take away our self-esteem, the profound confidence in our abilities, until, stunned, we start believing that we really are this empty dummy, the shell we have been reduced to also thanks to our unconscious and fierce complicity.

"Why did I let this happen?" "Why did I never react?" These simple questions become possible only when the worst is over, when "the die is cast" and the Rubicon is a thing of the past.[1] This book is dedicated to those who are tired of speaking badly and thinking even worse and who, together with me, want to change. The intent is to reopen a space between me who is writing these pages – the urgency is such it feels they are being dictated – and you who are reading them. It is in this space that an opportunity opens up, which certainly goes beyond the inkblots this book offers. It is an opportunity to really change together. The task is difficult and challenging, but it can no longer be put off.

For once, I have decided to write the preface not at the end but actually at the beginning of the book, and therefore, I confess, I have no idea what I will write. I simply don't know. If I did, I would have already written it. I can only anticipate to myself the intention of shedding light on some of the traps that the mind constructs and reconstructs like a silent spider, the ones we often fall into, even though we don't mean to. I can only anticipate that if it is important to speak well, to think well is even more important. The problem is that when we think we are never alone, we are always and often contaminated by others and by something else. The thoughts we formulate are not really ours; it's as if our mind preferred to flow in what has already been thought, lived, and felt. Also, I am not referring to the creative originality we try to pursue in the intellectual or scientific community, as here I am referring to everyday thinking, to the uninterrupted stream of thought that we process as the hours go by, throughout the day. Do we know what we are thinking about when we get up? And afterwards? Are the thoughts that enter and leave our minds in an unstoppable and continuous flow, like in a sandstorm, ours? Do they belong to us or do they come to us? From where? From whom? These pages are dedicated to all those who, like me, are tired of "being thought by their own mind", which, like a runaway horse, seems to swerve right and left, depending on the input of the moment. They are dedicated to those who wish to direct their minds towards streams of thought that really do belong to us, that make us feel good. In order to do this, we must learn how to disable the "traps" and free ourselves of what is "contaminating" before it takes hold and harms us.

This book is a second step in a trajectory that started when I wrote *Eco-words* in 2020. Some months later, I realised that speaking well was not enough, and that in order to fully understand the meaning of words we listen to, it is necessary to grasp the energy of the thoughts that produce them. The same words, in fact, can be ecological when they are uttered in a certain context, while in another they can be highly toxic. There was a moment, linked to a biographical event, in which I understood that thoughts can be much more important than words – yes, exactly that absurd and unchecked stream of thought, unleashed inside us every day, that throws us around like a furling mainsail.

A few weeks before the lockdown was imposed, I was in Genoa,[2] in the home of a very dear friend of mine called Lidia. We were spending a pleasant afternoon together when she received a message from a mutual friend we hadn't heard from for some time. This friend invited Lidia to her wedding; she informed her that she had decided, with her companion, to get married and the wedding would take place shortly (they had been living together for 20 years and had three children together). It was a "better late than never" type of wedding. I could see Lidia was taken aback. This message, in fact, was sent following two years of silence on the part of this supposedly mutual friend, during which Lidia had grieved the death of her mother and gone through a traumatic separation after being married for 20 years. So, not having bothered to ask her once in these two years how she was doing, this supposed friend was now inviting her to her wedding and wanted to share with her the joys and the success of her love life.

I was astonished and surprised by such carelessness and tried to comfort Lidia. She decided to answer nicely and say that, in the meantime, she'd moved to Genoa and could not be in Rome on the day of the wedding. The friend's answer to the news that Lidia had moved to another city was, "Well done! How brave!" Indeed, she was brave, because instead of behaving like a victim after the separation, she had decided to start a new life and move elsewhere. The two adjectives used by the friend seemed to be nice and encouraging, but who knows why, when reading them on Lidia's phone, I had a slight but distinct feeling of discomfort – we all know this feeling; it's what we usually experience when we listen to polluting words. The impression was that of a compliment, but I sensed that the energy behind these words was a different one; the intention that had generated them was different. Lidia wrote back, using the same gentle fierceness: "Well done! The two of you are also very brave!"

I am grateful to Lidia for sharing her bewilderment, and to this supposed friend because without her message, I would have never felt the urge to write these pages. This is how it became clear to me that I would write the sequel to *Eco-words* and that it would be another diary, almost a logbook of a long journey that I would embark on together with my mind (which from now on would be subjected to careful scrutiny) and with all the other minds I would encounter along the way. My investigation began. I wanted to understand how is it that my thoughts seem to get blocked on their own from time to time, giving way to a sort of horror film, in which the most terrible events and circumstances are displayed, with their recurring protagonists, along with myself, who are the people I love most. I came to understand that this was not an individual folly, and that what happened to me probably also happens to other people, so I started asking everyone I came into contact with. The unstoppable flow of mud and strange ideas, worries, fears, and shocks had to be observed and oriented towards new objectives and destinations that would make me and us feel good. Once again, I found myself listening, observing, and scrutinising myself while searching for signs and ideas that might help us all think differently.

It is not a coincidence that the idea which motivated me to write this book originated and developed in the months of the first wave of COVID-19: the virus caused a lot of physical harm; however, we are far from understanding the extent of the consequent psychological harm. The virus caused the death and sickness of many people; however, it didn't only affect our bodies; it also affected our minds, polluting them to such an extent with a wave of negative thoughts that suffocated us not only materially but also spiritually. The virus seems to have spread a black blanket over the entire globe, the blackness formed by the density of our thoughts, which together resonate at the same frequency. To make a different sound is almost a revolutionary act. Not thinking in synch is a true act of resistance. We must equip ourselves in our everyday life and literally learn how to reverse the stream of thought, monitor it, and stop it when it stuns us and takes us far away. We will not bow before the Goddess Despair; we will not yield to Mute Rage. We resist. As Queen Elizabeth, one of the longest-serving and most loved monarchs on the planet, said, referring to COVID-19:

Never give up, never despair!

Rome, 20 June 2020

xiv Foreword

Postscript

Writing a book is like setting off on a long journey with no destination. When one sets off, one does not yet know what the final destination will be, nor what the various stages will be beforehand. There are pauses, but when my fingers stop typing, everyday life speeds up and continues in a frenzy. Just over two years have passed since 20 June 2020. I continue to write these pages, but in the meantime, war has broken out in Ukraine. The Cold War, which seemed to be a nostalgic memory from a James Bond film, has returned to terrorise us in the evening news. We watch the news bewildered as we see Europe being devastated once again by missiles and bombs. Dark jokes circulate on the web about Putin being nominated for the Nobel Prize in Medicine. With fierce and base sarcasm, they point out how the war in Ukraine has brought about the mass healing from COVID-19, which, in fact, has ceased to be a national emergency in the media. Let's be clear: people still die of COVID-19, but now they continue to do so in silence, without appearing in the newspapers. In short, in 2022, we continue to die, but "on an equal footing" with cardiovascular diseases, cancers, and many other pathologies. Disasters continue, civilians in Ukraine are bombed and die by the hundreds, and immigrants drown in the Mediterranean Sea in desperate journeys to reach Europe. Pope Francis continues undaunted to make appeals that, unfortunately, too few listen to. In one of his speeches, he reminded us that home is the first place where we learn to love.

But if we continue to allow people's homes to be destroyed, does this mean we are also destroying the opportunity of millions of children to learn to love?

Remember: "Never give up, never despair!" Weren't we, wonderful 50-year-olds, the ones who boasted, for years, that we were the first generation not to have experienced war?

Milan, 20 June 2022

Notes

1 The Rubicon is a river in Italy famously crossed by Julius Caesar in 49 BC. In Italian, the saying "to cross the Rubicon" means one has reached a point where it is no longer possible to change a decision or course of action.
2 Genoa is a city in the north of Italy.

PREFACE TO THE ENGLISH EDITION

Pollution is not out there, but inside us.

Less than a year has passed since *Ecologia del pensiero* was published in Italian. However, the world seems to have completely changed in the meantime. War – for us Europeans, it was essentially the conflict in Ukraine – has re-fragmented into multiple wars scattered around the globe. These wars were already taking place, but the Israel-Palestine conflict now means we can no longer continue to ignore all of them. There is a huge gap between the peaceful daily life, with its comforts and supposed problems, which we experience in our affluent and opulent cities, and the world, the one that seems more real, more authentic, marked by war, terrorism, violence against women, torture against migrants and refugees, violations of human and civil rights, the persecution of ethnic minorities, homophobia targeting homosexuals, racism that targets everyone who is not "white", discrimination of disabled people, aggressions against other animal species, practices of destruction and annihilation of plant species, increasing climate and environmental pollution. New and additional barriers are continuously erected against someone or something, with various absurd claims pretending to legitimise them: "they" will take away our peace, jobs, resources, wealth, and, in short, our well-being. Natural disasters have multiplied, like warnings from Mother Earth to all of humanity. These warnings are forgotten not only by politics but also by civil society as soon as the calamitous event is over, only to be remembered again when the next disaster takes place. Young people despair and throw red or coloured paint at artworks, in what seems to be a ritual of compensation/restitution to nature. These monuments and paintings that have been stained, dirtied, and violated seem to be saying: "just as humans have damaged and

xvi Preface to the English edition

violated the works of nature, so we rise as silent symbols of living species, species that are violated and granted no voice". By symbolically and concretely staining the products of human creativity, the violations inflicted on Mother Earth – abused and polluted by intensive production and consumption practices – are denounced. But then, through a very surprising subversion of reality, those young people who are just trying to gain our attention for the systematic and intensive destruction of our planet become enemies; their voices of dissent and protest are annihilated and silenced by reducing them to "deviant voices": they become eco-vandals. In this way, following a very consolidated strategy of communication, after the source of the message has been delegitimised, the content of the message also loses its strength.

We are all inert and helpless spectators; we stand silently, dismayed, not knowing what to do or how to intervene. We are informed, at least partially, we know what we are causing, but like passengers on a high-speed train, we do not know how to stop it or how to get off and continue on foot.

This book has already changed since I wrote it one year ago: once again, I have modified the title, from the Italian *Ecologia del pensiero* (Ecology of thought) to *Eco-Thoughts*. So many disasters and wars, such as devastation, require a form of eco-thinking. It is from the ways we literally think about worlds that their social construction derives. When thoughts resound together, they are powerful vectors able to shape and transform reality. But going back to the fact that this book has changed: yes, books have a life of their own. Indeed, they escape our mind and then the hands of us authors to circulate freely in the world, following and tracing itineraries we could not even have imagined. I do not know whether this book is useful or worthy of the precious time it takes to read it. It is yet another book written as if it were a message of hope, as if these pages could fluctuate and transform themselves into concentric circles that grow wider. This book seems to be very much convinced it is useful, while I write these last (but first) pages, as if the safety of the entire planet could depend on a neologism: "eco-thought"; on the need to eco-think together, which implies not only the human species but rather joining forces of the eco-thoughts of all living species, as Donna Haraway (2016) proposed in *Chthulucene*. As if all the modalities – or at least many of the ones we rely on when organising our social life on this planet – were destined to be rethought, transformed, and challenged. We need eco-gazes on the world to be able to restore the beauty of our being thrown into the landscape we inhabit. Capable of reconnecting to the vibrancy of existence, to the ethicality of our feeling, and to what we share with other living beings; capable of "weaving"[1] the threads of the living together again, which the rationality of thought seems to have mistakenly severed. As beings cut off from the world, we need to restart nourishing ourselves with the beauty of nature and of art: if it is true that beauty heals the world, then what we must do at this moment is hang on to it with all our strength. It is the crack – the separation of internal and external – that makes evil possible. We must re-think this divide in terms of how porous its boundaries are, the gap between us and the world as a place of encounter, a space of interweaving. Today pollution is a central issue, however, pollution is not out there, but inside us. It nestles in our polluted and polluting minds. Our minds think toxic, asphyxiating thoughts – thoughts that are more poisonous than the air we breathe and the water we drink. It is precisely those thoughts that we need to go back to in order to reformulate them. This book aims to break down walls: those between people, between genders, between ethnicities, and between animal and plant species. But these walls run through us, they are carved in our flesh, they separate minds from bodies, children from parents, and ancestors from descendants. Time, however, is one, unique, multiple, and infinite, and space can expand to include us all – as if we were staring into it standing on the edge of a huge black hole. These pages are an invitation and a call; they are a manifesto for a new ecology of thinking capable of nourishing our minds and bodies, of reconnecting us to the earth we come from and to which, willingly or not, we will return. We could go back to hearing the song of nature, its sounds, and its multiple voices, without forgetting that we are also scientists; indeed, we can be both: we can go back to being poet-scientists. It is the spirit that feeds our thoughts that addresses us. Sitting on the shoulders of our ancestors and standing before our descendants, can we make a difference? These pages connecting us, dear reader, are already the difference we invoke. They question us, making such a small difference possible. However, we can only proceed with uncertain steps, for short stretches, insecure about our ideas, and humbly supported by our values. Perhaps it is true that we cannot save the entire planet, but at least we will have tried. I like to think that these verses by Goliarda Sapienza[2] can ideally be reconsidered as a cry that rises from Mother Earth and stands as an archetype of the feminine:

> You're killing me, but my face
> will remain as if
> glassed in your eyes.
> Sharp. At night
> Pinned down
> The eyelids will cry.[3]

Villadeati, 8 March 2024

Notes

1 The use of the term weaving is a homage to Tim Ingold (2000b).
2 Goliarda Sapienza was a Sicilian writer who lived between 1924 and 1996. She was also a theatre and film actress. She acted in Luchino Visconti's film *Senso*.
3 Sapienza (2013, p. 63).

ACKNOWLEDGEMENTS

I would like to thank all the colleagues and friends, whose conversations have nourished me and have subsequently converged in this book. Among them a special thanks to Tia DeNora, Christopher Mathieu, and many other colleagues from the European Sociological Association Research Networks on Sociology of the Arts and Sociology of Culture. However, I would like to express my deepest gratitude to two colleagues who have recently passed away, and whose work has had a significant impact on my own research: Vera Zolberg and Howard Becker. While I had a closer relationship with Vera and followed Howard's work from more of a distance, they have been indispensable references for many scholars of my generation. I like to think that they might read these words and smile with satisfaction at the affection and esteem reflected in them. I also thank Lia Luchetti for the invaluable assistance in editing the translation and Emma Catherine Gainsforth for the care and attention with which she translated – not only linguistically but also culturally – the adventurous flow of my writing, assisted by Edward Fortes. I extend special thanks to my publisher, Routledge, which continues to believe in my scholarly work. I am also grateful to Simon Bates, Emily Briggs, and Lakshita Joshi, who have supported this project from the beginning. Finally, extraordinary thanks go to the hills of the Lower Monferrato region in Italy, which inspired the way my thoughts progressed as I wrote, offering me shelter and comfort with their beauty. Those same hills remind me of a short but intense vacation spent with Vera and Aristide Zolberg many years ago, when we all still believed we would have lived forever.

"That which is closest to us
needs a tortuous path to manifest itself."[1]

In the first chapter, I analyse the flow of our everyday thoughts, trying to understand how to improve this flow, if and where it is possible. In order to do so, I start with a metaphor, one offered to us by the notion of landscape. I observe how the external "natural landscape", which becomes the context in which we process our thoughts, possibly resonates with the "landscape as the dwelling of the self" (i.e. the portion of external context that every one of us symbolically invests with meaning, that we identify with, and that for this reason influences our stream of thought), and how both these types of landscape resonate with the actual "mindscape" (i.e. the frame within which our thoughts and the related mental scripts take shape). In the last paragraph, I briefly discuss some of the possible boundaries inside which our thoughts take shape, and, in particular, I mention one of the fundamental places in which these forms are transmitted: the school. To identify an exhaustive list of such boundaries would be misleading; indeed, it would be an impossible task to attempt in the space of a book, let alone in a single paragraph. However, where I articulate these short reflections, I propose at least two that are bound to have ruinous effects on the forms our daily thoughts may take: (a) the idea that knowledge and cognition are boring, dreary, and factual; (b) the idea that theoretical knowledge and practical knowledge are disconnected and that they can therefore proceed separately. The first idea has damaging effects because it permanently distances us from the only proper tool we have to think clearly and live better, which is culture, in all its forms and manifestations. The second idea also has damaging effects because it creates a hierarchy in the domain of knowledge, and by establishing such a hierarchy, it legitimises another one between men and women, who excel in different areas of knowledge. In other words, once these foundations are laid, knowledge, far from being the driving force for promoting and enhancing all social and cultural differences, becomes the basis for legitimising social inequalities.

1

ARCHITECTURES OF THE MIND AND MINDSCAPES

> Ταράσσει τοὺς ἀνθρώπους οὐ τὰ πράγματα, ἀλλὰ
> τὰ περὶ τῶν πραγμάτων, δόγματα.
>
> Epictetus

A learned Greek man, a philosopher who was enslaved and lived in the 1st century A.D., handed these words down to us; we read them centuries later, as sharp and intact as if they were made of steel. However, for some strange reason, the sequence of signs cannot be activated in us until we incorporate it, i.e. we experience it directly. In short, it is not enough to write something down, let alone read it. How many times have we written or read in the pages of a book beautiful maxims that nevertheless remained trapped, forever clinging to the lines of those pages? How many times have we thought of important and compelling sentences that echoed in our minds and yet floated on the surface of our thoughts, fluttering, without being able to settle? In fact, if we really understood Epictetus, we would put an end to anxiety and depression once and for all, notwithstanding psychiatrists, psychotherapists, and the pharmaceutical industry. The happiness pill could be renamed the "Epictetus pill". All the same, what he claimed, so many centuries ago, is still valid:

> "Men are disturbed not by things, but by the views which they take of things".[2]

I wish Epictetus was my uncle, or at least a distant relative of mine.

DOI: 10.4324/9781003484592-1

4 Architectures of the mind and mindscapes

A dear friend tells me how desperate she is: she has just separated, she has two young children and her ex-husband, whose only desire is to live comfortably with his new partner, is fighting hard not to give her the financial support she needs. Barbara (this is not her real name) does not have a stable job, and in any case, she earns a little over 1,000 euros a month with a part-time job. In fact, the salary is not even that bad, but in Verona,[3] this amount of money is not enough, considering the rent she pays. Barbara is desperate; she cries on the phone. She has started seeing a therapist for support, and this therapist – who in my opinion is as fierce as her ex-husband – has diagnosed a severe depression, which seems to mean that a person who has two small children to support and an ex-husband who could not care less has absolutely no right to be sad. In addition to paying an expensive therapist, she should also be cheerful. The next day, I phone Barbara back. She tells me she cried for a long time but then decided to sleep on it. Today, nothing at all has changed since yesterday: the same insufficient salary, the same bast... ex-husband, the same small children to bring up, the same expensive city, and the same annoying psychotherapist. Yet Barbara is no longer crying. The emotional storm seems to have subsided. Her emotional system is no longer on edge. Barbara hints at a smile and even almost manages to joke with me, talking about her/our future as mothers. What has happened? Nothing. Nothing at all. Barbara has simply taken what is known as the "Epictetus pill" and stopped letting the very black future, which does not exist yet, spill over onto the present, which does exist and is not as threatening, at least not at the moment. All in all, she and her beautiful children are in excellent health, and, at least for this month, the bills have already been paid.

We are all "Barbara", at least once a month. This extraordinary and absurd phenomenon is familiar to us all. In the face of adversity, the mindscape that takes shape in our thoughts often jolts us from one rock to another, almost like a typhoon, and then, for no apparent reason, after a certain amount of time, we seem to return to our daily routine, at least for a while. What actually happens to us? Are these emotional storms rare events? Are they pathological? Do they only happen to us? Should we run to a therapist, or can we manage on our own? The point is that the same thing happens to the therapist, the person who is supposed to cure us and free us from this supposed illness, and this is why it is not a question of treating this as a pathology but rather of learning to cope with it.

This book intends to make a small contribution, to initiate a shared reflection among the readers and the writer, one that may enable all of us to "think clearly and live better", by sketching an auto-ethnography of our everyday life that may free us, as much as possible, from the evils of living. I am and remain a sociologist. I believe that what nourishes us at a young age shapes us forever.[4] So, it is from sociological theories that I draw to write the following pages. Indeed, is not sociology the discipline that, more than any other, is interested precisely in how symbolic forms influence the meanings we attribute to our everyday life?[5] Is it not for this reason that generations of scholars like myself have observed and studied how everything social dances with us, becoming inextricably intertwined with the trajectory of our lives? The point is that *when we think, we are never alone*,[6] so it is best that we try to understand this together.

1. Natural landscapes and mindscapes

The interconnection between mind and external space has been explored and investigated by numerous disciplines: neuroscientists have dealt with the problem, but also scholars in the field of aesthetics and psychoanalysts who view the landscape as a metaphor of our mind; as if in a play of mirrors, the external landscape and the horizons we grasp with our gaze were constructed by the eye while, at the same time, they continue to inhabit and resonate inside us like archetypes of our psyche, like magical places in which to take refuge. "Earth's geographies are inseparable from those of the mind, and between landscapes and mindscapes there are psychoanalytic, neuroaesthetic and, inevitably, poetic links", Vittorio Lingiardi writes in a very meaningful passage.[7] The author then highlights, somewhat dismayed, not only

> the destruction of landscape, but also its manipulation for commercial and advertising purposes, the shift *(that is,)* from landscape as artistic invention to landscape as advertising invention. Screen-saver landscapes with photoshopped mountains, blued seas, bleached beaches, combed deserts. From a single brushstroke to everyone's computer.

Lingiardi adds that "on the contrary, images should be salvaged, removed from the market of trivialisation and placed back at the centre of psychic experience". He claims to want to contribute with his writing to a process of restoration and proposes "a domestic effort aimed at both caring for images and preserving landscapes".[8] The author is well aware that landscape visions become psychic images, and, as such, we may add, they end up influencing the very maps of our mind. It is precisely from the observation of such a strong connection between the inside and the outside that I would like to start.

In the following pages, we will explore a spatial metaphor that represents our mind as a landscape, literally inhabited by the flow of our thoughts, a kind of Victorian mansion, with long corridors and many rooms. However, the notion of landscape also inspires another reflection: like a fresco on a wall or a painting on a beautiful canvas, our thoughts constantly map and draw "mindscapes" for us and with us, more or less realistic and truthful scenarios that accompany us in our everyday life; indeed, they literally represent the script of our everyday life.

6 Architectures of the mind and mindscapes

The notion of landscape is more suited to illustrate this argument than that of garden, since – as scholars in the field of aesthetics remind us – a garden is a type of landscape that always requires human intervention.[9] Moreover, a landscape is not appropriable; it has no boundaries, cannot be fenced in, nor can it be entirely owned by anyone.[10] In short, a landscape is better qualified than a garden to represent our mind because it implies a dimension of openness and transcendence with respect to the corporeality of individuals. From a sociological point of view, the idea of mind that seems to us most appropriate for the purposes of this argument is that of an open mind, exposed to the unexpected, to sudden and radical change; a mind, in short, that incorporates the inability to control its own entry and exit points; a mind with mobile and fluctuating boundaries; a space without walls, where the inside and the outside alternate seamlessly. Moreover, the mindscape seems to differ from the natural landscape in that it still comprises an arcane or conscious structure in which thoughts are harnessed. This structure is said to consist of our deepest beliefs, sometimes so deep that they are invisible even to ourselves. However, the difference is only apparent: the mindscape is much more similar to the natural landscape than we might expect. A natural landscape, in fact, does not exist outside our gaze; it is nothing more than the selection made by our eye. Like a photographer who decides to take that picture and portray that exact section of the landscape, our gaze decides, consciously or unconsciously, what to look at. There is no such thing as a neutral landscape, and there is no such thing as a gaze that does not carry with it the values influencing the decision to look. The same could be said of our mental processes: there is no such thing as a mindscape that does not carry with it the solid, grounded matrix of beliefs and deep thoughts that literally form and shape our stream of thought, bringing them into focus and rendering them memorable.

While writing these pages, I performed two small experiments. In the first, I asked myself what and how many thoughts flowed through me in the course of the morning, let's say a handful of hours, from 8 a.m. to 12 p.m. Only four hours. I realised that the number of thoughts exceeded my capacity to calculate and that, moreover, I was unable to remember them, except by making a special effort. The second experiment consisted of trying to understand in which direction my stream of thought would go. I realised that the mind seemed to proceed like a cart driven by a horse without reins, and that the pace of the cart and the horse seemed to depend on a deeper inner disposition, a sort of "vigilant stillness", to quote a well-known verse by the Italian poet Ungaretti. This vigilant stillness rendered the course creative and interesting, but as soon as this profound disposition was disturbed for some reason, it was replaced by a vigilant anxiety that made all turns and trajectories dangerous, threatening, and impervious. In short, the mindscape is, like a natural landscape, the object and conscious result of an inner decision of the soul's gaze, which decides where to rest and what to look at.[11]

2. "Everyday scripts": the arcane order of our ideas

A friend tells me about a recurring nightmare he has. It is a kind of daydream, not an actual dream. He has to attend an important and decisive work meeting, and everything goes wrong. He can't find the file on his computer, then screen share jams, he makes a comment that is rather inappropriate, and then realises that his microphone is not muted and that the colleague he is talking about can hear him. In short, it sounds like the script of a horror film adapted to his everyday life. But isn't that what happens to all of us from time to time? A sort of mental film that seems to start almost automatically, while we are sitting in the bath, totally unaware, or on the train, or sitting in traffic, or or or? It's as if every now and then our mind were composing an articulate and complex script with very specific details, so very accurate and realistic, in which none of the gruesome details are omitted or left out. In short, nothing is missing in these self-produced and self-administered films: while our mind wanders, the terrifying mindscape takes shape, and we are shocked by the vision of the film that we ourselves have produced. We pretend to forget the name of the director, though we actually know him or her very well, and are totally impotent as we continue watching the sequence.

Marcel Proust is to be credited with one of the most intense descriptions of a particular variant of such mental script, which involves the spilling over into the present of anxieties and worries located in the future, however near. In practice, this ingenious mental mechanism consists in producing anxiety and dismay in the *hic et nunc*, the here and now – while we are in a situation of relative tranquillity – by projecting the subject into the future, where something extremely unpleasant and painful is very likely to happen. By way of example, we may think of the ritual of the mother's kiss described so skilfully by the French writer. In Combray, in fact, the mother's kiss becomes the emotional trigger that initiates a sequence of anxious thoughts described by the narrator's voice:

> But the only one of us for whom Swann's arrival became the object of a painful preoccupation was I. This was because on the evenings when strangers, or merely M. Swann, were present, Mama did not come up to my room. I had dinner before everyone else and afterward I came and sat at the table, until eight o'clock when it was understood that I had to go upstairs; the precious and fragile kiss that Mama usually entrusted to me in my bed when I was going to sleep I would have to convey from the dining room to my bedroom and protect during the whole time I undressed, so that its sweetness would not shatter, so that its volatile essence would not disperse and evaporate, and on precisely those evenings when I needed to receive it with more care, I had to take it, I had to snatch it brusquely, publicly, without even having the time and the freedom of mind necessary to bring to what I was doing the attention of those individuals controlled

8 Architectures of the mind and mindscapes

by some mania, who do their utmost not to think of anything else while they are shutting a door, so as to be able, when the morbid uncertainty returns to them, to confront it victoriously with the memory of the moment when they did shut the door.[12]

In this case, it isn't even about the absence of the mother's kiss; rather, the fact is that the mother will kiss her son in the dining room, in the presence of others, not the moment before he goes to sleep, in his room. It is enough for the context of reception in which the boy is given this kiss to change to set off a sequence of anxiety and worry in the Proustian first-person narrative that prevents him from enjoying Swann's unannounced visit. Basically, when he hears Swann's voice, the thought that comes to mind is not: "I will enjoy Swann's visit or what he will say to me", which is the event taking place in the nearest future, but:

> I am worried about the later but certain consequences of this visit, that is, the fact that my mother will give me a kiss in the dining room, which means that when I am in bed, in my room, tonight, my mother's kiss will be a faint and less vivid memory and this will cause pain linked to her absence.

This is an emblematic case of the future spilling into the present and preventing the present from being fully experienced. Basically, what happens to all of us every other day.

Another description by Proust, one that is very useful to illustrate the concept of "mental script", is that of Swann's jealousy, of the suffering caused by his beloved Odette. The latter, more or less consciously, appears to be very good at provoking her lover's mental torments:

> One day he [Swann] was trying, without hurting Odette, to ask her if she had ever had any dealings with a procuress. Actually he was convinced she had not; reading the anonymous letter had introduced the conjecture into his mind, but in a mechanical way; it had met with no credence there, but had in fact remained there, and Swann, in order to be rid of the purely material but nonetheless awkward presence of the suspicion, wanted Odette to remove it. "Oh, no! Not that they don't pester me," she added, revealing by her smile a self-satisfied vanity which she no longer noticed could not seem justified to Swann. "There was one here yesterday who stayed more than two hours waiting for me, offered me any amount I liked. It seems some ambassador had said to her: "I'll kill myself if you don't get her for me." (...) I wish you could have seen the way I spoke to her; my maid heard me from the next room and told me I was shouting at the top of my voice. I said, "Haven't I told you I don't want to? It's a poor idea,

I don't like it. Really, I should hope I'm still free to do what I want! If I needed the money, I could understand…" (…) You see, your little Odette has some good in her, all the same, even though some people find her so detestable." Moreover her very admissions, when she made them, of faults that she supposed he had discovered, served Swann as points of departure toward new doubts rather than put an end to the old.[13]

The concept of mental script perfectly illustrates how the feeling of jealousy manifests itself: the jealous lover's distress usually builds up in a sort of hallucinatory state that produces a large number of images. A single detail of the person's daily life becomes increasingly threatening and turns into the pretext for the construction of a mental script, in which a person's worst fears and concerns become as vivid and realistic as real events. What must be emphasised here is that neither the veracity nor the accuracy of such script function as necessary cause. In fact, the mental film takes shape starting from a single real detail, which literally functions as the sufficient cause. The point is that this toxic way of working of our mind, which does not apply only to Othello but to all of us mortals – for no one is entirely immune to it – can manifest itself in many different formats: revenge fantasies, hatred, anxiety, worries, envy, insecurity, and a wide range of negative emotions that creep up on us and naturally tend to flood our souls to the point they almost drown us.[14]

Proust's touch of genius; however, the antidote to all negative scripts (at least with regard to the script of toxic love) is only a few pages away. Here Swann, who by now is no longer with Odette, recalls his love affair as if it were a distant dream:

But while, an hour after he had woken, he was giving instructions to the hairdresser so that his brush cut would not become disordered on the train, he thought about his dream again, and saw once again, as he had felt them close beside him, Odette's pale complexion, her too thin cheeks, her drawn features, her tired eyes, everything which – in the course of the successive expression of tenderness which had made of his abiding love for Odette a long oblivion of the first image he had formed of her – he had ceased to notice since the earliest days of their acquaintance, days to which no doubt, while he slept, his memory had returned to search for their exact sensation. And with the intermittent coarseness that reappeared in him as soon as he was no longer unhappy and the level of his morality dropped accordingly, he exclaimed to himself: "To think that I wasted years of my life, that I wanted to die, that I felt my deepest love, for a woman who did not appeal to me, who was not my type!"[15]

The key passage is "as soon as he was no longer unhappy"; in fact, the truth is that a fundamental characteristic of human beings is distraction, the

10 Architectures of the mind and mindscapes

inability to stay with the intensity of a single emotion for a prolonged period of time. Unless we are dealing with an event that is so traumatic that it has annihilated and paralysed us permanently, very often the perception of anxiety and suffering cannot be prolonged in time without interruption, because after a while we tend to forget, at least momentarily, how unlucky we always are – that, at least, is our impression. In fact, this mental script, the formation of this ominous representation, requires a great deal of attention and concentration. In other words, even though we might not want to admit it, if we actually pay attention, we notice that after a while, the game we are playing or the game we are taking part in, even though we might not intend to, actually becomes boring. It's like watching a play that after a while, no longer speaks to us and is no longer engaging. When our mind gets stuck, it might only be for a moment, but there is an opening, through which we are able to catch a small glimpse of what the next state of mind will be. The truth is that everyone who has experienced a toxic relationship knows very well that Swann is right – that years later, looking back, we will be amazed and wonder how was it possible to despair over Odette or Oddone, who was not even our type. I have always thought that Swann's conclusion should be included in the opening page of any treatise on how we fall in love and behave in a relationship; it would spare all those who read it and become convinced enough to accept his advice and take his word for it (after all, we are talking about taking Proust's word for it) months and years of youthful and/or senile anguish and distress, as the case may be. However, the truth is that this conclusion resonates, it sounds true only to those who have already experienced this type of anguish and distress in the past. Indeed, the miracle of our mind remains intact for the observer, for those of us who want to look at the processes that structure our thinking with a gaze that is both detached and participatory, as if our mind were playing with us and our emotions in an endless game of chess, leading us where it wants and swirling us around like a furling mainsail.

3. Flats, villas, and other dwellings: where the self resides

Many studies and various disciplinary perspectives understand space as the place in which meanings are constructed with reference, firstly, to the social definition of such space and its destination; secondly, with respect to the activities that take place in it and for which it is equipped; and, finally, with respect to the subjects who travel through it or inhabit it in a stable and continuous manner. Before considering private space, I would like to mention at least two reflections on public space that have focused on what is called the "place-lessness of the spaces".[16] The first one is a reflection by Marc Augè,[17] his well-known theory of non-places. The French anthropologist identified a specific type of space, that of airports or railway stations, which forces a functional and ahistorical relationship onto the subjects passing through it (inside Fiumicino airport in Rome, travellers about to leave for a certain destination are "destined" not to leave any biographical trace in that specific space, which is precisely a non-place). The second reflection concerns the notion of "orphan spaces",[18] public places that are literally constructed and socially organised in such a way as not to permit any kind of connection between space, biographical trajectory, and social use, a connection that is absolutely necessary for space to become a place and that is characterised by the sedimentation of meanings deriving from various assemblages of sense that have come into being over time. In the public domain, orphan spaces are the exact opposite of the dwellings of the self in private spaces, which we will discuss below. They are spaces that have been preventively deprived of the possibility of acquiring a specific configuration of meaning in relation to the biographical trajectories of their users. Adriano Olivetti, who theorised the spiritual life of the factory,[19] would have said that these are spaces that have been denied the possibility of cultivating their own spiritual life, severing the vital link between space itself and the historical subjects that pass through it. This concept of orphan space, which is illuminating in describing a certain public use of space, is an interesting point of reference from which to look at the social configurations of private space that constitute its opposite. Orphan spaces, in fact, are public places where no self can transit and remain entire. Provocatively, one might say that, in order to access a non-place, the subject must agree to be socially defined as a non-self, that is, someone who is a person regardless of his or her biographical identity: when I enter a railway station, I am a traveller in transit from Rome to Trieste (as certified by my train ticket), and in a certain sense, I agree to symbolically strip myself of my biographical identity. It is no coincidence that orphan spaces and non-places have multiplied in our contemporary world: just as the process of commodification has the secondary effect of reducing all products to merchandise, which therefore renders different products interchangeable, comparable, and commensurable, at least in the sense of their economic valorisation, so this effect of depersonalisation also extends to places, which take on the appearance of orphan places, becoming ahistorical and equivalent, insofar as they are conceptualised (exclusively or prevalently) on the basis of their functional definition. Underlying both processes is the fierce reduction of semantic complexity, which reduces everything to a functional dimension. The spiritual life of places (whether public or private) and objects is thus effectively obscured.

Already in *Eco-Words. The Ecology of Conversation*,[20] I began to reflect on the relationship between space and subjectivity, developing the concept of "spatialisation of the self", which alludes to the fluid boundaries of our subjectivity and to the fact that these can transcend the physical limitations of our corporeality. In other words, our "I" – far from comprising only corporeal physicality – also seems to extend to the spaces which, more or less

12 Architectures of the mind and mindscapes

intentionally, each subject invests with such a meaning and function: from one's car to the writer's desk, from the laptop to the scooter, from one's wardrobe to a mobile phone – the examples are infinite. What they have in common is that they have a specific importance for that subject, such that a violation or alteration of these spaces (real or virtual) is perceived as a symbolic violence, that is, as a violation of the extension of the self and its integrity. This notion actually helps us to better understand the emotional complexity of a subject's reactions to events that are perceived as "disruptive" when they occur inside spaces that are highly symbolic. For example, a mother might have the best intentions and act not out of curiosity but intending to protect, but if she reads her daughter's conversations on her mobile phone, what creates a surplus of violence in her daughter's perception of that behaviour, beyond the act itself, is precisely the violation of a virtual space, considered fundamental to her daughter's subjectivity. In this sense, virtual and real spaces can be equivalent: going through someone's chest of drawers or reading messages on a phone are acts that are perceived as being equally serious by the person who is subjected to them.

It should be noted that, during the pandemic and the lockdown that followed, the extension of subjectivity in domestic spaces in some cases considerably increased, enhancing the process of symbolic projection onto the spaces of our self. Alberto, a subject interviewed in the course of anthropological research on the consequences of the lockdown, who lives in a one-room apartment in the centre of Milan, described his experience as follows:

> The one-room apartment became an extension of my body and therefore also a place of the mind. I am everywhere now because I know every single detail. It has become a more intimate place, I am attached to it more than ever, almost affectively. The functions of the living space have remained the same but have become more important, meaningful, fuller, more aware, more necessary.[21]

Here I propose going back to the notion of the *spatialisation of the self*, already outlined in *Eco-Words*, and elaborate on it also with reference to the categories of time, as well as those of space. In fact, the self has a primarily temporal dimension that coincides, on the one hand, with its memory and, on the other, with its multiple representations of the present and future. This dimension also includes the concept of chain of thought, the strange connector that already David Hume[22] identified as the only possible support for the idea we form of ourselves as continuous beings enduring in biographical time. In this temporality of the self, the adverb *meanwhile*, as Paolo Jedlowski[23] observes, acquires a peculiar value:

> *Meanwhile* is also the name of the fact that each one of us is inscribed in a collective history: actions, speeches, desires repeated almost at the same

time in almost the same way by a multitude of others we do not know though we somewhat resemble them.

Jedlowski proposes a spatial metaphor for this adverb, which so uniquely characterises our subjectivity, projecting it into the co-presence of parallel stories and events:

> Rooms are by definition co-present. They are an articulation of space. You can be in one room; meanwhile, others exist. The corridor is the passage that brings this *meanwhile* into being, the place where you experience it. In a house it does what the adverb *meanwhile* does in a sentence, it promises connections. It is a passage.[24]

As mentioned earlier, the self is characterised by its own spatial dimension; that is, it extends into space far beyond our body. It is a sort of symbolic self that transcends bodily boundaries to project its beliefs, values, tastes, and inclinations outside itself into the world. That is, the self projects the cognitive and aesthetic organisation that characterises it into its sphere of proximity to make that portion of space, in which its physicality moves, more like itself. Perhaps it is also a way of domesticating the threshold, of rendering a leap *continuous (that is, 1, 1.1, 1.2, 1.3, ... 2)*, a gap that would otherwise have the appearance of a *discrete variable (that is, 1,2)*.

This border area is a kind of aesthetic-symbolic extension of the self, onto which the subject projects its inner world. It is evident that this symbolic space cannot have unlimited boundaries, but must nevertheless define itself through a series of external limits, which probably depend on more general factors (such as the culture one belongs to – we may think of the macroscopic gap in the perception of domestic spaces between Japan and the United States) or more specific ones (gender, generation, etc.). Continuing to use this metaphor, we might then ask: what are the dwellings of subjectivity; where does the self live? On closer inspection, we may answer that our self inhabits our home, though that would be too reductive and trivial with respect to the potential dwellings of subjectivity. The self may well inhabit a musical instrument, an example taken from a conversation with a mother who told me about her son's musical education in a Steiner school, emphasising a particular aspect: the way he took care of his instrument and the relationship that each student established with their own instrument. In her story, this relationship was clearly one in which the social and the material intertwined, performing practices and meanings of the learning environment itself:

One thing in particular struck me: something that happened during the last year of primary school, which made me realise how much these students loved music and their instruments. During an orchestra class, one of my son's classmates quarrelled fiercely with another student; the intensity of the fight was unheard of for children of that age. The quarrel led to one

14 Architectures of the mind and mindscapes

student kicking the violin that belonged to the other, and although the two had already beaten each other up badly, it was only then that the child who owned the violin burst into tears. The kicks and punches aimed at his body were nothing compared to the damage done to his beloved violin. Such a feeling would have been quite normal in the case of an older student, but the child in question was in fifth grade and had been studying the violin for just over a year.

The mother rightly focuses on the child's fondness and attachment to the violin. For the purposes of the present discussion, this example is illuminating: in this case, we might argue that the subjectivity of the child extends to the instrument itself, which in all respects becomes the *dwelling of the self*. This helps understand the tears and distress of the child, who experiences his companion's kick as a violation of his own subjectivity. How does the musical instrument reverberate the child's aesthetic and cognitive organisation of his world? Clearly, the violin also embodies a moral order that echoes the one the child's family world view is based on: the repudiation of violence, the care objects deserve, the harmony of beauty, and the value of music are some of the traits grounding the moral order that the kick has just shattered. Tears are a response to the violation of the order that has been attacked and that must literally be repaired with the mediation and intervention of the adult world. What is at stake here is not only love for music, but also an inner moral order, one the entire symbolic world of the child rests on.

If we consider the metaphor of the dwelling, it is evident that the conception of home we have in mind is not at all irrelevant with regard to such processes of subjectivation. When Prince Tancredi in Luchino Visconti's famous film (1963), inspired by Tomasi di Lampedusa's novel,[25] makes the Leopard say that "a palace where you know all the rooms isn't worth living in", he immediately transports us into another world, where the perception of space and the way people inhabit it are different. Large dwellings are particularly appealing for many of us; they seem to act as a nostalgic reminder of a way of living of the past. The successful British TV series *Downton Abbey* comes to mind, based on a symbolic equivocation of the history of a lineage and/or of a house.[26] Watching and re-watching the episodes of the series, it is not easy to understand whether we are more interested in the stories of the characters or in the furniture and style that shape everyday life, made possible by the very fact of inhabiting those spaces. What keeps us glued to the screen is the sense that the house is a possible symbolic abode of our subjectivity, not so much the countless and cloying adventures of its protagonists. For much of the Western world, a large house with a garden and/or park continues to represent an ideal model of dwelling, as if our self could express itself more fully in large spaces. The aristocratic traditions and the sumptuous lifestyles associated with them, passed down to us by both our genetic and cultural DNA, continue to exert a powerful fascination that would be incomprehensible, for example, for a Japanese citizen, for whom a large house might appear to be *too* large and probably also uncomfortable. The point is that when our self is allowed to spread out and suggest beauty in the organisation of the spaces closest to us, it is as if something were opening up, capable of expanding and rarefying the passing of time in everyday life. A place that we perceive as oriented and organised by our canons of beauty functions as a *dwelling of the self*, and when it becomes an extension of our inner world, it helps us express it. In other words, the *dwellings of the self* become the places of our creativity, of our well-being, and of our inner balance. They are the places where we can enter into dialogue with our ancestors and feel their closeness and protection. They are the places where the cheaters and evil-minded are exposed, because in the end, they are the places of our inner self. No matter whether luxurious or modestly furnished, what matters is the feeling that guides our hands as we organise them. The choices made in these spaces become at once the furniture of the space and the decor of the mind. When we have the honour of being invited by others to enter a house that is also a dwelling of the self, we observe how the furniture is arranged, the layout of the décor, and, as if by reflection, catch a glimpse of the intentions of the person's soul.

As Lingiardi points out:

> The world of objects, the way we choose and use them, constitutes an extraordinary vocabulary that allows us to express the aesthetics of our Self. Objects, environments and landscapes have specific evocative effects that help shape our inner world (...).[27]

In the last few decades, we have witnessed a trend develop that is particularly interesting with regard to what we are discussing.[28] The art of tidying our home has been described as a strategy for inner change by countless authors from a variety of disciplinary fields.[29] A series of books, mostly intended for the general public, often manuals for practical use, which, however, seem to reflect a kind of popular wisdom. In particular, Margareta Magnusson[30] addresses the way homes are tidied according to the Swedish tradition and offers a series of reflections on a specific theme: tidying a home as an individual and practical activity that consists in sorting the objects of one's own existence as one approaches the moment of departure from this world and, at the same time, tidying as a social activity (which involves communicating to one's loved ones what they should do with material objects), which means sorting one's family and social relationships. According to this tradition – in Sweden it is called *döstädning* – as an act of love and respect towards our loved ones, we should help them understand what to do with all the objects belonging to us in advance, so as to make this painful and tiring practical aspect unnecessary after our death. It involves communicating with a series of detailed instructions, given also many years before our future death, on how

16 Architectures of the mind and mindscapes

we wish all our material possessions to be used and distributed. Not only the most important ones, as one would in a normal will, but also individual items of clothing or objects we own. In short, people explain to their loved ones how they would like their house to be emptied. *Döstädning* also seems to be understood as a preventive act aimed at facilitating the grieving process associated with death. Also, in this case, there is a close connection between ordering a subject's physical space and ordering the symbolic space of their social and family relations. *Döstädning* also helps the subject to better process his or her own impermanence in the world. In short, it is a small but real act of responsibility towards those we love and who will outlive us.

But let us return to the relationship between domestic space and subjectivity: if the home and the space in which a subject spends part of his or her everyday life are to be understood as true extensions of his or her subjectivity, if our concept of self ceases to coincide with the physical boundaries of corporeality, then an obvious – and not surprising – consequence of this is that inner and outer change go hand in hand. A messy bookcase – *our* messy bookcase – seems to prevent us from thinking clearly and from having well-organised thoughts. A house in which the bathroom is neglected seems to prevent us from taking care of our bodies as we should and/or would like to. If caring for the self and caring for its extension in space were intimately connected, and if this theoretical hypothesis were to be proved correct, then *we could care for places in order to care for people*, and *care for our own places in order to care for ourselves*. Those who have the privilege of being able to choose whether to do the cleaning themselves or have others do it experience that unique feeling connected to space when it has been cleaned and cared for by our own hands. As if we alone had the power and ability to recreate the inner connection between us and our domestic space. This experience is more easily observable when we can *choose* to do the cleaning ourselves, rather than being forced to clean on a daily basis.

Once again, it is Proust who offers an example of the symbolic consonance between space, time, and subjectivity, with uncle Adolphe's house, which seems to be a real dwelling of the self. In the *Recherche*, uncle Adolphe is a brother of the narrator's grandfather, an officer who has retired with the rank of major. His house emanates a sense of darkness and coolness mixed with a feeling of *ancien régime*. Unlike previous examples, in this case we focus on a particular afternoon ritual of uncle Adolphe's, whose function it is to oversee the timing of the visits that take place in the house:

> Once or twice a month, in Paris, I used to be sent to pay him a visit as he was finishing lunch wearing a plain loose-fitting jacket and waited on by his servant who was dressed in a work jacket of striped duck, violet and white. (...) we would pass through a drawing room in which no one ever stopped, where no one ever made a fire, whose walls were ornamented

with gilded moldings, its ceilings painted with a blue that was meant to imitate the sky and its furniture upholstered in satin as at my grandparents', but yellow; then we would go on into what he called his "study," whose walls were hung with some of those engravings depicting, against a dark background, a fleshy pink goddess driving a chariot, standing on a globe, or wearing a star on her forehead, which were admired during the Second Empire because they were felt to have a Pompeiian look about them, (...) And I would stay with my uncle until his valet came to him from the coachman to ask what time the latter should harness up. My uncle would then sink into a deep meditation while his admiring valet, afraid of disturbing him by the slightest movement, waited curiously for the result, which was always identical. At last, after the greatest hesitation, my uncle would unfailingly utter these words: "At quarter past two," which the valet would repeat with surprise, but without disputing them: "At quarter past two? Very good... I'll go and tell him..."[31]

Uncle Adolphe's afternoon ritual records the eternal return of the same response that marks the passage of time during his nephew's visits: the act performed by the uncle and his valet, which repeats itself each time, always the same, and signals the end of the visit on the stage of their daily routine, symbolically serves to prevent possible further unexpected events from taking place in that space – which is precisely the dwelling of the self. The little ritual, both extravagant and fascinating, is not a useless and senile eccentricity, as it actually has the important function of capturing and freezing for a moment the irruption of the unpredictable in the passage of time, with a short dialogue that reduces it to an orderly and compliant flow. In such space, time must repeat itself in an identical way: the same line uttered with curiosity by the incredulous valet, who always seems to be reassuringly surprised, serves to rid the space of the unpredictability of destiny, fastening it to a small part of the same, which is able to repeat itself always in an identical way. In this short conversation, Proust draws a picture of the symbolic and cognitive organisation of uncle Adolphe's entire world; those words are the décor of his soul. Listening to the brief exchange, we catch a glimpse of uncle Adolphe's yearning for the eternal fixity of a gesture; we sense his desire for immortality.

4.   The school of thoughts: brief notes on school violence

When reflecting on processes of socialisation, we tend to emphasise how fundamental they are in the formation of values, beliefs, and lifestyles of future world citizens. Perhaps we tend to overlook or take for granted the area that has to do with how the architecture of our cognitive processes is formed. Where and when is the complex architecture that supports our structures of

18 Architectures of the mind and mindscapes

relevance formed? How and when are the thoughts that will carry us into the adult world shaped? These questions have been the focus of a wide-ranging debate that has involved the cognitive sciences, psychology, pedagogy, and also sociology. Perhaps the latter offers the perspective most able to show and prove that *when we think, we are never alone,* to rephrase a famous comment by Maurice Halbwachs[32] on the process of memory. The stream of thought, in fact, sometimes seems to flow through us like a gentle breeze, sometimes like a real typhoon. But where do we learn to think, shape our thoughts, where do we learn what to think about? It goes without saying that there are a number of crucial transitions from family to school and that, depending on the situation, these overlap in different ways. The following pages offer some thoughts, by way of example, on some of the areas profoundly influenced by school.

A first issue, for example, concerns our conception of knowledge and the ways in which this knowledge is acquired. Even though all generalisations end up presenting a tendency in its most extreme form and never really account for the complexity of different contexts, it is nevertheless worth recalling that the divide between theoretical and practical knowledge should not be taken for granted; simply accepting the fact that it is possible to educate competent and qualified citizens of the world while completely ignoring a range of practical skills and knowledge has a number of significant consequences. As early as primary school, we learn and are taught that there are two types of knowledge – one is first-class while the other is second-class – and that all technical and practical skills always belong to the second category. The extreme consequences of this distorted view are evident in everyday life, every time we meet adults who master ancient Greek but who are not able to fix an electrical appliance, grow a vegetable garden, or sew a pair of trousers, or, on the contrary, whose ability is remarkable in these areas but is lost when they are given a simple literary text. This creates a divide that is neither cognitive nor merely cultural between groups of people who not only possess different types of knowledge and skills but literally *see* the world differently. The splitting of different types of knowledge, the separation between theory and praxis, seems to correspond to a way of marking the world: in one domain there are those who can think, in other those who can do. This condemns our stream of thought to sterility and our stream of actions to meaningless repetition. It is as if we were, from the start, making half-men and half-women, who are incapable of doing one thing or the other, who believe, moreover, that their partiality is a totality. This misleading representation causes more erudite people to believe that practical knowledge is irrelevant, and less erudite people to ignore the fact that what they don't know is indeed important. The split between *knowledge* and *know-how* therefore seems to create two types of hypertrophic beings: beings with a big head but no hands, and beings with big hands but no head. In any case, while this conception has resulted in a significant increase in knowledge because of specialisation, it has also meant the disappearance of a general vision.

Byung-Chul Han[33] also addresses the problem of hands when he writes about "the handless human beings of the future". He is actually referring to the contrast between the subject who operates in the virtual world of information (i.e. using only his fingers on the keyboard) and the subject who experiences by using his or her whole hand. It is, however, interesting that this idea of a symbolic and practical loss of a way of doing things that is connected to a manual and bodily dimension is widespread, even though it is approached from different angles.

Another issue, closely linked to the previous one, concerns the connection between passion and knowledge. In *L'ora di lezione* (Lesson Time) by Massimo Recalcati,[34] this issue is defined in terms of an erotic dimension of teaching. The author effectively grasps a central question: how is it possible that knowledge can be – or even must be – boring? Why is knowledge not related to a joyful and passionate dimension? Is it possible to share and acquire knowledge in motion, a type of knowledge that is not static, but that literally sets our conscience in motion? What are the Lego bricks that should be used during a class? Over the years, first as a student and then as a professor, I have come to believe that the key ingredient is not so much the notions to be conveyed, but the attitude needed to conquer minds. At a time when the number of books available both online and offline is soaring, when the ways and opportunities to access almost unlimited stores and repositories of notions are multiplying, it seems to me that the teacher–learner relationship and the inverse relationship, between learner and teacher, must undergo a radical transformation: this relationship must and can be rethought and should be inspired by an idea of citizenship skills, especially in the case of the humanities (the scientific areas present a very different case). Citizenship skills are taught and learnt thanks to a kind of vivid, vital knowledge,[35] thanks to the shared awareness that education aimed at beauty is the only means to achieve the globalisation of good ideas. Why not imagine a kind of Socratic Oath for all school teachers of all levels, something similar to the Hippocratic Oath, able to stress the importance of the pedagogical relationship?

School violence perpetrated by teachers on learners continues to be a problem, especially in countries where the majority of the schools are public, which means students lack the additional protection they gain as paying clients. Although it concerns a very small minority of teachers, it ends up discrediting the reputation of the whole teaching staff, which is actually generally excellent. Violence is not only psychological; it is also the type we are probably more likely to recognise. Also, the failure to arouse passion and interest for a part of knowledge that is viewed as foundational in a particular school could be considered as a partial form of "neglect". Teachers who systematically fail in the teaching process because of their incapacity

20 Architectures of the mind and mindscapes

and end up conveying the idea that the subject they teach is useless, boring, or incomprehensible are not respecting the pedagogical agreement between them and their students.[36] This causes damage that will affect the lives of pupils for many decades. Especially in primary school, but often also in secondary school, subjects are literally embodied by people: if the science or maths or history teacher fails and causes her or his pupils to feel repulsion rather than fascination, the consequence of this will be a lifelong disaffection with that entire portion of knowledge. In a school system such as the Italian one, which boasts excellent teachers in all grades and types of schools and has produced an important body of work in the field of pedagogy (such as the work of Maria Montessori, to name but one), studied all around the world, we can no longer tolerate a small, inactive minority that betrays a fundamental ecological mission: to be a school of knowledge, of citizenship skills. A family friend, the father of a seven-year-old girl and a sixteen-year-old boy, told me the following story:

After applying for a new job, I moved to another city with my family. We changed schools; we changed everything. With my kids, we went from Trieste to Florence, which for us was a bit like going to another continent. My eldest son began attending a new high school and made new friends; fortunately, everything turned out fine. It seemed to work out. But then she arrived, the horrible art history teacher, the one who was supposed to make him fall in love with Brunelleschi, Leon Battista Alberti, and Michelangelo: well, we are in Florence, so if she couldn't do it, who could? From the start, it was all so terribly boring. She explained insignificant details; she was not able to convey a passion that she herself did not feel. When it was time to test the students, she would ask our son's classmates to recognise an artwork from a tiny detail, as if it were a TV quiz. They had to study the titles of the artworks, the date, commissioner, a whole series of detailed notions that multiplied endlessly, just adding one artist to another. Was this excruciating activity of learning everything by heart really the goal to be achieved? Was there nothing else? Our son was not up for it and challenged her. He accurately analysed the perspective used for the different haloes of the saints painted in a work by Beato Angelico. He basically introduced a creative digression, as, having studied painting, he knew how to distinguish one perspective from another. The teacher, however, did not approve; who knows, perhaps the lesson risked becoming interesting. And so, instead of praising the creativity of a pupil who did not accept to be crushed under this massive number of notions, she had no choice but to accuse him of plagiarism: "Next time", she said annoyed, "you must include the complete list of art history websites you consulted". Dear professor, why did you decide to be a teacher if you have so little admiration for your students?

At some time during our studies, we have all encountered mediocre teachers who, by being strict, were pretending to have competences that were not

Architectures of the mind and mindscapes **21**

there, teachers who were ready to trade the scientific reputation they did not have for the self-esteem of their pupils, which they therefore had to progressively undermine. Subjects that were actually easy and interesting ended up becoming linguistic battlegrounds; exams and class assignments turned into complex quizzes with no solution. I still remember a terrible Italian teacher in a famous Milanese classical high school who literally managed to terrorise her students with intricate quizzes on all the most unlikely details of the *Iliad* and the *Odyssey*. Those texts became hateful, but above all, they remained mute and incapable of conveying anything relevant. Why is it so important for the future lives of these male and female students to remember the names of the children Andromache had after Hector's death? Is this really the ultimate goal we wish to pursue in a high school when we propose reading the extraordinary pages of the *Iliad* and the *Odyssey*?

Thinking back to those years, in which I, like everyone else, sometimes happened to run into one of these teachers, makes me want to propose the institution of a sort of social sanction: in addition to school violence, abuse of attention should also be acknowledged. It's actually not that difficult to spark interest in others and arouse passion for a subject. I remember a young science teacher who never gave up when she noticed her students becoming bored. She was very good at it. When she saw someone getting distracted or struggling to stay concentrated, she used to say with a smile: "Are you bored? What a pity! Come on, maybe you'll like the next topic more. Don't give up!"

I would like to return briefly to the issue of teaching centred on superficial factual notions and the relative aridity of knowledge. It's almost as if we hadn't realised that a silent revolution has been taking place for a few decades now – one that has been taking place in the storehouses of knowledge. In the age of computers and artificial intelligence, it is no longer necessary to remember all the details. No human being can compete with the capabilities and possibilities of a computer in this domain, nor should one attempt this. Why focus on details, on an immense amount of knowledge, when it can be stored effectively by any computer and consulted when needed? The skills that should be acquired in the area of knowledge should, therefore, be others. Artificial intelligence and its progressive employment in our daily lives can free us from what now are pointless tasks, such as mastering all the details of a culture whose ever-increasing dimensions far exceed the mnemonic capacity of any of us. If an ordinary computer becomes a prosthesis of our ability to think and speak, we all become cyborgs capable of mastering cultures of vast dimensions, concentrating all our energies and intentions on the organisation and interpretation of these details. The personal computer has become a friend and an indispensable travel companion that frees us from an obsessive number of notions, enabling us to go back to having original thoughts and being passionate. The terrible Italian teacher, whose name I can unfortunately still remember, was not only incapable of teaching; she had not

22 Architectures of the mind and mindscapes

even realised that over the years the knowledge to be taught and learned had changed, that competing with a computer is a challenge that makes no sense, one that we are bound to lose. It is as if we had decided to continue imparting knowledge that is arranged according to the cognitive schemas of a computer to the younger generation of students and then were surprised by the fact that they failed in this absurd task and continued to perform in less excellent ways than a computer. Knowledge arranged to suit a computer cannot also be suited to the human mind; it is like trying to win a race by running alongside a Ferrari. Knowledge could be organised in a way that enhances our skills so they may dialogue with those of a computer. The extreme attention to isolated notions that characterises some kinds of knowledge is the latest trend in teaching that mistakes the cognitive schemas of artificial intelligence for those of the human mind, condemning young minds to failure and annihilation. As Dawna Markova[37] would say, the most important educational challenge continues to be to understand that "it's not how smart your child is, it's how your child is smart".[38] When knowledge is embodied, when it is literally incorporated by a learner, then we meet our true masters:

> They are the teachers we will never forget, who have left a permanent mark. This is evident if we look at the etymology of the Italian verb *insegnare* (to teach), which means to leave a mark, a sign, in the learner. We will never forget these teachers not only because of what they taught us, because of the content of their speech, but first and foremost because of how they taught us, because of the enigma of their speech that cannot be solved, their charismatic and mysterious power. That is what matters most in the education of a child or of a young person. This does not have to do with the content of knowledge, but with how the love of knowledge is conveyed.[39]

Notes

1 Calasso (2021, p. 14).
2 Epictetus (1890).
3 Verona is a small town in the north of Italy.
4 Von Glasersfeld (1981); Garfinkel (1963, 1967).
5 Spillman (2019).
6 This expression is a reformulation of the famous statement by Maurice Halbwachs (1925): "One never remembers alone".
7 Lingiardi (2017, pp. 7–8).
8 Ibid., p. 25.
9 D'Angelo (2021, pp. 5–8).
10 Ibid.
11 A similar reflection is developed by Lahman (2018).
12 Proust (2003), e-book version.
13 Ibid., p. 362.
14 See also Ahmed (2015).

15 Ibid., p. 373.
16 Ingram (2018, p. 1).
17 Augé (1995).
18 Ingram (2018).
19 Olivetti (2012).
20 Tota (2023).
21 De Matteis (2021, p. 107).
22 Hume (1896).
23 Jedlowski (2020, p. 24).
24 Ibid., pp. 39–40.
25 Tomasi di Lampedusa (1958).
26 In Italian, *casata* (lineage) and *casa* (house).
27 Lingiardi (2017, p. 27).
28 New definitions of space have also been proposed in relation to architecture; see, for example, Norberg-Schulz (1971) and Norberg-Schulz and Norberg-Schulz (1980).
29 Magnusson (2017) and Tatsumi (2017).
30 Magnusson (2017).
31 Proust (2003), e-book version.
32 Halbwachs (1925).
33 Han (2022, p. 10).
34 Recalcati (2014).
35 Tota and De Feo (2022).
36 A pioneering study on this topic is due to Rosenthal and Jacobson (1968).
37 Markova and Powell (1992, p. 1).
38 The intention here is certainly not to deny the importance of exercises such as learning poems and literary texts by heart, which are absolutely fundamental, as they can provide our thoughts and conversations with the rich and necessary vocabulary needed to fully express ourselves. Rather, the intention is to propose a broader reflection on the sterility of certain forms of teaching centred on isolated notions, also criticised by many scholars in the field of pedagogy.
39 Recalcati (2014, p. 104).

In the second chapter, I consider a series of forms of verbal pollution, among which: the enemy within, the obscuring of emotions, external sabotage, the use of nicknames, verbal microaggressions, and techniques for constructing unreality. Secondly, after illustrating some of the sociocultural characteristics of time perception in contemporary society (referring to the work of numerous scholars who have extensively dealt with the topic), I proceed to illustrate some forms of pollution of temporal perception, which include the flooding of the future into the present, the autopilot syndrome, and various forms of domestication of the wild future. In the third part of the chapter, I revisit the concept of the spatialisation of the self to illustrate some possible pathological forms of organisation of domestic space, such as disposophobia and decluttering. These should not be understood as being mere expressions of individual psychological pathologies; indeed, I suggest we consider them as extreme (and certainly pathological) forms of resistance to consumer society and to the fierce marketing of desires the latter promotes. In the fourth part, I introduce the concept of Self-Home (based on Didier Anzieu's Skin-Ego) and argue for its utility and explanatory potential. Finally, in the last part, drawing inspiration from Alejandro Diaz's work Happiness is Expensive, I analyse the compulsive and pathological phenomenon by which we seem to believe that the market is the exclusive place where we may find a possible solution to all our problems and desires, also referring to the concept of "identity badges" proposed by Zygmunt Bauman.

2
FORMS OF SYMBOLIC POLLUTION[1]

1. Speech pollution

The words we listen to during childhood, when our identities are fragile and still being shaped, leave indelible marks on us, both positive and negative. It is almost as if the streams of words we listened to as children form a sort of magical and imperceptible layer that accompanies us for the rest of our lives like invisible armour. In it, we may grow up feeling happy and protected or, on the contrary, trapped and imprisoned, unable to respond, as petrified victims of the repeated violence we have been exposed to. Indeed, we may say that the words we listen to in childhood are our destiny, in the sense that they will inspire and shape both the words we listen to when we become adults and those we learn to speak. Being familiar with something – something that resonates *with*, together – is what solidifies a path, a stream of words and thoughts. It is the habit of joy, happiness, success, and care; or, on the contrary, the habit of verbal violence, invisibility, humiliation, judgement. The problem is our vantage point, the point from which we observe what we experience, which is always inside us. This means that if we are used to being denigrated, treated badly, or humiliated, we will end up thinking that such situations are normal, i.e. we will not classify them as "humiliation" or "abuse". Being familiar with those feelings is what makes them "normal", it is what makes them invisible to the subject experiencing them. Once they become invisible, those conditions – despite being extreme for an external observer – become a sort of steel cage, from which it seems almost impossible to escape. Escape is all the more impossible the tighter the grip of the fierce and unyielding guardian that inhabits us. In other words, we are our worst enemy. And this enemy is inside us. The worst acts of sabotage – the ones that

DOI: 10.4324/9781003484592-2

26 Forms of symbolic pollution

are more likely to succeed – are the ones we plan ourselves. This, however, is a long and silent journey, one that starts in childhood and continues in adulthood.

Everything begins with the words and thoughts of someone else – words and thoughts we listen to – that feed us at an age in which it is impossible to say no. As adults, we find ourselves in the same position of submissiveness and consternation every time we hear someone utter the same sequence of words. If our father spoke toxic and poisonous words, these will be deposited in our subconscious memory, and whenever another adult male utters similar words, we resonate, petrified, assuming the old submissive posture – as if under the influence of a terrifying spell – the one we adopted the first time we heard them. This is how, inadvertently, as adults, we find ourselves in improbable and hilarious situations. The plumber attacks us, and instead of telling him to get lost, politely bringing him down a peg, we feel crushed and endure the verbal violence. The point is that we are not actually dealing with the plumber; we are answering our father once again and for the one hundredth time, as we have been forever frozen in the trauma being repeated by these words. There are parts of us – adult and conscious parts – that we perform in the world, while other parts – childish and traumatised – we do everything we can to ignore. Trauma, however, demands to be listened to; it demands to be looked at and embraced by the rest of our subjectivity. Otherwise, it turns into an unrelenting tyrant, an invisible and undisputable despot that intervenes in all of our interactions. What we must ask is: can I and do I want to be only and exclusively my trauma, or my traumas, for the rest of my life? Can I also be something or someone else? Speaking of this, Stefano De Matteis uses an interesting metaphor that helps understand how the vulnerability that comes with suffering can become the object of a conscious choice:

> This is what the lobster dilemma consists in: to leave one's armour behind, to realise it is temporary, stop using as trenches the certainties that in the present only make us suffer, and expose oneself to risk, having the courage and strength to choose vulnerability. Indeed, vulnerability turns out to be a moment of extreme and fundamental strength. It is a decisive step. Because it brings about change and is the prelude to the reconstruction of a new life.[2]

Also, with regard to the concept of limitation, he adds:

> Limitation is the implicit world available to us, and the explicit possibility we have of overcoming our being finite. Going back to the initial metaphor: the lobster's armour is part of "its" nature, while a limitation is an integral part of "our" cultural nature, it helps us become a human being.[3]

1.1 Daily conversations and strategies of manipulation

In the following pages, I will illustrate a series of examples taken from daily life and literature.[4] With these examples – I hope they are insightful – we will examine some of the possible pathologies that social interaction is exposed to.[5]

a. "The strategy of the mongoose"

"The strategy of the mongoose" is a metaphor that is often used by business consultants to indicate a specific mode of hunting: it refers to predators, such as the mongoose, that camouflage how dangerous they are in order to get as close as possible to their victims and then use this proximity to launch their final and decisive attack. Mongooses are usually very successful predators, and their attack technique is rather sophisticated. It is not surprising, therefore, that in the corporate sphere, this metaphor is widely used to describe the behaviour of colleagues or competing adversaries in economic markets. It is now a question of verifying whether this metaphor can be applied to the broader sphere of everyday life. In fact, as we shall see, there are many "mongooses" around (with all due respect to this highly intelligent animal).

A dear friend – I will call her Giulia – retired after a long career as a lawyer. By then, she was living alone and decided to move to a small town in the Maremma area of the Lazio region. She told me the following story, which, in my opinion, perfectly illustrates the strategy of the mongoose. Debora was a rather beautiful woman who lived with her husband, Alfonso, in the town Giulia moved to. She seemed to be somewhat unhappy because of how marginalised she felt in such a small town. For a long time, she had been employed in odd jobs; she had also worked as a maid in the house where Giulia lived. Meeting Giulia, who was much older, proved to be an important opportunity for social emancipation. Giulia would lend her books from her library; she spoke to her about life in a big city, and Debora seemed to take in everything Giulia and the world she belonged to had to offer. After a while, Debora was able to open a small bar in a village close nearby together with her daughters – this had been the dream of her life. In this period, a close friendship seemed to form between the two women. Also, Debora's husband offered to take care of Giulia's garden. And so he worked as a gardener for a couple of months, charging very little or even refusing to be paid. Giulia insisted on paying for the work or on increasing the hourly wage they had agreed on, but he would smile and say: "You always want to pay…"

One day, out of the blue, both Alfonso and Debora became unreachable. Giulia phoned and sent messages, but no one answered. My friend didn't want to seem pushy and always let at least a month go by before trying again. Many months passed. Finally, one day Debora answered a phone call (from a number unknown to her); it was from one of Giulia's friends, who asked her why she was

28 Forms of symbolic pollution

not answering her phone. Debora made up some trivial excuse. The picture that emerged in the meantime was very different. Debora and Alfonso, far from being real friends, had pretended to be friendly by offering to help Giulia so she would think highly of them. Their sudden disappearance, without reason or explanation, was intended to lure Giulia into a kind of psychological trap: Giulia would have tried to contact her supposed friend and found herself in a kind of strange energy circuit; she would have begged for the other woman's attention. Giulia, however, did not fall into the trap and simply stopped trying to contact them.

b. When I don't want to hear the answer: Adantina's unstoppable monologue

My dear great-aunt Elvira, who kept to herself and liked solitude, spent the last years of her life in a large mansion on Lake Maggiore. She had a trusted maid, a young woman in her forties called Adantina. Adantina came from Romania but had lived in Italy for many years and spoke Italian fluently. In fact, she also spoke Italian at home, with her Romanian husband and their two children, who were still very young. After giving birth to her second child, Adantina gained a lot of weight, so much that she could barely move around while doing housework. All the weight she carried around with her seemed to be a kind of solid armour separating her from the rest of the world, and particularly from her terrible husband, a handsome and greedy man who was only interested in money and in seducing other women – he constantly cheated on his wife. This unhappy marriage made Adantina suffer a lot. Over the years, she had developed a discursive strategy of her own, with which she kept herself company while waxing the floors and polishing the silver in my great-aunt's large house. In fact, since the latter refused to participate in any form of conversation, preferring to read, Adantina had solved the problem by speaking to herself: it was like watching something out an American sitcom. Adantina's solitary conversation went something like this: "Here we go, let's clean the kitchen. Gosh is it filthy…" "Where is the hoover, Mrs Elvira?" She would suddenly ask, hoping that because she needed to find the indispensable appliance, my great-aunt would finally decide to answer. But because my great-aunt Elvira was familiar with the techniques the women used to lure her into conversation, she stubbornly kept silent. After a few minutes of deafening silence, Adantina would suddenly pretend to be surprised seeing the hoover in its usual place – as if she had just found it after an exhausting search, as if, instead of an old hoover, she were seeing an old friend. She would exclaim:

Ah there you are! I found you finally. Where were you? … Now, let's see, what shall we do? Shall we clean the tiles first or the floor? I know, let's do the tiles with the rag, it should be here … where's the rag? The rag?

Changing the subject, she would add: "Who knows if the sky will clear today … it's been so windy for so long". "Is it lunchtime already?" She muttered to herself as soon as she was hungry. "I wonder what tasty food there is for lunch today. Actually, I wonder will we eat at all in this house", she said irritably. The hours went by like this in the large house, with my great-aunt Elvira pretending to read the adventures of Fabrice del Dongo[6] while Adantina pretended to converse with her, in a duel made of dialogue and silence.

On those rare occasions when I happened to witness this incredible monologue, Adantina entertaining herself for hours on end, every minute of every hour of every morning spent in that house, I always wondered what would have happened if somebody had actually answered her. In other words, I wondered whether she ever considered a possible answer, and I always came to the surprising conclusion that no, in fact, Adantina would have been very disappointed if someone had taken the trouble to answer her, because surely the answer would not have been as good as her own. The truth was that Adantina did not talk to herself because no one wanted to talk to her; this may have been true in the beginning (in conversations with her nasty husband), but over time the situation had changed considerably. Adantina spoke to herself because she did not want anyone to give her answers she did not like. With her unstoppable monologue, she had creatively solved the problem by going to the root causes.

c. When the tone of voice makes a difference

My phone rings. I don't recognise the number, but I decide to answer anyway, as if under a sudden spell. And there she is, on the other end: that voice, the malignant tone I can recognise instantly. It's her. I can't believe it; it's a horrible family friend. My paternal grandfather was from a beautiful town in southern Italy, and I inherited this relationship with Esterina directly from him. She is the only person in the world I know whose tone of voice is always unmistakeably judgemental. Practically everything she says is said in this tone. The unlucky interlocutor – unfortunately, in this case, me – knows what to expect: he or she will be scolded, reprimanded, very quickly put in the position of having done something wrong, and will have to feel guilty about this. Esterina is like the main character in a horror story: whatever she says, her conversation is pathological. Her words flow like a raging torrent; they are toxic, even though they seem to be kind: "Good morning, it's Esterina!" And you might say, "Dear author, what's so toxic about that?" The tone is. As she utters these words, she is implying: "I know you haven't recognised me". She calls me while the coronavirus is raging in Italy, more than 4,000 people have died, mainly in Lombardy, where, as far as she knows, I still reside. But instead of asking me how I am, she tells me off for never calling her. I would like to answer: "Perhaps you should ask yourself why", but I'm trapped in my false "politeness", prisoner of the bad thoughts that come from the past, which make me feel I am chained to my tedious good manners. The conversation

30 Forms of symbolic pollution

continues and, as expected, quickly deteriorates. I tell her that I have moved to Rome and am naive enough to tell her that I work at the university. At this point, something astounding happens: Esterina misunderstands me and thinks I am in politics, so she asks me – something that happens in the worst Italian comedy films – to find an employment for her two hopeless children. Seeing how embarrassed I am, she insists: "I'll wait. Find them a job and let me know". I cannot bring myself to be rude. I invent an excuse and hang up.

Esterina is like a lethal weapon in an *Armageddon*, her tone of voice, the way she expresses her thoughts, her every action is aimed at manipulating the other, at taking control, at all costs. Her poisonous liquid is made of gifts, pretend interest, and seemingly good intentions, but her kindness is the bowing head of the demon that permanently inhabits her and turns all the members of her family into potential victims, either to be tamed or to be hurt. According to our dear family friend in this world, there are only friends and enemies: the people she has already succeeded in enslaving are friends, while those who resist strenuously and do not allow themselves to be tamed are enemies. For years, I prudently kept my distance, counting on the more than 1,200 kilometres that separated our houses. If I had a magic wand and knew how to use it, I would turn her into a wise birch, unable to utter a single word. Esterina has taught me that the tone of voice with which one speaks can transform even the kindest words into stones.

d. The art of answering the "real" question

In everyday life, it sometimes happens that we hear questions or overhear parts of a conversation in which a subject states something, intending to say something else. In such a circumstance, to be effective, we must listen with our inner ear, because relying on the mere physical sound of words is not enough.[7] Our inner ear is the curious state of mind that allows us to grasp what is rustling between the lines of a conversation, to go beyond and behind the words of another person and understand their deepest intentions. Exercising this ability to listen becomes the most effective way to avoid the development of pathological communication, which is otherwise inevitable. In fact, the interlocutor – who says A, meaning B – constructs a semantic ambiguity, an interactional contradiction that is enough to initiate a pathological type of conversation. However, sometimes a small miracle takes place: the listener manages to dodge the blow by answering the real question. A good example of this dynamic is a scene in the 2010 film *Loose Cannons*, directed by Ferzan Özpetek. In one of the most important scenes of the film, Tommaso's grandmother (played by Ilaria Occhini) says to her loyal maid, who has just showed her affection: "You're so ugly". Instead of taking offence, the young maid answers: "I love you too, ma'am". It is as if the young maid were able to speak the delicate language the wise but rude lady uses to

Forms of symbolic pollution **31**

express herself. Instead of demonstrating her affection, the woman is only able to say: "You're so ugly". It sounds like the dialogue of two crazy people, while in fact it is a profound dialogue, in which the question and the answer are separated by other parts of a silent conversation taking place between the most intimate feelings of the two women. What we say with words does not always coincide with our feelings, and the notion of lying is not enough to describe these cases. It is not, in fact, a matter of lying but rather of using "bad words".

The art of answering the real question being posed allows us to give a real answer to the person speaking to us and to do so effectively, though, most importantly, it requires an act of empathy and understanding on our part. In other words, it means asking ourselves: "What is her problem? Why is she using such aggressive words?" before answering.

In a very successful play, the Sicilian comedian Teresa Mannino recounts what happens every time she returns to Sicily and is reunited with her family. She tells us, in a funny way, how her various aunts, grandmothers, and cousins react to the fact she is slim, as if there were something to be ashamed of, which is commented on every time they meet. She is constantly told: "Are you eating?" "You must eat something!" "Are you on a diet?" "Why aren't you eating?" "You look unwell" "C'mon, you must eat, eat something!" This is all repeated with a slight Sicilian accent that transforms simple sequences of words into small and precious linguistic–cultural cameos. What is their problem? Why does Teresa's beauty and her being in perfect physical shape cause these reactions? We have all happened to witness this type of conversation between an overweight woman and another younger and thinner woman. What is surprising is that it only takes a few seconds for the woman who is *thinner* to become *too thin*, at which point an endless list of offensive comments follows. Also, in this case, we must ask ourselves: "What is the problem?" How often would we like to answer: "Don't worry, you are already beautiful, as long as you are happy with your size and weight". However, this is actually not possible, because the truth is that our interlocutor, who cannot come to terms with the fact that she is overweight and is therefore asking us to put on weight together with her, would feel hurt – indeed, very hurt. All the same, if we are able to guess what the problem is, the conversation becomes more effective and allows us to respond with a slight smile, the twitch of an eye, which alone is able to reveal a world. The point is that women and men are neither too fat nor too thin. Our weight is exactly what we want it to be; above all, nobody wants their actual and desired weight – which we choose daily when deciding what to eat – to be the subject of conversation, to be judged or evaluated by whoever feels like it. The standard cannot be externalised, it cannot be decided by others. So who should be making this decision? Once again, the conversation is being infiltrated by the malignant

32 Forms of symbolic pollution

adverb, and we should ask: "Too much according to me or you? How dare you? Why don't you keep your 'too much' to yourself?"

e. Small external boycotts and other manipulations

This dynamic can take many forms, but it always translates into our interlocutor rejecting the point of view we are expressing. In practice, we are asked what it is we desire, but if this desire does not conform to that of the other speaker, our desire is annihilated. Moreover, this dynamic is often accompanied by an outright boycott of the project we have just shared with this person.

I am on holiday; I'm staying at Viola's (an invented name) with another dear friend. We are on her beautiful terrace overlooking the sea at Venice Lido. Our hostess is setting the table for lunch and asks us would we like some wine. We answer together: "Thank you, but absolutely no. We want to be able to work in the afternoon". Viola frowns slightly but says nothing. When we sit down, I notice with amazement that not only are there wine glasses next to the water glasses, but that sure enough, Viola has filled them to the brim. My friend and I look at each other with a smile of understanding. During lunch, we don't touch the wine, and as soon as Viola goes into the kitchen, still smiling, we pour it back into the bottle.

A young colleague of mine, who knows I am writing this book, tells me a story.

She has just arrived at her mother's sister's house. She is slightly overweight, and without wanting to go on a proper diet, she has decided to avoid sugar. She has therefore eliminated fruit juices with added sugar and prefers to drink water. During the conversation with her elderly aunt, she tells her about this decision. After about five minutes, her aunt goes into the kitchen and comes back with a glass of fruit juice (obviously containing a huge amount of sugar) poured especially for her. My friend, not wanting to be rude, waits for her aunt to return to the kitchen and uses it to water the geranium next to her, which sincerely thanks her.

The most famous literary boycott is probably the one described by Marcel Proust. It has to do with the way the narrator's great-aunt interferes in the relationship between his grandmother, Bathilde, and his grandfather: his grandmother, wishing to look after her husband's health, has forbidden him to drink spirits, but great-aunt Bathilde, who wants to humiliate her, keeps offering his grandfather some cognac. As soon as she does so, she calls Bathilde back from her walk in the garden, just to witness the woman's desperate and vain attempt to prevent the grandfather from drinking the cognac she has just poured.

When these garden walks of my grandmother's took place after dinner, one thing had the power to make her come inside again: this was (…) if my great-aunt called out to her: "Bathilde! Come and stop your husband from drinking cognac!" To tease her, in fact (she had brought into my father's family so different a mentality that everyone poked fun at her and tormented her), since liqueurs were forbidden to my grandfather, my great-aunt would make him drink a few drops. My poor grandmother would come in, fervently beg her husband not to taste the cognac; he would become angry, drink his mouthful despite her, and my grandmother would go off again, sad, discouraged, (…). This torture which my great-aunt inflicted on her, the spectacle of my grandmother's vain entreaties and of her weakness, defeated in advance, trying uselessly to take the liqueur glass away from my grandfather, were the kinds of things which you later become so accustomed to seeing that you smile as you contemplate them and take the part of the persecutor resolutely and gaily enough to persuade yourself privately that no persecution is involved; at that time they filled me with such horror that I would have liked to hit my great-aunt. But as soon as I heard: "Bathilde, come and stop your husband from drinking cognac!", already a man in my cowardice, I did what we all do, once we are grown up, when confronted with sufferings and injustices: I did not want to see them; I went up to sob at the very top of the house next to the schoolroom (…).[8]

How many Proustian great-aunts and how many grandmothers like Bathilde have we encountered, without ever having the courage to try and answer with a comforting smile?

f. The importance of a name: masks and nicknames

I would like to touch on something I wrote about in *Eco-Words: The Ecology of Conversation*, something I believe is very important, which I have decided to go back to after reading *Ecologia dei media* (Ecology of the Media) by Fausto Colombo, which came out in 2020. In particular, I am interested in the issue he addresses in relation to the dimensions of recognition connected to a name and their relationship with nicknames. In our religious culture, it is the ritual of baptism that permanently secures a subject's name. It seems that the ritual and the attribution of a name are what initiate the process of identity formation of the newborn in its community of reference. In fact, sociology has taught us how subjectivation always involves the process of recognition. Goffman[9] explains this very well in some of his works, as do the exponents of symbolic interactionism. In short, without recognition on the part of others, no self can develop. In fact, subjectivity is not solitary; it is essentially social. Fausto Colombo takes inspiration from the gospels and

34 Forms of symbolic pollution

reminds us that in John (20:14–16), when after the Resurrection May Magdalene meets Jesus without knowing he has risen, it is precisely her name that allows Jesus to reveal himself to her:

> At this, she turned around and saw Jesus standing there, but she did not realise that it was Jesus. He asked her, "Woman, why are you crying? Who is it you are looking for?" Thinking he was the gardener, she said, "Sir, if you have carried him away, tell me where you have put him, and I will get him". Jesus said to her, "Mary". She turned towards him and cried out in Aramaic, "Rabboni!" (which means "Teacher").[10]

In the following passage, Colombo emphasises that by feeling recognised and seen, Mary Magdalene, in turn, becomes capable of recognition. The crucial transition here has to do with the identification process that goes from the more generic "woman" to the name "Mary": in this transition lies the difference between an ordinary member of a class and a specific subjectivity. When saying "Mary", the proper name of the woman who is standing in front of him, Jesus actualises and literally creates – in this space and moment of time, *hic et nunc* (here and now) – the relationship between that woman and himself. It is worthwhile noting that the success of Luca Guadagnino's 2017 film *Call Me by Your Name*, and of the novel it is based on, by the Egyptian writer André Aciman, can no doubt also be explained by the sense of disorientation created by the title with reference to the very foundations on which subjectivity rests: calling another with the name of the person who is speaking is so disorienting it almost interrupts the free flow of our thoughts.

Mutual recognition, in fact, is the founding act of sociality, at least in our cultural tradition. In this sense, it is reasonable to question the use of nicknames: if identity is concealed and recognition is hindered, at least in the ways in which we normally grant and receive it, what happens when we interact in forms that involve masking subjectivity? I am not arguing that using a nickname is itself polluting, simply that it entails a fundamental change in communicative interaction consisting of the depersonalisation of the subject. Perhaps the most appropriate analogy is a masquerade ball: conversing and interacting with others using a nickname and exhibiting social traits that are different from the ones we really possess is a bit like attending a party wearing a mask, which disconnects our behaviour from our "face" – a term that must be treated with the complexity assigned to it by Goffman.[11] When subjects *have no face*, they are freed from the responsibility that goes with individuation, i.e. they can converse and act independently of their biographical history. They can do and say things that do not conform to the image they have constructed for themselves in the course of their biographical journey, and that has been acknowledged over time by significant others who know them. An online nickname and an offline mask worn at a masquerade ball serve, in fact, above all, to modify the way others, who potentially know us, perceive our own self. A nickname and/or a mask therefore liberate subjects from their previous biographical histories, creating a space in which subjectivity is suspended. In such a space, a subject can be free to act and/or use words that would be in stark contrast to the self-perception this person wishes to maintain among significant others. However, this suspension is twofold and operates as a sort of two-faced Janus: if on the one hand it seems to free the subject from habit and open up new opportunities, on the other it renders the person fragile and exposed because now this person is no longer supported by his or her biographical history. While certainly limiting, our history nevertheless protects us. This is why, by depriving us of our name, a nickname also deprives us of the possibility of being recognised: no one can call us by our name; no one can call us "Mary". Suspended in a social realm that is almost a limbo, *we can speak, say things, but cannot actually be anything*. The words we are free to use will never be part of our biographical history. A nickname may even become a dangerous pretext, a way to *spit* anger, pain, and hatred at other people. In other words, a nickname is not itself pathological, just as masks do not induce violent behaviour when they are worn. However, it is fair to say that a nickname can open a breach and foster pathological forms of communication when it is misinterpreted.

Is this not, in fact, part of everyone's daily experience on the web? Does not the expression "keyboard warrior", now part of an acquired vocabulary, refer precisely to the stark discrepancy that we have all on occasion observed between the level of aggression expressed in a face-to-face interaction by a given subject and the escalation of aggressive behaviour that becomes possible for that same subject in an online communication? If the words being uttered can be detached from the biographical history of the subject, if they no longer feed this history, they become empty, they have no weight and carry no consequences for the speaker. No one is obliged to take social responsibility for these words. To put it differently, they are *cowardly words*.

This dynamic must be analysed thoroughly in order to fully understand its functioning: words uttered by a biographical subject feed both the "face" of the person they are addressing and that of the subject saying them. This is a fundamental aspect of all instances of face-to-face interaction. If we take away the "face" of one of the speakers (the one uttering these words) with a nickname, these words become cowardly, as they tend to feed only the face of the one who receives them. I can, therefore, use slandering expressions with impunity, without running the risk of being socially sanctioned the way slandering generally is: having concealed my subjectivity with a nickname, I have severed the link between my slandering behaviour and the possibility of using that behaviour to construct the social identity of slander around my person. As Goffman would say, my career as a slanderer, that is, as a criminal, cannot be initiated by anyone, simply because no one knows

36 Forms of symbolic pollution

who I am. However, there is another possible career that any one of us can pursue against those who take advantage of nicknames: it is the career of a coward, a person with no authority or morality, capable only of being judgemental, who is protected by the anonymity that defies all responsibility and authorship.

g. Pathological invitations

In everyday life and in our professional life, we receive all kinds of invitations. Often, they are not genuine invitations. There are, in fact, at least two types of invitations: (a) positive ones, in which the speaker expects the other person to accept them; (b) pathological or reverse invitations. The latter mostly consist of words expressed out of courtesy or need, with an opposite intention. In this case, the expectation is that the invitation will be refused, but because of how it is formulated, the responsibility for refusing the opportunity being presented falls solely on the person who is supposedly being invited. In the professional sphere, unfortunately, pathological invitations are more frequent than one might think. A colleague of mine who teaches geography at a university in northern Italy, a scholar whose work is of international relevance, told me the following story, a good example of a pathological invitation in an academic context.

In the middle of August, Roberta (an invented name) received an e-mail inviting her to attend a conference in September. We must bear in mind that academic conferences are organised months in advance, and, given the reputation of the colleague in question, it was highly unlikely that with only a few weeks' notice she would be able to attend. Moreover, the e-mail was sent to her during the summer holidays, and clearly the sender was counting on the fact that it would probably take her some days to read it. However, by chance, my friend opened it the following day. Also, the colleague who had delivered the reverse invitation justified the timing, saying that the conference programme had only been confirmed at the end of July, which was clearly only intended to make her manipulative strategy more effective, as the justification was only intended to render the false invitation convincing. This unacceptable proposal, in fact, was accompanied by a poster of the conference listing all the names of the participants, though the e-mail pointed out that it had not been made public yet. On the poster were the names of at least ten other colleagues who had evidently been contacted well in advance and had therefore had plenty of time to confirm their participation. This poster was even more offensive than the e-mail, as it clearly showed that my colleague was the last person to be invited, even though her work on the issues addressed by the conference was internationally recognised. This lousy colleague did not even bother to indicate the session or role my geographer friend might have been interested in. A reverse invitation, in fact, has the sole purpose of placing the exclusive responsibility for a refusal on the person who is apparently being invited. A pathological invitation also aims to convey the message that the person being invited is actually not welcome and will not be welcome in the future. It does this by using the invitation format to convey the exact opposite, which is "you're not welcome!"

h. Obscuring emotions and suspending empathy

Thus the metropolitan type of man-which, of course, exists in a thousand individual variants, develops an organ protecting him against the threatening currents and discrepancies of his external environment which would uproot him. He reacts with his head instead of his heart. In this an increased awareness assumes the psychic prerogative. Metropolitan life, thus, underlies a heightened awareness and a predominance of intelligence in metropolitan man. The reaction to metropolitan phenomena is shifted to that organ which is least sensitive and quite remote from the depth of the personality. Intellectuality is thus seen to preserve subjective life against the overwhelming power of metropolitan life, and intellectuality branches out in many directions and is integrated with numerous discrete phenomena.[12]

As early as the beginning of the last century, Simmel had already understood the correlation between urban contexts and the type of psychic life that would be enhanced by these contexts. Massimo Cerulo[13] turns to Simmel to analyse the relationship between emotions and late modernity, taking his reflections further. Most importantly, he speaks of "a controversial feeling" and proposes reconsidering the concept of "generalised anaesthesia",[14] effectively combining it with Lacroix's[15] reflections: "A bulimia of strong sensations goes together with an anaesthesia of sensitivity. People are very emotional but can no longer actually feel anything".[16] This phenomenon seems to have reached such a level of intensity, it results in the general pollution of all social relations and in a sort of widespread blackout of our perceptive and interpretative capacities. It is worth insisting on this tendency, which has been described on several occasions by numerous scholars[17] and from a plurality of disciplinary perspectives: we are targeted by so many information flows, profoundly challenging and intimately destabilising, we react by drastically reducing our capacity for empathy. In 2022, Barbara Kruger presented the installation *Untitled* at the edition of the Venice art biennale called *The Milk of Dreams*. Visitors were immersed in an environment with huge words written on the walls that read (Figure 2.1):

38 Forms of symbolic pollution

FIGURE 2.1 *"Untitled"* by Barbara Kruger, Venice Art Biennale called *The Milk of Dreams*, 2022.

IN THE BEGINNING THERE WAS CRYING.
PLEASE CRY.
IN THE MIDDLE THERE WAS CONFUSION.
PLEASE CARE.

With this installation, the artist decided to place the visitors in the centre of the room and overwhelm them with these giant messages in an attempt to spark awareness and awaken them from their state of numbness. The effect was immediate. The contrast the installation created between the dimensions we are used to and the ones the artist forced upon us created a sense of cognitive vertigo that shook the audience and prompted reflection.

The intensity and frequency of the horrors we come into contact with on a daily basis produce in us a sort of habit and a sense of repulsion. This is a perfectly understandable psychological defence mechanism, one that is even healthy; however, if these feelings increase disproportionately, they trigger dynamics that are eventually capable of blocking the mechanisms of social production of trust and solidarity, which means the potential erosion of the very fabric of civil society. The fact that our connection with the Other is systematically severed, empathic expression suspended, means that in the long run, our capacity to think and feel is undermined, our ability to connect with others annihilated, and our self-displaced. When we are no longer able to feel compassion, that is, when we are no longer able to feel anything with the Other, we begin to drift, no longer grounded in the social and moral fabric whose weft connects us to one another. When these threads are broken – which might mistakenly seem like an act of protection and defence – our identity begins to crumble. If we stop feeling sorry, if we stop caring for others, we are giving up an essential and constitutive part of our humanity – the one that more than any other is worth preserving. The progressive oblivion of empathy, its weakening in individual and collective consciousness is an irreparable loss, one we cannot afford. It is a silent, insidious form of symbolic pollution affecting relationships, one we must resolutely guard ourselves against. In this perspective, the crimes of fraud, extortion, and intentional harm, especially when they take advantage of people's good faith, are extremely serious because they undermine both the victim's and the witnesses' ability to trust. Taking advantage of people's good faith means trampling on the right of people to be naive, to trust and rely on others. When this right is denied and the community, made up of direct witnesses or people who have heard about the crime, reacts with complacency and complicity rather than aversion and social repugnance, a culture of indifference, oppression, and injustice spreads and permanently pollutes the social fabric of our relationships.

1.2 Techniques for constructing unreality and verbal microaggressions

As Watzlawick[18] points out, there are numerous techniques for constructing unreality, and some are particularly effective in producing a cascading effect and finally a very strong disapproval of the "targeted" subject. During a qualitative study of pathological relationships between therapists and patients that I was involved in some years ago, one of the patients interviewed told me the following story:

I had been in therapy for over a year (I later discovered that my therapist was not qualified for the job). This therapy was "totalising" and the therapist acted as if he wanted to teach me how to live. I was an established architect

40 Forms of symbolic pollution

and had worked for a successful firm for many years. I was going through a very difficult period of my life due to the illness and then premature death of my husband, and I had turned to this therapist for psychological support. He had been suggested to me by his wife, who was a client of my firm. However, the effects of this therapy soon proved to be devastating. Instead of helping me work through my traumas, this therapist used our sessions, which became more and more frequent, to extract professional and personal information from me, which he then used against me and my family members to extort money from us. One of the manipulative techniques he systematically used was to "complicate simple matters". When I told him I had to make a simple phone call to a worker on a construction site, he gave me countless recommendations, as if I were facing the most difficult test of my career: "Make sure you stay centred. Breathe, relax, don't be afraid, don't become anxious". I listened to him in amazement, I could not understand why I had to take all these complicated precautions and follow these instructions to perform simple and routine tasks. In time, I began to realise that listening to such absurd and inappropriate instructions was undermining everything I was intimately confident about. I began to wonder whether I should actually follow his advice, until I eventually ended up thanking him for his way of taking care of me. In fact, this alleged therapist was using a number of techniques for constructing unreality: he constructed for me problems and obstacles that did not exist only to target my self-esteem and demonstrate his infallible ability to solve imaginary problems of his own making. The side effect was that I became more and more dependent on him.

This is an extreme case, but there are many examples of verbal microaggression[19] that occur almost invisibly in daily life and have to do with ethnic issues or sexual discrimination. As Wing Sue and Spanierman point out, these microaggressions can have devastating long-term effects. They often intersect with both the techniques of constructing unreality already mentioned and with various techniques of victim blaming, as the following example shows.

I am sitting in a café in the centre of Rome when I overhear the following conversation between a woman and, presumably, her partner, who are sitting at the table next to mine. The young woman is telling her partner, who is much older, about something unpleasant that happened at work. Her boss questioned her competence and put her in a bad light in front of some colleagues who are particularly hostile towards her. She seems to be shaken by this event and fears that something similar may happen again in the near future. Her partner seems to be understanding and affectionate, but then suddenly he says: "Of course, you poor thing, it had to be you!" This short sequence of words is like a shot in the ear, I turn around, risking to seem rude, to see the effect on the young woman's face: her lips twitch, and the expression on her face changes almost unnoticeably. I hear her voice fading as the conversation goes on; she

Forms of symbolic pollution **41**

is still complaining but is less determined. The mild poison that has been given to her at the most appropriate moment seems to make its way through her person, affecting the way she perceives herself: it is slowly starting to work. I can almost hear the sound of her thoughts as they come to her: "What if it were true... Does everything always happen to me? Is there really something wrong with me? Something that inevitably turns me into a kind of intended victim?" The older partner notices my inquiring gaze and probably also the poorly concealed anxiety it betrays; he looks at me. He seems complicit, as if he were expecting me to become an ally, as an older woman, as if I were capable of seeking some sort of unreasonable and merciless revenge against this woman in her prime, much younger and more beautiful than me. But I stare into space; my gaze is cold and distant. I offer him no possible form of alliance.

1.3   Ethnography of a polluting mind: the "enemy within"

There are many techniques of self-sabotage. Self-sabotage techniques are definitely the most effective because we do everything ourselves: when we are the targets we can be as fierce as we want, there is nothing stopping us.

A few years ago, I decided to take up martial arts. I was already in my fifties, so it was not a decision to be taken lightly. Nevertheless, I was passionate about it and very determined. Due to a series of circumstances, I found myself in a school with a family of masters; they were all Japanese and spoke very little Italian. They trained me almost in spite of myself in the ancient arts of karate. I soon began to perform kicks and pirouettes, katas with fantastic and unpronounceable names, with a group of students, almost all Japanese, who performed these complex katas with the ease of true samurai. Months and years went by, and one exam after another, I came close to obtaining my brown belt. Karate has taught me a lot: I have learned to move my arms and feet in spaces around my body that I did not know were accessible to me, to move and breathe synchronously, to sense the intentions of my opponent during a fight as if it were a dance, and understand that strength is never rigid but the effect of fluid hardness, that the trajectory of a punch is essential to determine how effective it will be, that balance depends on the mind and on the heart, in short, it has taught me a lot about myself. One of the most interesting discoveries, however, is how to deal with "the enemy within". In fact, I soon realised that the limitations I experienced in physical movement were closely related to the limitations my mind set for me. When the teacher showed us a new movement to perform, a mass of sentences would crowd my mind: "I'll never make it", "if I kick a pirouette like that I'll get stuck in mid-air, I'll never hit my opponent", and so on. In short, it was all about confronting my age and society's expectations regarding the movements and trajectories appropriate for a body that age. But appropriate for whom? The thoughts crowding my mind were *social, not individual*. In other

42 Forms of symbolic pollution

words, I was not thinking, for instance, that I had a particular pain in a particular part of my body and that this particular kata might therefore be impossible for me. The thoughts crowding my mind could have been thought by someone else (in the sense that they were social, not personal thoughts), because they concerned a hypothetical anyone, to whom I had to conform regardless of my specific psychological and physical abilities, but simply because I belonged to the 50-year-old age group. "Who was it that was doing this thinking?" Exactly who was it? I decided to call him "the enemy within", for he was not at all likeable, let alone cooperative. I soon realised he was very similar to a jinx, and that the quieter he was, the happier I was.

Unfortunately, the *enemy within* is someone we all know. It is the shrill little voice that in the middle of a very stressful performance wakes up and encourages us by saying: "You're never going to make it", or afterwards, "I told you you were never going to make it..." In short, it is the friend we would all prefer never to have met. So what should we do? How should we speak to and disempower the enemy within? There is no one way; above all, there are no indications that apply to everyone. Each of us must find our own way. Let's say that laughing about it can be an effective remedy, and if this does not work, at least we have laughed. Moreover, the enemy within can also have a positive function, sometimes reminding us that we have got ourselves into a situation that is beyond our reach and that a dignified U-turn may be the best solution. In short, sometimes it might even turn out to be a nice nuisance. Though, who knows why, as a woman, I invariably imagine that my internal enemy has a male voice... ☺

2. Pathological forms of time perception

> We do not inherit the earth from our ancestors,
> we borrow it from our children.
>
> *Native American proverb*

The human condition in late modernity has been the focus of numerous theoretical reflections that have emphasised how in this epoch temporality has acquired a specific form.[20] As early as 1989, for example, Harvey noted that the contemporary condition is characterised by a disproportionate and increasing temporal acceleration, which even then seemed to imply the distinct loss of a sense of future. In 1970, an important book by Toffler was published titled *Future Shock*. In the reflections by these scholars, the present seems to evaporate as it seems to be tragically compromised and relegated to some near past, at the very moment it is being experienced. According to Bauman,[21] we all inhabit a liquid world in which liquefied materiality corresponds to the increasing fluidity of all relationships, which also affects the way we experience them. Even spatio-temporal categories seem to become liquid; time seems to move so fast it exceeds the human capacity to grasp it: "Speed, not duration, matters. With the right speed, one can consume the whole of eternity inside the continuous present of earthly life".[22] But where else does this speed come from, if not from the comparison between real and virtual, online and offline? Also, it is worth making a small digression in order to recall that depending on the name we decide to give this dichotomy, very different scenarios and arguments emerge, which may even separate different generations of citizens. What I mean is that for those born in the 1990s and after, the distinction between real and virtual seems less relevant than the one between online and offline, because the latter better describes everyday experience. It is only us – I would say the over-fifties – who feel nostalgic about the opposition between real and virtual: we inhabit the Web, adapting to it unwillingly, pretending to be enthusiastic and navigating with great ability, often disoriented – like dinosaurs stranded in the Po Valley – and often asking our smiling and merciless children and/or grandchildren to solve the problems we have once again gotten ourselves into using the computer.

But let us go back to what are supposedly the causes, or at least the contributing causes, of this reckless speed. They must certainly have to do with common experiences, or at least with experiences we have witnessed in the media. Two types of mediated or direct experience come to mind, though there must be many other examples: the speed of rockets travelling through space, and the closer, more familiar speed of our personal computers.

Our personal computer is a sort of "brilliant friend" we welcomed into our homes and slowly contributed to transforming into a monstrous and tyrannical being, as we absurdly and masochistically continue to measure ourselves against its performance. It almost seems like subjects inhabiting contemporaneity (at least in the Western world) perceive as a looming and external threat the temporal flow of the machine *par excellence*, the man-god created in the image and likeness of his own mind – the computer. Indeed, the creature has ended up overshadowing its creator: a computer seems to be so much faster than the human mind that it ends up exerting a discomforting fascination, basically leading us to forget that it is nothing other than a machine, whose functional and performative characteristics can in no way be treated as a benchmark for human performance. This has an undesired and unforeseen consequence, one that backfires when we become subjugated by this speed, now an unrealistic model that imposes an external tyranny, which turns into a standard with which to measure all present and future cognitive activities. If contemporary temporality is a sort of unassailable immediacy, which seems to devour and cannibalise all other possible present durations, this is probably because we erroneously compare the temporality of our thoughts with what seems to be the computer's temporality, and in this comparison we are bound to get lost. The speed we have created turns into an external yardstick, one that is tyrannical and cruel, that no human

44 Forms of symbolic pollution

mind is able to compete with. Unless we start practising a form of ecological thinking. In fact, we must learn how to think *our* own thoughts again, and remember that *thinking slowly* can be a quality, as Franco Cassano argues:

> Slow thinking will provide shelter for the refugees of fast thinking when machines begin to shake more and more and knowledge will no longer be able to calm the shaking. Slow thinking is the most ancient seismic construction. Starting from now, we must walk, think by foot, slowly observe the houses, understand that when they become crowded they become vulgar, and wish for the sea behind them to become visible again. We must contemplate the measure which can only be conceived by walking (...).[23]

It is as if, after inventing high-speed trains, we had suddenly decided that everyone had to try and run at the same or at least similar speed: is this not absurd? We have to imagine a group of desperate little people trying to run as fast as a high-speed train. Why is it that, in many ways and in many different contexts, we let the speed of a computer become the standard against which we measure the pace at which we process social experience?

At present, it seems that one of the most difficult daily tasks for everyone is to keep our mind in the same temporality our body is in. The connection between our thoughts, the speed of which is constantly and mistakenly measured against the virtual world, and the body thinking such thoughts has been severed. The mind–body dualism seems to have reached its peak. The point is that in order to experience such a speed we are obliged to lose our body, or at least to partly suspend its functioning. In fact, if we want to travel at a speed of 600 kilometres per hour, we must sit, not walk. Let me be clear: this is not a Luddite argument against the use of machines. We are all happily cyborgs.[24] The point is that by only sitting, by transforming ourselves into cyborgs, we extend the experience of this split between body and mind, of losing our body, into the rest of our daily lives, when we could be present in our body and with our body. The point is that we are all cyborgs, as Donna Haraway understood many years ago. If we try putting down our mobile phones, half of our daily tasks will seem impossible. One wonders: how did we live before smartphones became so widespread? Many of us have spent at least half of our lives without using a mobile phone, so we know it is possible and even enjoyable. Yet, the individual and collective memory of such a social experience seems to have been damaged; it seems to have crumbled. Even my own generation seems to have forgotten how to live without a smartphone. Does this have to do with nostalgia? Absolutely not. In fact, we get on very well with smartphones. What must be decided in a contemporary world in which we already are cyborgs, whether we like it or not, is: do we want to become hybridised with technology *happily* or *unhappily*?

Forms of symbolic pollution **45**

These brief comments, also inspired by the work of some scholars, can help us put together a picture of the cultural and social conditions that overall characterise the perception of time in our contemporary world and allow us to examine some of the specific forms of pathological time perception we experience daily.

2.1 When the past is present

This pathological form of time perception is something we are all acquainted with, in the sense that each of us has, at least once, dealt with and perseveringly nurtured a part of our past that is highly traumatic and toxic. For years, we have watered and fed it inside of us with loving care, hoping it would produce its seasonal poisonous fruits – sadness, depression, anxiety, insomnia, despair, insecurity, low self-esteem, and every other possible form of suffering. It is similar to what happens in *Sleeping Beauty*: something occurs that exceeds our emotional and cognitive capabilities. Our system responds with defensive mechanisms that freeze the event and everything around it. Time and space around it are suspended while we wait for a day in the future to arrive, the day we will have the strength and resources necessary to process the trauma (this is when Prince Charming arrives and manages to cut through the bramble bush and save the beautiful princess). It is worth noting that in the fairy tale, it is a kiss that saves the princess and unfreezes the castle and the surrounding forest, bringing everyone back to life. An act of love is needed to heat the ice that froze the traumatic moment in time and space, turning it into marble. In the fairy tale, trauma is symbolised by the witch's curse. The enchanted castle lies in a spatial elsewhere (inaccessible to all except the hero because of the thick, horny vegetation hiding it from view) and in a non-time (linear time is suspended here; everyone is frozen in the action they were performing when the spell was cast). In fact, the time and space of trauma are suspended and placed in an elsewhere governed by different cosmic laws. I have already argued[25] that this fairy tale can be interpreted as a metaphorical representation of the functioning of the unconscious, whose life is fundamentally regulated by the emotional flows of an individual. However, these flows seem timeless, capable of surviving intact for entire decades. In other words, there are past traumas that remain firmly fixed in the present, stubbornly intertwined with it, unwilling to leave, forming a *living past* inside us. Since they are not linguistically, discursively, and emotionally processed by the traumatised subject, they remain there, invisible and cumbersome, like enormous boulders preventing the present from unfolding. The present cannot unravel; it is entangled on all sides, caught on the hook that has become rusty over time, which nonetheless is strong enough to hold the entire scroll of our existence together. We cannot move forward; something hinders the course of events, forcing it to play what we may call the game of

46 Forms of symbolic pollution

eternal recurrence. We will go back to the notion of sustainability of trauma and the importance of practising an ecology of the past in the following chapters. However, I would like to anticipate a reflection here:

> Memories are understood to occupy a meaningful distance (although spatial and temporal distances vary materially and symbolically) from actual events that have, essentially, ended. This distance can come in several forms: temporal, spatial, cognitive, emotional, and experiential. But while memory studies often articulates the ways that, for example, event-precipitated trauma can continue, the event itself is over.[26]

Yet, we may add, the event persists and feeds on every subsequent representation and/or narrative. Therefore, trauma is not solely constituted by the event that produced it; it is elastically shaped by all the narratives and/or representations working together that we have constructed around it.[27] This is, in essence, the fundamental aspect of the theory of the restlessness of events developed in 2010 by Robin Wagner-Pacifici and subsequently combined with quantum theory.[28] In an essay written some years ago,[29] I argued that by applying the theory of the restlessness of events and that of quanta to the concept of bodily memory, we can better understand how trauma continues to live in our subjectivity. The crucial point is that trauma is alive; it is vital. If the past floods into the present, there is a vital force that persists precisely in this act of flooding. Subjected to denial, kept beneath the surface, rendered invisible, and withdrawn from the dimension of words, this past feeds itself; it becomes stronger and lives a life of its own, independent of the subject, similar to a cyst growing uncontrollably under the skin, detached and beyond the control of the ego. By denying the possibility of naming it or by removing trauma from the verbal dimension, the subject simultaneously denies the possibility of coming into contact with it or of entering into dialogue with this part of himself or herself, which is therefore relegated to the subconscious, which is like the basement of a house. This is evident if we look at the research of many psychotherapists. Gerard Fromm,[30] for instance, emphasised how trauma seems to fall "outside of social discourse", thereby posing a problem of transmissibility in family memory between one generation and the next. In the aphorism 341 in *The Gay Science*, the impression is that the nature of the demon mentioned by Nietzsche is precisely that of the cyclicity of the temporality of trauma:

> What if some day or night a demon were to steal into your loneliest loneliness and say to you: "This life as you now live it and have lived it you will have to live once again and innumerable times again; and there will be nothing new in it, but every pain and every joy and every thought and sigh and everything unspeakably small or great in your life must return to

you, all in the same succession and sequence – even this spider and this moonlight between the trees, and even this moment and I myself. The eternal hourglass of existence is turned over again and again, and you with it, speck of dust!" Would you not throw yourself down and gnash your teeth and curse the demon who spoke thus? Or have you once experienced a tremendous moment when you would have answered him: "You are a god, and never have I heard anything more divine". If this thought gained power over you, as you are it would transform and possibly crush you; the question in each and every thing, "Do you want this again and innumerable times again?" would lie on your actions as the heaviest weight! Or how well disposed would you have to become to yourself and to life *to long for nothing more fervently* than for this ultimate eternal confirmation and seal?[31]

Nietzsche's conception, inspired by Stoic philosophy, removes human condition from linear time and throws it into the abyss of the eternal recurrence of cyclical time. However, if we were to make use of Nietzsche's thinking and ground it in a pragmatics of everyday life, we might perhaps adapt it to our own purposes (hoping Nietzsche will not take offence) and consider that this conception of time describes one part of temporal experience in particular: precisely that of traumatic time. There is a film ingrained in the cinematic imagination of many of us that, perhaps more than others, stages the tragic cyclicity of traumatic time: *Memento* (2000), written and directed by Christopher Nolan and inspired by a story by his brother Jonathan Nolan, *Memento Mori*. The protagonist, Leonard Shelby, suffers from a mnemonic disorder called "anterograde amnesia", caused by a dramatic event, and is condemned to be unable to remember anything that happens to him for more than 15 minutes. This disorder, which he tries to deal with by writing notes for himself and leaving them everywhere (also on his skin), causes him to cyclically relive events he has already experienced, imprisoning him inside a kind of circular traumatic plot. In short, a real biographical nightmare, in which the subject seems to live his existence trapped in a sort of infinite game of Snakes and Ladders, in which, at the end of each sequence of moves, the player must return to the starting square.

2.2 The time machine: what if the future floods the present?

One of the most common pathological forms of time perception involves the future flooding the present every time we get caught in a vicious mental script. I am quite certain that as soon as I describe one, you will all start thinking, "Oh, yes, that often happens to me…"

Usually, these mental scripts start suddenly, at a moment when we are not fully aware. In fact, generally, we cannot remember the moment in detail.

48 Forms of symbolic pollution

The mental exercise consists of imagining a little devil that starts these mental scripts for us and inside us. Very often, when we wake up, we have the strange feeling that the crowd of strange thoughts, so vivid they seemed highly plausible, came from somewhere outside of us. It leaves a strange aftertaste, and waking up, we begin to regain control of our mind, which seemed to have been on autopilot throughout the duration of the mental script. We will call this pathological form of time perception exactly that: *the autopilot syndrome*. How exactly does it work? It can happen at any moment when we are awake, often before falling asleep or when waking up, or in a moment of distraction. There needs to be a moment when we are not fully vigilant, that is when, as if by magic, the film starts and we find ourselves watching the story of our lives on an imaginary mega-screen. Below are some mental scripts recounted to me by some acquaintances and friends who agreed to share with me – for a scientific cause – some sequences of these mental visions. Usually, it is factual reality that offers the starting point.

Andrea is terrified of insects. He owns a beautiful house in the Tuscan countryside. He tells me about a particular fear he often fantasises about. Here is the sequence of mental images he sees going by in his mind when he is awake: I am in the bedroom. I am about to go to sleep when suddenly I see a huge, hairy black spider on the wall. As soon as it realises it is being watched (instead of wisely running away like its spider friends usually do), it jumps onto me and bites me. I feel a sharp pain in my shoulder and collapse onto the bed. I scream my partner's name, but she's watching TV, and the volume is loud, she can't hear me. Meanwhile, I realise the spider is poisonous; everything becomes blurred, and I lose consciousness. When I wake up, I'm in hospital, in very bad conditions.

Erika is German; she lives and works in Milan and is always late. This defect is a problem, because in Milan, punctuality is a social value. Sometimes, when she has an important appointment, the following mental script starts in her mind: I have to get up at 7:30, but the alarm doesn't go off. At 8, I realise I'm late, so I try to leave the house as quickly as I can, but while drinking my coffee, ready to go, I stain my white shirt. When I open the wardrobe to look for a shirt the same colour I realise all my shirts are either dirty or need ironing. Since I don't have time to iron a shirt, I have to change the other clothes I'm wearing, and suddenly I have no idea what to wear. The only outfit suitable for the meeting seems to be the one I had chosen. I begin to panic. In the end, I find another dress and arrive at my appointment half an hour late. I am reprimanded by all my colleagues.

We could go on like this indefinitely: some people have a flat tire, others cannot remember the speech they have to deliver, and others cook the wrong dish even though they are Michelin-starred chefs. In short, there are infinite mental scripts. There is no need to continue with the list; by now, it should be enough for each one of us to think about the ones we are familiar with.

Forms of symbolic pollution **49**

We could say that mental scripts are a way of dealing with our fears, of staging them so as to be able to watch them and try to control them. Or we could say that they are just a way to become even more terrified. Or we could simply decide that when they start, we should try and be ourselves again and, using the imaginary remote control that changes the channels of our mental screen, decide to look for a program we truly enjoy.

What all possible variants of *the autopilot syndrome* have in common is a pathological form of time perception: we seem to suddenly become engulfed in our own mind, literally immobilised in front of a mega-screen looming over us, and for a handful of seconds we have this very strong feeling of not being able to escape. When I was little, my mother always read fairy tales to me from a book called *The Swing of the Stars*. I remember one of these stories very well; it was about a journey to the land of dreams, from where wonderful and horrible dreams were sent to the children around the world. Mental scripts generated by the autopilot syndrome are like bad dreams – very bad dreams – only they are usually very short, very vivid, and take place in a state of wakefulness. It is a particular state of wakefulness: we are awake but absent, caught in a plot that engulfs us and seems to come from outside. When the future invades the present and terrifies us with more or less terrorising scenes, we are sort of unconsciously aware. Our mind seems to be militarily occupied by alien images, fantasies, sounds, and words, which anticipate events that have not yet happened and probably never will. The predominant emotion provoked by this pathological way of perceiving time is anxiety. In a book written in 1995, the psychologist Lisa Capps and the ethnolinguist Elinor Ochs analysed the ways in which panic is constructed (the main emotion provoked by these mental scripts), and showed that panic is the result of a process that detaches us from the world: suddenly, we are alone with our thoughts, disconnected from common sense, uprooted and isolated from everything. All the possible future effects of something that is not actually present begin to invade, and this invasion arrives from the future into the present, literally paralysing the subject who is placed at the centre of the script, trapped in the plot like the prey of a spider caught in a thick web, one that paralyses and prevents all movement. As soon as there is a glimmer, a crack able to reconnect the mind to the present, an opening forms in the web, and the script begins to fade, to vanish as if by magic. Significantly, Meg, who is the patient suffering from anxiety attacks quoted by the two authors, says:

> Sometimes I get to the end of the day and I feel exhausted by all the "what if this happened" and "what if that happens." And then I realise I spent the entire day on the couch – that it's just me and my own thoughts driving me crazy.[32]

50 Forms of symbolic pollution

2.3   *Domesticating the wild future: black swans and other unresolved issues*

In a book published in 2007, Nassim Nicholas Taleb revolutionised the international language of prediction using the metaphor of the "black swan". As we shall see, this metaphor is of fundamental importance to further develop our argument. In this book, Taleb emphasises the importance of studying rare events and considers uncertainty as the fundamental disrupting element in the analysis of all types of phenomena:

> This may seem like a strong statement – that we need to principally study the rare and extreme events in order to figure out common ones – but I will make myself clear as follows. There are two possible ways to approach phenomena. The first is to rule out the extraordinary and focus on the "normal". The examiner leaves aside "outliers" and studies ordinary cases. The second approach is to consider that in order to understand a phenomenon, one needs first to consider the extremes – particularly if, like the Black Swan, they carry an extraordinary cumulative effect. (...) Almost everything in social life is produced by rare but consequential shocks and jumps; all the while almost everything studied about social life focuses on the "normal," particularly with "bell curve" methods of inference that tell you close to nothing. Why? Because the bell curve ignores large deviations, cannot handle them, yet makes us confident that we have tamed uncertainty.[33]

A "black swan" is therefore a rare and unpredictable event capable of disrupting all our plans and altering the course of events in ways entirely unforeseen and unimaginable (e.g., the social and economic consequences of the COVID-19 pandemic). The black swan is a symbol of our anxiety about the future, as it embodies uncertainty, the fallacy of all possible predictive mechanisms. One of the fundamental problems that human nature must confront, in fact, is anxiety about the future, the fear of what is to come, and the consequent desire to foresee, to know in advance what will happen, even if only in a vague and undefined way. The attempt to read ahead, to foresee the future, can take multiple directions. Without intending to provide an exhaustive list but aiming to offer only a few examples, I will highlight some below. A very common way of *taming the future* is to take refuge in probability theory. The calculation of probabilities, in fact, makes it possible to anticipate how likely the occurrence of a given event is and even estimate the margin of error of this likelihood. In other words, it is possible to predict how likely an event is compared to another with a certain degree of accuracy. However, in a 2021 book, *Zero Virgola Io* (which means "zero point me"), Luca Pietromarchi recounts his experience as a COVID-19 patient and notes how little statistical calculation was relevant when the event in question (illness) became part of his personal experience. Probability theory is very effective when applied in conjunction to the law of large numbers, but when it is referred to as personal experience, it loses significance. In other words, knowing that the probability a person has of dying in a plane crash is one in ten million is of little help if I am sitting on a plane that is about to crash, and this observation is in line with what Taleb says when commenting on the behaviour of the bell curve.

Another way of domesticating the future involves identifying macro-trends, lines of development that provide insights into the formation of certain unfolding trends without necessarily grasping the specific details of this formation. In simpler terms, when we are unable to foresee the exact future, it is enough to understand its main trends, accepting that it is not possible to know the details. This approach has a number of variants; for instance, some more or less esoteric perspectives stress that these trends are traces of energy that can be identified in family memories and stories. Alternatively, this trend is a historical cycle linking one life to a younger one, creating a sequence of connections which, although invisible to the human eye, may be grasped by the superhuman gaze of someone capable of seeing better than others.

Myth provides us with one of the most tragic and intense examples of such figure: Cassandra, the daughter of King Priam and Hecuba, who receives the gift of prophecy from the god Apollo. He promises to teach her to see the future in exchange for her love. She initially agrees, but after receiving this gift, she refuses Apollo. In retaliation, the god condemns her to never be believed. Cassandra thus represents the tragic condition of a seer who is not able to communicate to others what she foresees. Her story is a tragic one, as she represents the inability to communicate. Indeed, she is a silenced seer, a half-goddess who is rejected by the gods and misunderstood by humans. Cassandra has inspired generations of scholars and writers. Among them, I would like to mention Christa Wolf, who thought of Cassandra as one of the first female figures reduced to being treated as an object. She appears to us as a woman who knows the mysteries of the universe to the point of mastering the art of prophecy. Her wisdom, however, provokes the envy of both divine and human men. In Christa Wolf's book,[34] Cassandra becomes a feminist *avant la lettre*, and her story is told by patriarchal myth, which literally tears her to shreds.

The fact is that any strategy aimed at restricting and controlling the swinging of the metaphorical pendulum that represents our life trajectory is likely to be mostly ineffective. Taleb's black swan perfectly embodies the unforeseen and unpredictable event that crushes us and is impossible to avoid. In my view, it is not about discovering a more effective strategy to control events – one that finally works. Rather, it is about acknowledging how impossible and inadequate this way of thinking is, one grounded in a set of individual, collective, and social expectations. To a certain degree, being part of

52 Forms of symbolic pollution

a social community implies the belief in a shared and guaranteed set of social expectations that individuals may rely on. While this constitutes a common foundation of sociality, which fosters a sense of belonging to a community that shares certain values, beliefs, and lifestyles, it is crucial to be aware of the fact that this is merely a social agreement, not an ontological certainty. And that adherence to the social pact, which entails a series of duties, also entails a series of rights and protections. The point is that this pact is grounded in a fragile social convention that must be continually upheld and reproduced. In essence, beyond the expectations that individuals belonging to a social community legitimately form, it is generally more prudent to learn how to keep one's balance while surfing the waves. It is a bit like surfing or windsurfing, in fact, to use a sports metaphor: one must learn how to fall and get back up again, knowing that before long another wave will knock us down.

There is a force, an inner confidence, that may come from God, the universe, oneself, reason, or any other element, depending on our personal beliefs and values. Without this force, without the support of this type of confidence in life, individuals find themselves in the grip of despair. The fluid and unpredictable trajectory of life, at times fierce in its course, becomes untenable. In contemporary times, the process of disenchantment of the world (already observed by Max Weber)[35] and the progressive rationalisation of knowledge have significantly eroded the set of shared belief that supported individuals throughout their life and helped them manage the anxiety that comes with being able to represent the future. Several years ago, Alberto Melucci[36] wrote a book with a subtitle that read *Il futuro è adesso* (The Future Is Now). Its message was multifaceted: on the one hand, it invited readers not to postpone choices and desires that could be realised here and now; on the other, it encouraged them to recognise that one's posture in the present can determine one's future trajectory. An ecological proposal may involve surrender – an active, vigilant, aware kind of surrender. Surrendering to life, in fact, far from being a negative approach, can become a way to stop swimming against the current. It means accepting that the path we identify as preferable for ourselves, for others, or even for an entire institution, may not necessarily be the best one. We might be wrong. This is an issue I have already addressed in *Eco-Words*, but it presents itself here with the same urgency, as it is one of the most crucial aspects of our entire existence. It intersects our daily lives, forcing us to make and unmake plans and projects, entering, like a little devil, our tidy, festively adorned rooms and causing great havoc. The only thing we can do, when we see the little devil approach, is decide whether we want to despair or accept it and deal with it. Our grandmothers wisely suggested "making a virtue of necessity", and grandmothers, as we know, are always right. Is there reason in the universe? Is there a divine plan supporting us? Indeed, when we see the horrors of war, forced migration, and the torture inflicted on migrants, when we witness children's tears and contemplate all the evil of living, we entertain doubts about the adequacy or even the existence of this divine plan. The Italian poet Montale conveys the evil of living when he writes:

> I have often met the evil of living: |the gurgle of the strangled brook, |the papering of the parched leaf | the fallen horse, dying. |Of good I found little more than the omen |disclosed by the divine indifference: |the statue in the drowsing, | noon, and the cloud, and the hawk soaring.[37]

Borrowing Montale's words to further evoke a series of reflections, we may say that the solid and quiet stillness of the statue and the distance from which the cloud and the hawk observe human affairs seem to be necessary conditions for subjectivity to be able to open up to the evil of living. There are sophisticated reflections on this by eminent theologians, though for a humble ethnography of everyday life such as this one it is not easy to relate to them. Perhaps a recent comment by Pope Francis may assist us here – a very simple and enlightening sentence, namely that God is omnipotent *in love*.

Another reflection worth considering concerns the growing importance and widespread use of concepts such as resilience[38] and antifragility.[39] It is no coincidence that in 2022, the Italian national economic recovery plan was called PNRR, which stands for Piano Nazionale di Ripresa e Resilienza (National Plan for Recovery and Resilience). The term "resilience" has entered public discourse relatively recently and essentially comes from the research of Werner and Smith,[40] according to whom a resilient individual is an individual able to resist trauma and remain unchanged. Resilience can be defined as the ability to recover quickly after illness, change, or a series of unfortunate and negative events. Originally, this term designated the property of a material that allows it to return to its original shape after being compressed, bent, or stretched. To a certain extent, resilience has to do with the concept of elasticity. In the mid-1980s, a number of scholars from various disciplines – educators, psychologists, psychiatrists, sociologists, and social psychologists – published a series of longitudinal studies (Shonkoff and Meisels)[41] on preschool children raised in particularly adverse conditions (divorced parents, parents with mental disorders, situations of sexual abuse). What emerged was that some groups of children had a particular ability to survive the most difficult conditions – they were indeed resilient. The National Plan for Recovery and Resilience thus refers to this property, originally attributed to specific types of materials and later extended to the personality traits of certain individuals. It is evident that the emergence and widespread use of terms such as resilience and antifragility in public discourse, which views them as values, also represent a long-term consequence of the progressive weakening of faith in divine providence, which the process of disenchantment of the world, described by Weber, also contributed to.

54 Forms of symbolic pollution

In contemporary times, unable to rely on divine providence, we find ourselves theorising the need for widespread and novel resilience, both individual and collective. It almost seems that the task of producing the antibodies necessary to cope with the evil of living is being externalised: if many can no longer rely on their faith in God or the universe, it becomes necessary to socially theorise the desirability of a new model of humanity capable of autonomously withstanding the blows dealt to us by life, capable of enduring without being hurt, and, above all, without requiring someone else to repair the damage caused. In this regard, it must be noted that the concept of antifragility differs from that of resilience: while resilience is the ability to withstand shocks and remain unchanged, antifragility thrives in disorder and improves in moments of crisis. Moreover, antifragility is immune to all processes of error prediction and is shielded from adversities. According to Taleb,[42] in fact, antifragility enjoys a singular property: it puts us in a position to ride the unknown, to do things without understanding their meaning, even doing them well. In this sense, theoretical reflections on resilience only partially intersect with the concept developed by Taleb. We may say that, to a certain extent, reflections on resilience and antifragility seem to address the *restlessness of events* proposed by Robin Wagner-Pacifici[43] from the subject's perspective, offering a key to understand how to "ride" disorder without being overwhelmed. In both cases, the perspective of control is questioned – the idea of linear progression, of a development that can be predicted from the beginning, the idea that errors and leaps forward are rare or residual events. In this perspective, the opposite is true: an error is an illusion in the definition of the observing subject; it is merely a deviation from the original plan conceived by the mind of the observer and existing solely and monadically in that mind. Destiny is the trajectory of an arrow shot randomly from the past into the future or, vice versa, from the future into the past. Ultimately, this arrow defines us as an enchanted trace, the only possible one among all the trajectories that have opened and closed as we moved forward. The destination is therefore the journey itself, as many teachers, writers, scholars, and poets have reminded us numerous times.

Taleb[44] proposes thriving in disorder by using the concept of "antifragile", according to which, in order to innovate, one must "try to get in trouble. I mean serious, but not terminal, trouble".[45] He also stresses another aspect: what kills some makes others thrive, meaning the fragility of one part of the system becomes the antifragility of another part. The idea that Taleb intends to overturn is that chance is risky and should be eliminated or at least reduced. Mistakes, in fact, are a constitutive and important part of human existence: those who never allow themselves to make small mistakes are more likely to make big ones. The point is not "not to make mistakes", but not to make irreversible mistakes. In this sense, according to Taleb, we should be wary not of those who make a mistake but rather of those who continue

Forms of symbolic pollution **55**

to make the same mistakes. An error, in fact, is an opportunity to learn new information and apply it to the system:

> Yogi Berra once said: "We made the wrong mistake" – and for John all mistakes are wrong mistakes. Nature loves small errors (...), humans don't.[46]

The author proposes a theory of action able to positively overcome what he calls "the teleological fallacy"[47]: the curious illusion we rely on, according to which we know exactly where we are going and even where we were going in the past, and the belief that "others have succeeded in the past by knowing where they were going".[48] As the author states:

> The error of thinking you know exactly where you are going and assuming that you know *today* what your preferences will be *tomorrow* has an associated one. It is the illusion of thinking that *others*, too, know where they are going, and that they would tell you what they want if you just asked them.[49]

Instead, Taleb proposes a theory of action based on option, that is, the ability to change course. Has it ever happened to you to become attached to a situation – it might just be a particularly beautiful café where you have breakfast or a nice bookshop or something similar – and come to believe that they are indispensable parts of your daily life, that without them life would not be as good? What inevitably happens, however, is that these nice parts one day are no longer there; they simply get replaced with other different but equally beautiful and enriching ones. In fact, even though Taleb does not mention this explicitly, his reflection is about impermanence and how we decide to deal with it in our life.

2.4 A brief digression on the concept of control: from design to growth

In his book *Planting Our World*,[50] Stefano Mancuso stresses that a city cannot be understood as being solely the result of urban planning; the concept of design is not enough to explain the notion of city but must be complemented by the notion of growth. Growth expresses the magnetic and vital force of living things, while design, at least in the sense suggested by Mancuso, seems to refer to the imaginative creativity of our minds. This, however, is a static representation in which we know the initial and final form, while with the model based on growth, we only know the starting point: birth. In an essay on the dissolution of the distinction between body, mind, and culture,[51] Tim Ingold revisits this distinction, differentiating between the activities of

56 Forms of symbolic pollution

making and *weaving*, emphasising how design is a static form of construction that contrasts with dwelling as a dynamic form of growth, as opposed to the idea that there is an original and pre-existing model, one that is entirely mental, to be developed. The concept of individual, as defined by Ingold, is particularly useful here. He states:

> (...) the human being emerges not as a creature whose evolved capacities are filled up with structures that represent the world, but rather as a centre of awareness and agency whose processes resonate with those of the environment. Knowledge, then, far from lying in the relations between structures in the world and structures in the mind, mediated by the person of the knower, is immanent in the life and experience of the knower as it unfolds within the field of practice set up through his or her presence as a being-in-the-world.[52]

It seems to me that the opposition between growth and design identified by Mancuso (very similar to the opposition described by Ingold), with reference to the plan of a city is useful to focus on an aspect that further clarifies the previously discussed relationship between subjectivity and models of resilience and antifragility. The human condition is characterised by a vitality that cannot be grasped by any static representation (by design, to quote the distinction made by Mancuso). In this context, Simmel's traditional distinction between life and form also comes to mind. The trajectory of our future is one of growth: our future grows crooked and twisted, like a tree, bending, stretching, and straightening, depending on atmospheric and environmental conditions. We cannot trace this course in advance, or, more accurately, we certainly can, but only as an exercise of imagination, as a strategy to externalise and give form to our ideas, not as a realistic description of its development. The truth seems to be that life is a journey, and we cannot know in advance what its intermediate stages or its final destination will be. The problem is that it can also be a very dangerous journey: in this case, if it is true that for some, God is dead, we are socially required to become resilient and antifragile. As if socially, we were being told:

> Well, since some of you are non-believers and are therefore no longer supported by faith, you must become resilient in order to function socially the same way; in the meantime, consumption will not decline and economic development will continue to thrive.

It is reasonable to believe that in the near future we will see ads selling products that increase resilience instead of eliminating wrinkles, abdominal swelling, or excess fat. It is actually interesting to try and imagine what these products might be. In short, resilience is not necessarily a property of ecological thinking; it can also function in an "instrumental turn" if used by a system that must exert increasing forms of control over individual consumers in order to continue growing at an unsustainable rate. Now let us go back to positive and nourishing forms of resilience.

In a recent book, Tia DeNora[53] develops the concept of hope, which is understood as a predisposition to thought and action that requires being socially supported and enhanced. The condition of a person who is hopeful can be described, according to the author, as the human condition of someone who is prepared to keep their gaze fixed on a horizon that, though indefinite, maintains its magnetic attraction. The hopeful person constitutes the ideal-typical image of someone who, being resilient, can afford to hope, and, being hopeful, acquires and maintains their resilience. According to the wisdom of the ancient Romans, *spes ultima dea est et omnium rerum pretiosissima, quia sine spe homines vivere nequeunt* (hope is the last goddess and most precious of all things because without hope, people cannot live). This ancient maxim that has been passed down through the centuries by our ancestors depicts one of the possible postures of subjectivity: on the one hand, we surrender to the events in life by developing the ability to be elastically resilient; on the other, we keep staring at the horizon, which is barely visible – we can hardly make out its shape. Yet, it is by staring at the almost unknown horizon that our destiny unfolds like an arrow travelling towards infinity, though we know that at least in part we are able to determine its direction. It should be noted that this active conception of hope is also emphasised by the philosopher Ernst Bloch,[54] who sees hope as a form of "militant optimism" that "overcomes the existing horizon in the direction of 'the horizon of the future' – a future already prefigured in the objective potential of reality".[55]

Going back to the distinction made by Stefano Mancuso with regard to how plants grow, this model, unlike design, can also be rather unsettling because growth can be crooked and may produce burrs and deformations, while our mind prefers to think in terms of projects that develop in a straight line, that are flawless, and that contain no errors. As I have argued in *Eco-Words*, error is the deviation that our gaze records between a plan and what actually exists. Errors are constructed by our mind; they are the outcome of an arbitrary evaluation process that we subject a vital and rich piece of existence to, claiming to know what is best or, alternatively, what things should be like. An error is basically the photocopy of an incomplete and limited drawing that our gaze projects onto the world, only to look away each time, alarmed by the fact that existence is so vast and complex that it cannot be grasped by any gaze, let alone ours. Error is the annoyed comment of those who turn away from the vertigo of life. Clearly, I am using the term error to refer to personal events, small mistakes we make every day. These reflections do not apply in any way to the concept of crime, which is something completely different.

58 Forms of symbolic pollution

3. Pathological forms of domestic space organisation

I would like to return to the issue of the spatialisation of the self to illustrate some possible pathological forms of domestic space organisation and then argue that the concept of Self-Home may be useful in providing an even more effective explanation. In the modern world, subjectivity has become rooted in space, and the home has become a symbolic place where the self can express itself. However, this concept must be understood as being historically and geographically determined, which is why its explanatory potential is limited to a series of specific periods and places. This does not mean that the spirit of the home and the desire to take care of domestic spaces are not to be found in a more distant past, but that the explanatory principle of this concept cannot be applied indiscriminately to every place and culture. A first and very evident exception is the case of nomadic communities that have developed forms of spatialisation of the self very different from the ones being considered here. I will therefore refer to the Western culture of many European countries and especially to contemporary times. I would like to briefly mention two opposite forms of pathological organisation of domestic space in order to shed light on how the latter is connected to subjectivity. The first is disposophobia, a compulsive disorder in which a person is afraid of throwing things away and ends up creating piles of waste that accumulate in domestic spaces; these become uninhabitable as there is basically no room left for the subjects residing in these spaces. Here is an example of disposophobia taken from a true story, told to me by a philosopher, a colleague of mine.

Giovanni (an invented name) had rented out a small apartment in the countryside near Rome to a man in his fifties who was separated and worked in a post office. This man, we will call him Luigi, had a son in his twenties who visited every week. It seems that because of the lockdown, Luigi experienced a mental breakdown, and for many weeks, even after the lockdown had been lifted, Luigi refused to go out. Because he was on sick leave, a doctor visited periodically. This doctor, however, was always greeted with an excuse at the doorstep and was never allowed to enter. Meanwhile, the neighbours who lived in other apartments in the same building began trying to reach Giovanni on the phone: they complained about the pile of garbage that had formed in his small garden next to the apartment and about the horrible smell coming from inside. After months of negotiation, Luigi (who had not paid rent for a long time) finally agreed to leave. When Giovanni and the neighbours entered the apartment, they could not believe their eyes: the three small rooms of the flat, as well as the corridor and the bathroom, were absolutely filled with bags of rubbish, and mice and insects roamed freely. The windows had been sealed from the inside with wooden boards nailed to them, so they could not be opened. This also allowed Luigi to accumulate waste and form piles the height of a person. The bathroom was so full of trash that it was totally inaccessible, which made one wonder where and how

Forms of symbolic pollution **59**

did Luigi take care of his vital needs and personal hygiene. There were traces of food everywhere. The bed was covered by garbage bags. Even though the flat was so filthy, Luigi's son, legally an adult but still very young, had continued to visit at least once a week. It took a team of cleaners almost a week to clear the house. Because there was no ventilation, surfaces everywhere were covered in mould, up to at least a metre and a half from the ground. The walls had to be plastered and repainted. The bidet and toilet were replaced as they could not be cleaned. The kitchen cabinets were rotten as the extreme humidity had ruined the wood. The situation was unbelievable. It was hard to imagine how a person could live in such filthy conditions. Yet Luigi had a beautiful and fairly new black car, which he kept clean and in perfect order. This is why nobody could have imagined that the space he lived in was in such a state. When Giovanni tried to ask Luigi for an explanation in the presence of his son, the two of them seemed to have no idea what he was talking about; they seemed to be completely unaware of what he was alluding to. It became clear that, according to both Luigi and his son, the state of the apartment was not at all exceptional. It seemed they could not tell the difference between the extreme squalor of this space and the hygienic conditions one would expect to find in a house.

Disposophobia is the behavioural opposite of compulsive decluttering. People affected by pathological decluttering throw away all types of objects, including essential items, to keep their physical and mental space in order – only to find themselves repurchasing those same items immediately afterward. It is no coincidence that these behavioural disorders are rather common in contemporary times, as they appear to be closely linked to some of the fundamental trends in our society. In *Liquid Life*, Bauman underscores how the driving force of consumer society lies in the almost instantaneous obsolescence of the goods or services purchased by citizens:

> The past of each identity is strewn with rubbish tips on which have been dumped, daily, one by one, the indispensables of the day before yesterday which turned into yesterday's awkward burdens. (...) The art of marketing is focused on the prevention of the closing of options and the fulfillment of desires. (...) the emphasis here falls not on arousing new desires but on extinguishing the "old" (read: those of a moment ago), in order to clear the site for new shopping escapades. (...) Denizens of the liquid modern world need no further priming to obsessively explore the shops in the hope of finding ready-made, consumer friendly and publicly legible identity badges. They wander through the winding passages of the shopping malls prompted and guided by a semi-conscious hope of bumping into the very identity badge or token needed to bring their selves up to date, and by a gnawing apprehension that the moment when a badge of pride turns into a badge of shame might otherwise be overlooked.[56]

60 Forms of symbolic pollution

In this perspective, disposophobia and, conversely, compulsive decluttering should not be understood as being simply terms to describe disturbing psychotic figures, as they seem to indicate tragic figures almost inevitably generated by the functioning of consumer society, which has prevailed in late capitalism. Though a person suffering from disposophobia may be seen as an outcast, an antisocial neighbour who imposes a burden that is too heavy to carry for any established form of peaceful coexistence, from a sociological point of view, this person is also a sort of tragic hero who resists extreme consumerism and who, for this reason, is affected by an illness consisting of an extreme and impulsive form of conservationism. In cultural and symbolic terms, people who are affected by disposophobia refuse to take part in the race to produce waste, and this is why they end up being severely ill. Their obsessive disorder disturbs us because by compulsively accumulating waste and presenting it all at once, they force us to confront the hidden amount of waste we produce and dispose of every day, carefully filling a number of different bins. Compulsive decluttering, on the other hand, is simply the other side of the coin: the speed with which declutterers discard all their possessions far exceeds the speed suggested to us by the marketing of desires. This excess produces an experiential and cognitive gap, one that is capable of jamming the system. In other words, the hypothesis is that these two forms of pathological behaviour should not be looked at only through the lens of individual psychology, as they are also socially generated: these pathologies are disturbing precisely because they reveal – the way a monstrous grin does – some of the most pervasive and perverse dynamics that characterise consumer society.

Both of these pathological forms of behaviour have to do with how we arrange the objects we own in our domestic space. They are, in fact, pathological forms of organisation: disposophobia saturates space to the point it becomes physically impossible to inhabit it, while decluttering empties it completely, making it equally inhospitable and unsuitable for normal domestic life. Speaking to my colleague, the philosopher, many months after the events had taken place, he recalled the experience of the tenant, whom he affectionately nicknamed "the slob", and told me that, in his opinion, Luigi had ultimately agreed to leave the apartment simply because *there was no more room*, not enough physical space for him to inhabit the apartment with his body, and not being able to free up space by simply throwing away his garbage, he had been forced to move. So whereas the space of a person who suffers from disposophobia becomes too full, the space of a person obsessed with decluttering becomes too empty. These two pathological ways of organising space, which are somehow connected to the deeper logic of consumer society, shed new light on the concept of home as the dwelling of the self, or more directly, on the concept of the Self-Home.

4. From skin-ego to Self-Home[57]

In 1985, the French psychoanalyst Didier Anzieu,[58] building upon Freud's notion of *envelope*, introduced the concept of skin-ego, which he had already outlined in an article published in 1974. In this earlier work, Anzieu defined the skin-ego as the set of representations constructed by infants during the development phases which allow them to conceive of themselves as unique subjects, starting from the tactile experiences they have with their bodily surface, that is, their skin. Anzieu went back to this concept many times, emphasising the underlying physicality and materiality connected to the development of the idea of subjectivity.[59] Drawing on his psychoanalytic work, Anzieu employed this concept to shed new light on masochistic pathologies, for instance, the case of patients who inflict pain on themselves by cutting their skin. These cuts correspond to wounds of the ego, of memory, lacerations in the subject's psychic self, which cannot be expressed using the verbal fabric and are therefore expressed indirectly, through bodily tissue, by means of masochistic practices. Going beyond these interpretations, which may be more or less convincing, Anzieu's theory posits a strong correlation between the subject's corporeality (as understood in his or her subjective representation) and the subject's psychic ego. Moreover, the skin-ego is a concept of great interest because it leads one to reflect on the notion of boundary, which, in the case of subjectivity, is not a simple one. During the process of socialisation, as children, we all learn to distinguish our self from the world: where do I end? The underlying and commonly held notion is that I end where my skin ends. We generally view our skin as the barrier between ourselves and the external world. This is a practical solution to the existential problem of separating self from non-self that informs our daily lives. However, there are some spiritual traditions, as I have previously mentioned in *Eco-Words*, that suggest that the boundary between individuality and the outer world should be reconsidered and viewed not as a discrete variable but as a *continuum*. In other words, we transition from a me, my own self, to something that is a bit less me, and then to a me which has very little of me, and so on. In more radical versions, some of these perspectives have emphasised the continuity between subject and environment, postulating a kind of strong connection and thus hypothesising that there is a shared energetic consonance between the subject and its environment, which allows the subject to resonate with the environment. This raises a series of quite complex questions. For instance, a subject should always take responsibility for the environment surrounding it, even though the outcomes of this are not always entirely desirable. If a subject resonates with the surrounding environment and is, therefore, surrounded by the environment it resonates with, how should cases of severe violence inflicted on a victim be interpreted? The easiest option, one that unfortunately is rather common, is the horrible practice of victim blaming, which cannot

62 Forms of symbolic pollution

be endorsed by any civil society that considers itself democratic. Other issues that complicate the way we tend to practically distinguish between self and the rest of the world arise from Oliver Sacks'[60] studies on phantom limb syndrome, whereby patients with amputated limbs continue to feel this limb decades later, posing a serious challenge to our representation of the boundary between ourselves and the world. It is worth noting that the perspective adopted here is an entirely pragmatic one, which underlies an ethnography of everyday life. The aim is not to find the correct theoretical definition, one that is universally valid, but simply to observe how individuals manage in their daily lives and the types of distinctions they use to address such problems. If we continue our reflection on the problematic nature of the boundary concept applied to the subject and corporeality, we may introduce the notion of Self-Home, as a possible extension of the ego. In other words, the Self-Home could be understood as the extended representation that the subject has of its psychic life, which is projected onto a space-container of variable dimensions. In this sense, we may speak of how the subjects' psychic self in rooted space. As Emanuele Coccia writes:

> Every household is the fruit of this movement. We project ourselves in the space closest to us, and we make of this portion of space something intimate: a portion of world that has a particular relation to our own body, a kind of ordinary, material extension of our body. Our relation with our digs is exactly one of the immersion: we do not stand before them the way we stand before objects, we live in them as a fish lives in the sea.[61]

When we are in our home, we are that space, and that space is our extension. The concept of Self-Home allows us to grasp the immersive and non-divisive state, which is a necessary condition for everyday well-being. So what is notion of Self-Home useful for? Firstly, it may help us better understand a series of social phenomena that we currently underestimate. For instance, if we take such a notion seriously, the case of an elderly person who is forced to abandon his or her home – the place where the representation of his or her Self-Home is rooted – can be understood in all its complexity. During the various phases of the war in Ukraine, we listened to interviews on the news with elderly people who refused to leave their homes, preferring to face the extreme consequences of war and most certainly death. The notion of attachment to one's domestic space does not allow us to understand such behaviour, which seems unreasonable and unjustifiable. However, if we take the notion of Self-Home seriously, we may grasp the correlation between domestic space and the subjectivity of a person. It is important to note that the Self-Home is not necessarily the physical house of a subject. For this coincidence to occur, the subject must invest symbolically in a specific space, rooting his or her psychic life in it. There are houses that become *dwellings of the self,* regardless of their aesthetic qualities or dimensions. The subjective relationship between the ego and a specific space is what transforms a space into a Self-Home, transferring to the space the sacredness an individual is capable of. It is also true that the Self-Home manifests itself; it can be seen. When a space has become a place of the soul, it communicates well-being, care, and affection to anyone who simply passes through it or stays in it. Furthermore, the Self-Home allows us to reflect on a series of issues, such as the traumas suffered by those who are "forced" by history to leave their homes, or the difficulty of integration and participation in community life in a host country for migrants whose right to a home is repeatedly denied. Or again, the problem of boundaries between the subject and the external world, which becomes more complex and problematic when seen through the lens of this concept.

There are a number of correspondences between the Self-Home and Tim Ingold's[62] reflections, such as when he defines the home as a real "living organism".[63] According to Ingold, in fact, it is the process of dwelling that makes building possible:

> The philosopher Martin Heidegger expressed the very same point through an exploration of the notions of building and dwelling. Opposing the modernist convention that dwelling is an activity that goes on within, and is structured by, an environment that is already built, Heidegger argued that we cannot engage in any kind of building activity unless we already dwell within our surroundings. "Only if we are capable of dwelling", he declared, "only then can we build".[64] Now dwelling is to building, in Heidegger's terms, as weaving is to making in mine. Where making (like building) comes to an end with the completion of a work in its final form, weaving (like dwelling) continues for as long as life goes on – punctuated but not terminated by the appearance of the pieces that it successively brings into being. Dwelling in the world, in short, is tantamount to the ongoing, temporal interweaving of our lives with one another and with the manifold constituents of our environment.[65]

Reflections of this kind, inspired by Heidegger's phenomenology, seem to address the issues posed by the Self-Home in a specular manner, starting from the side opposite the subject, namely from inhabited space: the home as a living organism. In both concepts, these reflections respond to the need, on the one hand, to transcend the physicality of the walls surrounding and structuring a particular physical space (rethinking the home as a living organism and not simply as an organised set of bricks, tiles, etc.), and, on the other hand, to transcend the physicality of a body that does not seem to represent the only possible "envelope" of the subject considered here in an extended dimension (that of the Self-Home). In this sense, Ingold's *home as a living organism* and the *Self-Home* proposed here are complementary concepts.

64 Forms of symbolic pollution

5. The market as a "solution" in everyday life

Consumer society has made us used to the marketing of desires, contributing to perpetuate the false belief that the solutions to the problems we face on a daily basis can be found on the market, i.e., with the mediation of money and the purchase of a new good or service.

> In such a [consumer] society, the roads are many and scattered, but they all lead through shops. Any life pursuit, and most significantly the pursuit of dignity, self-esteem and happiness, requires the mediation of the market; and the world in which such pursuits are inscribed is made up of commodities – objects judged, appreciated or rejected according to the satisfaction they bring to the world's customers.[66]

Basically, in consumer society, all problems can be monetised and can be broken down into the sum of different goods and/or services needed for their solution. The process that conceals the real nature of the goods and/or services that are progressively purchased is made possible by the fact that, through marketing and advertising, we have become accustomed to the idea that a good is not merely a product but rather the solution to an identity claim that can be obtained with a good and/or service. These goods and services are nothing other than "identity badges".[67]

Another author who has exposed this type of mystification is Ivan Illich.[68] Many years ago, he denounced the *iatrogenesis* in health systems and the fact that, although health institutions are supposed to sell only treatments and drugs, they have institutionally incorporated the claim to sell health. This confusion persists today and has become even worse, as it now constitutes the hegemonic model for the purchase and sale of goods and services regulated by the market. The outcome of this is invisibly in plain sight. Women are a particularly attractive target for these types of communication and advertising strategies. Even sanitary pads can be treated as a representational device that promises to solve what it calls the problem with emotional instability caused by a woman's period, if only she buys this specific product. Now she can even allow herself to be slightly emotionally unstable during her period because that particular brand supports and reassures her: "You are valuable, despite your period". The response to this has to be: "How kind! I hadn't thought of that. I'll buy them right away!"

There are plenty of identity badges for older women as well: sanitary pads for what is said to be their incontinence (they might not suffer from it now, but they will, sooner or later), girdles for their belly, bras that make cosmetic surgery unnecessary, creams that eliminate wrinkles, creams that eliminate rashes, and others that make grey hair disappear. In short, ageing must be concealed at all costs; we are all supposed to live to 100 with the face and body of an 18-year-old. Not to mention the various health issues: there are remedies for going to the bathroom, others for not going to the bathroom, remedies for losing weight while eating or without exercising, remedies for sleeping, and others for staying awake and focused. Remedies to please one's partner. Remedies for a happy sex life. In short, there are all sorts of remedies for living. Men are as fortunate as women; indeed, the marketing of desires is equally fierce: there are men with prostate problems, men who are deaf, and men who cannot see; young men who sweat too much; and others who have acne. Not to mention body hair, which always seems to be in the wrong place, whether it is men (bald but who still need to shave) or women who undergo sadistic rituals to have skin as smooth as silk. The market is a massive reserve capable of dispensing beauty, health, and happiness. At the Swiss University of St. Gallen, in one of the main corridors, an artwork by Alejandro Díaz is exhibited called *Happiness is expensive*. Another version of the same artwork (which is straight and not curved) was displayed at the Museum of Art at the Rhode Island School of Design (RISD) in Providence, in the United States. I have always thought that the University of St. Gallen was the perfect venue for the exhibition of this artwork, as it is a faculty of economics (Figure 2.2).

But why must the remedies for the problems we deal with every day be necessarily found on the market? Why do I need a cream to make my

FIGURE 2.2 *"Happiness is expensive"* by Alejandro Díaz, Swiss University of St. Gallen.

66 Forms of symbolic pollution

skin more beautiful but not a few extra hours of rest or a healthy trip to the woods? Why are subjects reduced to the dichotomy worker/consumer? Why, if I am not working, am I expected to wander anxiously through the aisles of a shopping centre as if I were a gold prospector? Why do I have to accumulate all these goods and own so many pairs of shoes – more than the number of days I can wear them? Where is Serge Latouche's *frugal abundance*?[69] How do we deactivate all these compulsive behaviours? They are fed constantly by an unstoppable flood of images and messages that cause visual and moral pollution at the same time while reinforcing a deceptive idea of happiness, human dignity, and existence in general.

Quoting Kiku Adatto, Bauman writes:

> Childhood turns into a preparation for the selling of the self as children are trained to see all relationships in market terms' and to view other human beings, including friends and family members, through the prism of market-generated perceptions and evaluations.[70]

To conclude, I would like to quote the insightful words of Thich Nhat Hanh, a great Vietnamese thinker and spiritual leader in the Buddhist world. These words help us reconsider all the acts of daily consumption from a perspective of ecological thinking:

> How can you tell what communication is healthy and what is toxic? The energy of mindfulness is a necessary ingredient in healthy communication. Mindfulness requires letting go of judgment, returning to an awareness of the breath and the body, and bringing your full attention to what is in you and around you. This helps you notice whether the thought you just produced is healthy or unhealthy, compassionate or unkind. Conversation is a source of nourishment. We all get lonely and want to talk with someone. But when you have a conversation with another person, what that person says may be full of toxins, like hate, anger, and frustration. When you listen to what others say, you're consuming those toxins. You're bringing toxins into your consciousness and your body. That's why mindfulness of speaking and mindfulness of listening are very important. (...) You absorb the thoughts, speech, and actions you produce and those contained in the communications of those around you. That is a form of consumption. So when you read something, when you listen to someone, you should be careful not to allow the toxins to ruin your health and bring suffering to you and to the other person or group of people.[71]

In other texts, Thich Nhat Hanh extends these reflections to all other forms of consumption.

Notes

1 The term "domestication" here represents a tribute to Goody (1977).
2 De Matteis (2021, p. 11).
3 Ibid., p. 81.
4 Important contributions on this kind of studies are by Schulz von Thun (1981) and Zeldin (1998).
5 A very important contribution in this direction is by Strate (2022).
6 Fabrice del Dongo is the main character of *The Charterhouse of Parma*, a novel written by Stendhal in 1839.
7 The performative nature of words has been firstly studied by Austin (1961).
8 Proust (2003), e-book version.
9 Goffman (1961a, 1961b, 1963).
10 Colombo (2020, p. 89).
11 Erving Goffman (1959, 1967) deals extensively with the concept of "face", defined on several occasions as the image that represents our self and which is socially produced and reproduced during social interactions. The acceptance of our face by our interlocutor in a specific interaction means that we are recognised as reliable members of that community and as worthy of trust.
12 Simmel (1950, pp. 410–411).
13 Cerulo (2009, p. 90).
14 Hillman (2004).
15 Lacroix (2002).
16 Lacroix cit., in Cerulo (2009, p. 99).
17 Cerulo (2009).
18 Watzlawick (1976, 1981), Watzlawick, Weakland and Fisch (1974), and Fisch, Weakland and Segal (1982).
19 Wing Sue and Spanierman (2020).
20 Bergmann (1992); Franck (2003); Wittmann (2013).
21 Bauman (2000).
22 Bauman (2005, p. 7).
23 Cassano (1996, pp. 14–15).
24 Haraway (1991); Latour (1994).
25 Tota (2023).
26 Wagner-Pacifici (2016, p. 22).
27 On this point, see Zohar (1990), Culbertson (1995), Narvàez (2013), and Tota (2016).
28 Ibid.
29 Tota (2016).
30 Fromm (2012, p. XXI).
31 Nietzsche (2001, p. 194).
32 Capps and Ochs (1995, p. 25).
33 Taleb (2007, p. XXIV).
34 Wolf (1983).
35 Weber (1919).
36 Melucci (1994, 1996).
37 Spesso il male di vivere ho incontrato | era il rivo strozzato che gorgoglia, | era l'incartocciarsi della foglia riarsa, era il cavallo stramazzato. | Bene non seppi, fuori del prodigio che schiude la divina indifferenza: | era la statua nella sonnolenza del meriggio, e la nuvola, e il falco alto levato. English translation: Montale (1994, p. 37).
38 Werner and Smith (1982).
39 Taleb (2012).

68 Forms of symbolic pollution

40 Werner and Smith (1982, 2001).
41 Shonkoff and Meisels (2000).
42 Taleb (2012).
43 Wagner-Pacifici (2010, 2016).
44 Taleb (2012).
45 Ibid., e-book version.
46 Ibid.
47 Ibid.
48 Ibid.
49 Ibid.
50 Mancuso (2023).
51 Ingold (2000a), e-book version.
52 Ibid.
53 De Nora *et al.* (2022).
54 Bloch (1959).
55 Gili and Mangone (2022, p. 8).
56 Bauman (2005, pp. 33–34).
57 Although the concept of Ego-Home derives from a re-elaboration of the concept of *Moi-Peau*, which in English has been translated as Skin-Ego, I have chosen to translate Io-casa with Self-Home to avoid the Freudian meaning of the term Ego that would be misleading here (TN).
58 Anzieu (1995).
59 The notion of subjectivity has been extensively investigated from very different perspectives: for example, Mead (1934), Korzybski (1950), Laing (1959), Gardner (1983), Lasch (1984), Elster (1985), Strate (2000), and McCraty (2016).
60 Sacks (1985).
61 Coccia (2018), e-book version.
62 Ingold (2000b).
63 Blier (1987).
64 Heidegger (1971).
65 Ingold (2000b, pp. 347–348).
66 Bauman (2005, p. 107).
67 Ibid., p. 34.
68 Illich (1974).
69 Latouche (2014).
70 Bauman (2005, p. 115).
71 Nhat Hanh (2013, p. 5).

In the third chapter, I shift the focus from words to images and introduce the concept of "visual pollution", arguing that it is both useful and effective in providing an explanation, also highlighting the complexity its application involves given a correct interpretation of the conclusions reached by audience theories. These theories suggest that different individuals, when faced with the same iconic text, see things that are at least partially different. Furthermore, I propose simultaneously considering that we are the images we see, and that we tend to see what we are. When applying the concepts of pollution and sustainability to the social imaginary, I claim that: (a) without images, the self cannot contemplate itself; (b) while it is not always true that we are the images we see, it is certainly true that the images inhabiting our thoughts derive, with a very high degree of probability, from the contemporary social imaginary in circulation; (c) therefore, at least some of the images we see tend to become a structuring and constitutive part of our inner world, in that we certainly are the images we think. A short digression follows on Marc Augé's "war of dreams", which serves to illustrate how imaginaries become the Lego building blocks of society, used to construct and/or dismantle highly toxic ideological formations such as racism, homophobia, or sexism (in more technical terms, these are the resources employed to "naturalise" social inequalities). Hence, I emphasise that visual pollution simultaneously has an individual and a collective dimension. I also claim that the images we think can be considered as the aesthetic forms of our self; they are the elements with which we furnish the dwellings of our subjectivity. In the second part of the chapter, I demonstrate how certain television series have significantly contributed to shaping the social imaginary we refer to in our daily lives. The images from television series, in fact, serve as the elements with which we furnish the dwellings of our subjectivity, constructing a shared heritage of ideas, values, beliefs, and lifestyles. We draw upon this heritage to think, converse, dream, speak, smile, and co-exist. Therefore, the practical question that arises is: what kinds of imaginaries do we want to expose ourselves to daily? I clarify that only individuals are capable of identifying the type of imaginary that is right for them. A negative imaginary may have a cathartic quality for someone, while for another person it can become highly polluting. In this sense, the concept of visual pollution is a useful tool to carry with us in daily life but should not be understood as a tool for censoring authorship or limiting the creativity of visual texts. In the last paragraph, I conclude with a brief theoretical digression on the concept of intersectionality.

3

VISUAL POLLUTION

1. From words to images

We are the food we eat, the air we breathe, and the water we drink. Today, concepts such as environmental, noise, and electromagnetic pollution have become familiar and are widely used in public discourse. As we have repeatedly stressed, radical constructivism and phenomenology[1] have taught us that *we are the words we hear*.[2] In this sense, our subjectivity seems to be grounded discursively; its foundation is a collection of discontinuous perceptions, as David Hume[3] put it. The Palo Alto Mental Research Institute, in fact, demonstrated that words nourish and sustain individual identities (and collective ones) and that some words make us ill: listening to them for long periods of time under certain conditions (a situation of double bind, for example) can lead to serious personality disorders, such as schizophrenia.[4] Therefore, some words – or rather discursive structures – are capable of undermining subjectivity and permanently polluting the institutional life of an organisation or a community. But does this only apply to speech? How do images work? Are images as powerful as words? Indeed, today, the fundamental resources we use to interpret reality and give meaning to our existence include images. For this reason, Sartori speaks of "homo videns",[5] hypothesising that contemporary men and women experience the world – his or her world – predominantly through the visual dimension. For contemporary subjects, images constitute fundamental cognitive material. In this sense, should we claim that *we are also the images we see*? This question is theoretically and methodologically very complex for several reasons. The first is that while it might be true that we are also what we see, the exact opposite continues to be true: that is, *we see what we are*. In other words, the

DOI: 10.4324/9781003484592-3

72 Visual pollution

process by which we attribute meaning is never independent of the subject actualising it. In part, this was anticipated many years ago by the theorists of the School of Constance and continues to hold true in contemporary times. We may think of a notion such as *Erwartungshorizont*, developed by reception theory,[6] understood as the horizon of expectations that contributes to the production of meanings of a literary text, which may also be a visual text in the present perspective. Elsewhere, I have argued that subjectivity plays a predominant role in the social processes through which we literally construct the meaning of a work of art.[7] And so, when we look at a painting, is it right to say that this painting (i.e. its representation, the way we judge it, the way we feel when looking at it, the way we will remember or forget it, the specific processes that activate memory that it will or will not set in motion for us in the future, the ways in which it will or will not contribute to shaping our subjectivity) also contains a portrait of us? In part, this is correct, since it is we and only we who will be able to grasp its nuances, see its details, and attribute a specific meaning to it. However, this can also be said of an image used in advertising, of a selfie, or of any kind of visual text. This enormously complicates any reflection on "visual pollution", which I have obstinately worked on for more than a decade,[8] as it also introduces the next topic: if I see what I am, it is also true that different subjects looking at the same image will see different objects because the meaning of what they see will tend to vary, even just slowly or slightly. In this sense, how is it possible to continue speaking of visual pollution?

1.1 We are not the images we see, but rather the images we think

Concentrating on images, on the one hand, we are attempting to implicitly explore the possibility of interpreting them in terms of public ethics – by introducing the notion of visual pollution, we are also trying to understand what impact the social imaginary has on the democratic fabric of civil society. On the other hand, we are also trying to understand how a number of specific images eventually, or potentially, end up polluting us. Can we speak of a sustainable imaginary?[9] One that is constituted by collections of images that do not contribute to structuring or preserving discriminating ideological formations, such as racism or sexism? And even if it were possible to foresee such an imaginary, would it actually be a viable political option in today's world, as some rather questionable initiatives seem to believe – we may think of the mayor of the city of São Paulo, who in 2006 banned all advertising posters in the city. If it is true that we are also what we see, how can we learn to "defend" ourselves and only see and show the images we think are worth seeing? And again, are some images really capable of polluting our minds, our representations of the world we live in, of other people we interact with? Can images intervene in the delicate processes that constitute reality, investigated by scholars who termed them "self-fulfilling prophecies"?[10] Can they, in other words, contribute to provide truth value to the subjects' preconceptions or expectations, so that what these subjects think is real ends up becoming *really* real, as they conform and inform their actions to their thoughts? Does a racist or sexist image really constitute a threat, or is it mostly harmless, because what counts is how free we are in the act of decoding? What role do the media and social media play? Ultimately, in fact, the media, traditional and otherwise, continue to be among the greatest producers of images of our time. These questions have no clear-cut or simple answers. And so, we are left with a great many questions, which are rather difficult to answer. Though this is not a good enough reason to stop asking and thinking about them.

The concept of visual pollution makes it possible to document how this imaginary is at the centre of social conflicts, especially in contexts such as the present one, in which the nature of experience has become divorced from the requirement of co-presence.[11] In other words, what we see on our computer screen is capable of touching us in a profound and intimate way, to the point that it becomes part of our subjectivity. However, this means *can*, not *must*. What we are witnessing is, in fact, a real "war of dreams",[12] in which images are important, as they are powerful vectors of sense and meaning, but in which also real subjects are important, the people seeing those images.

According to Van Dijk,[13] through texts (including iconic ones, we might add), we can learn or unlearn racism. But let us return to our main question: why should or could images have a polluting effect, even though this might just be a side effect? The images we see in advertising are entertaining, the same as imagery in cinema or television series; they make us dream and provide us with the necessary material to represent ourselves and our dreams. So in what sense can they pollute, and in what way? We have learned from environmental studies how to fight acoustic, atmospheric, light, electromagnetic, and environmental pollution. The concept of pollution, however, has not yet been extended to the symbolic domain. The hypothesis is that some images are like fine dust; they are capable of polluting our minds, or rather of polluting the social representations of certain phenomena that we process in our minds. Such images therefore have the capacity to direct our future course of action with respect to the phenomena they represent. According to this hypothesis, images have the ability to structure and consolidate social formations, such as racism or sexism.

Such an idea, however, raises a number of relevant theoretical and empirical questions: firstly, we need to consider the nature of open text – quoting the concept developed by Umberto Eco – of all visual texts. In other words, we cannot assume that there is a shared intersubjectivity underlying the way an image is decoded by its users. What is highly "polluting" and negative for some may not be so for others who belong to different social groups. But the issue regarding the multivocality and multidimensionality of a text

74 Visual pollution

cannot be solved simply by attributing greater semiotic power to a minority that could potentially be discriminated against by an image. Put differently, one does not solve the problem by stating that a certain image spread by the media is highly racist if, and only if, it is recognised as such by the minority that it discriminates against – for example, Native American. This solution, analytical and political at the same time, is in fact based on a misleading assumption, which has also been found for a long time in much gender studies literature: not all Native Americans who look at that image will necessarily decode it in the same way. If we combine the concept of visual pollution with the results of audience theories, the question acquires a very different theoretical consistency and complexity. We may think of Stuart Hall's[14] classical model and the different modes of decoding it sets out. Given these premises, it is evident that the concept of visual pollution is only effective to the extent that it can be combined with various degrees of freedom in the decoding processes of actual spectators and viewers. It should be noted, however, that there are points of no return also in the case of the social imaginary produced by the media and social media, i.e. there are thresholds that cannot be crossed without provoking a clear and shared social reaction. In other words, there is a common-sense notion regarding the social acceptability of images to be found in the media that, for example, makes it possible to unanimously condemn paedophile images. The concept of visual pollution is therefore articulated, on the one hand, by taking into account the way users interpellate images and, on the other, by tracing symbolic boundaries beyond which images become *illicit, illegitimate representations* that must be censored. Once again, however, tracing these boundaries is not at all a simple operation, in the sense that these boundaries are far from being static; they are produced and reproduced both socially and institutionally. For this reason, they are not necessarily stable but rather dynamic and fluctuating. Moreover, they are constantly challenged by artistic codes and practices; we may think, for instance, of the subtle differences between eroticism and pornography. In fact, establishing the difference between an erotic image and a pornographic one is not always a simple and clear task; the degrees of intersubjectivity with which images can be decoded vary considerably. A large part of contemporary art photography, for instance, was born challenging and questioning the concept of social acceptability of our common imaginary. The boundaries, inside which the dividing line between licit and illicit images takes shape, are produced both socially by the judgments and reactions of real users and viewers and institutionally, for instance, by film or television censorship commissions. These commissions are further proof of how much power is assigned to images in a given cultural and social context. But what is the actual weight of images?

Applying the concepts of pollution and sustainability to the social imaginary, borrowing this metaphor from environmental discussions, means assuming that images in the media and images in general weigh and count more than common sense is willing to accept. It means thinking that "the future we want" depends on the ability to combine environmental sustainability with symbolic sustainability. In other words, we are not only the food we eat, the air we breathe, or the water we drink; we are also the words we hear and, above all, the images we see. Perhaps it is worth pausing here in order to develop a further reflection on this point: even though we might not be able to agree that ultimately we are also the images we see (since we are the first to recognise that we also see what we are and, moreover, that different subjects see different things when confronted with the same image), we can nevertheless agree that it is based on the images we see that we presumably select and process the images we think. So perhaps it is not entirely true that we are the images we see; however, these images undoubtedly constitute the social reserve we draw from when processing the images we think. Nor can we reasonably assume that the images which inhabit our thoughts do not become a structuring and constitutive part of our inner world, since *we certainly are the images we think*.

1.2 The war of dreams or the power of images

I draw all the time, also when I am not drawing because I am writing or concentrating on not doing anything (...). Writing abolishes time, compressing or dilating it. In drawing one finds the most concise expression. (...) Often graphic representations are drawn poems; and many poems describe contours, they are the fading tones of chiaroscuro. (...) Graphic work is more precise. It cannot be fooled by the sound of words. Compared to the unambiguity of lines, verses are threatened by the chatter of possible interpretations.[15]

This is how Günter Grass describes the complex relationship between words and drawing – the delicate interweaving of written text and image. According to the writer, these are almost complementary dimensions of expression, strongly interrelated and influencing each other, which nevertheless retain specific peculiarities. Drawing evokes the powerful plasticity of images, with which a written text cannot compete. Drawings, as well as images in general, activate perceptive and cognitive modalities that grasp the emotional rather than rational structures of representation. This is why they are so effective in processes of social legitimisation. But what is the social power of the imaginary? What is its specific role as an arena in which to compete and advance different values, as a place and space in which to socially construct subjectivities and individual and collective identities?[16]

Augé's *The War of Dreams*,[17] or war of images, constitutes a field of investigation where very different disciplines and analytical categories have tested

76 Visual pollution

their hypotheses. These disciplines and categories, despite the wide variety of perspectives they offer, share a common focus on the general forms of mediation with which social actors literally shape their *Weltanschauungen* (worldviews), their perceptive and discursive universes. Images literally become resources for the negotiation of the definition of the real; they provide the time and space in which competition takes place to shape subjectivities. Indeed, as Crespi points out, taking up the technical notion of the symbolic proposed by Cassirer, "symbolic mediation also always has a dimension that is constitutive of subjects".[18] In this sense, the imaginary is what establishes the order of what is possible and probable, materially structuring the boundaries of what we are able or unable to think.

Without images, the self cannot think itself. All forms of social inequality require established repertoires of images with which they can legitimise themselves. From this point of view, unequal images can only describe unequal opportunities. In this perspective, the concept of visual pollution refers to images that function as a starting point for the social legitimisation of discrimination. Media images "pollute" insofar as they are able to make inequalities seem "natural", when they are in fact politically and culturally determined. An image is sustainable if it does not univocally represent the hegemonic interests of the dominant classes but is able to articulate sites of dissent and opposition, giving voice to the images and discourses of minorities. In Paolo Genovesi's 2016 film *Perfetti Sconosciuti* (Perfect Strangers) Peppe, played by Giuseppe Battiston, and Lele, played by Valerio Mastandrea, swap mobile phones before taking part in a strange game during a dinner with friends. At the end of the film, we discover that these scenes have actually been only imagined by one of the protagonists because Rocco, played by Marco Giallini, makes sure the game cannot be played. In this imagined version of the game, at a certain point, following a series of misunderstandings, we discover that Peppe is homosexual. The other guests are angry because he never told them; they have been friends for ages, so they ask for an explanation. At this point, his friend Lele intervenes and answers for Peppe: "I'll tell you why he never told us. This evening I was gay for two hours, and I can tell you it was not pleasant". Genovesi addresses the gap between someone's real homophobia and the tolerant and universalistic attitude this same subject may fake. In this sense, it could be argued that, in relation to the particular topic of homophobia, Paolo Genovesi's film contributes to the dissemination of a sustainable, non-discriminatory series of images.

In reference to the war of dreams, the contribution of Stuart Hall[19] is fundamental, because according to Hall, images lend themselves better than words to the construction of effective and legitimate worlds. Images can shape cultural hegemony in the Gramscian sense in ways that would be unthinkable with written texts. Hall explains that this is because with images, the relationship between signified and signifier – to quote De Saussure's well-known distinction – is not as arbitrary as it is with words. While the word-cat is conventionally used to designate the living-being-cat (in Italian we say *gatto*, in English *cat*, in German *Katze*, in French *chat,* etc.), the image-cat shares many more characteristics with the living-being-cat: a tail, whiskers, two eyes, fur, four legs, etc. However, it does not purr, meow, or scratch. Stuart Hall tells us that the conventional relationship that exists between the image and the animal is less arbitrary than the one between the word and the animal. The theory Hall developed many years ago with reference to images continues to be useful today, as it allows us to analyse how effective processes of construction of hegemony are when they involve the use of visual texts. Images are literally *soaked* in hegemony, as values can be better concealed and made to circulate neutrally. Images construct worlds in which users have less freedom compared to words. In the process of decoding, a written text is much more open. A visual text, on the other hand, is relatively less open, and for this reason, it lends itself less to subversive, divergent, and oppositional readings. Images play a fundamental role; they are powerful, and they can function by effectively constructing worlds and parallel realities. As imitations of reality, they can be so faithful that they may seem to coincide with it. The process of naturalising hegemonic discourses seems easiest when it involves visual texts; these are the most effective tools in the formation and transformation of cultural hegemony. On the one hand, images support and shape the institutional discourse of media producers; on the other, they influence and delimit all the possible meanings of the social practices of their users. So if what we have just described seems to be a reasonable hypothesis, why is it that we care about the food we eat and the water we drink, but we do not seem to care about the images we see?

1.3   *The imaginary at stake in social conflicts*

A further brief theoretical reflection is needed to better clarify the role of social visual representations in the production of inequalities, discrimination, and the toxic culture we would gladly do without. Images, in fact, constitute one of the fundamental terrains on which to compete to socially construct gender, ethnicity, generational identities, and social class. A useful concept for proceeding in the analysis of what constitutes a sustainable imaginary is the concept of colonised image introduced by Augé in his essay *The War of Dreams*. The author describes how the clash between peoples has often been accompanied by the clash between imaginaries:

> Anthropology has been interested in the individual imagination, in its perpetual negotiation with collective images; in the making also of those images or rather of those objects (sometimes called "fetishes") which appeared both as producers of images and as social connection.

78 Visual pollution

Anthropologists, moreover, have had the opportunity (...) of observing, through situations coyly described as "cultural contact", how confrontations of the imaginary accompanied (...) conquests and colonisations, and how resistances, withdrawals and hopes took shape in the imagination of the vanquished for all that it was lastingly affected by, and in the strict sense imprinted with, that of the victors.[20]

According to Augé, a culture is only alive to the extent that, by encountering or clashing with otherness, it manages to transform itself, to bring into play its processes of symbolisation and institutionalisation. If we take into account a naive observation of the daily news in Italy, for instance, we might ask ourselves whether this means that in the face of the forced migration across the Mediterranean sea of thousands of young and old men, boys and girls, and women (often pregnant, sometimes as a result of rape occurred during their journey to migrate), a living culture such as ours could and should welcome, care for, help, try to support, and, on the other hand, creatively and vitally incorporate pieces of other migrant cultures.

Culture also serves to render the processes of production of meaning thinkable (through the use of symbols that culture makes available) and manageable (through institutions). The analysis of hyper-modernity, to which much of the French anthropologist's work is dedicated, mainly concerns moments of cultural contact, when the series of symbolic forms and the imaginary of different peoples meet. Such moments represent crucial and delicate phases in which the identities and othernesses of a people or social group are recast, in which the relations between dream and power, between the dominant imaginary and the colonised imaginary, are laid bare. The point is that the imaginary functions as the reservoir of our dreams and projects. *It traces and influences (to the point of delimiting) the boundary of the images we are capable of thinking*. While we have repeatedly stressed how complex it is to apply and refer to the concept of visual pollution, we must also realise that it is very unlikely that all the junk imagery we are exposed to on a daily basis has no effect on us. If words are so powerful, why should we be immune to images?

Moreover, how colonised and/or homologated is the imaginary circulating in our society? Cultural nomadism, which many scholars have spoken of, is like the other side of the coin of this globalisation of harmful images, of these drives towards the homologation of the available imaginary that seems to be transported from one society to another without any form of cultural rootedness. "A practice of the intervals, of the interfaces, and of the interstices",[21] which Rosi Braidotti spoke of many years ago, represents precisely the other side of the coin with respect to homologation: it is in the exercise of marginality, frequenting transit zones, and placing oneself at the edge of the world that the homologating regime of stereotypes spread by the media and by social media can be subverted. In this perspective, the homeless self seems to respond to the delocalisation of experience produced by the media with the conscious and reflexive delocalisation of its own borders. Faced with an imaginary that appears to us to be increasingly colonised, the most effective practices of resistance consist in placing oneself at the margins, in fragmenting the preconfigured repertoires of meaning, and in frequenting with awareness other possible imaginaries. Only by doing this may our social imaginary become truly sustainable.

Going back to Stuart Hall's theory[22] on the greater power images have to represent reality, we see that this same power can also be polluting, if and when images function as a way to legitimise and "naturalise" social inequalities. Images are therefore, by definition, the perfect materials for constructing forms of cultural hegemony, as they conceal values and disguise alternatives. Visual pollution and a sustainable imaginary become all the more pressing the clearer the role played by social imaginary becomes, which is what is at stake in conflicts between different groups. What must also be considered is the new forms of experience made possible by the media and social media, namely, experiences that are uprooted and disconnected from the *hic et nunc*, the here and now. What we see on our computer screen has the potential to become part of our everyday life. But how does it concretely happen that I am – or rather, can become – *also* what I see? To rephrase it in a more theoretically complex way: how do the processes of interpellation, to use Foucault's words, that subjects put into practice with respect to the images circulating on the web or to be found in advertising and television series work concretely? Why do some images turn more easily than others into material for the construction of identity? How much freedom do we actually have when coming into contact with stereotyped images of ethnicity, gender, and social class that a certain advertising campaign keeps presenting to us? In other words, why is it that given an imaginary animated by models with potentially anorexic physiques who become the undisputed icons of female beauty, only a few – fortunately, it is only a few – adolescents actually become anorexic, identifying with these skinny and basically sick bodies that are paraded on national and international catwalks? From our point of view, this is not a trivial question, nor is it merely a theoretical one. If we do not understand how and what happens in concrete terms, if we do not have the conceptual tools to fully grasp these mechanisms, we will not be able to understand how to "do better".

The symbolic order is made up of all the repertoires of images that are available to us: this does not mean that if I see a model who is very thin and is potentially anorexic on the cover of "Vanity Fair", I – a young teenager from a marginalised context – will necessarily fast, but it is equally true that the images used by the media and cultural texts (it could be a book by Donna Haraway or the series *Sex and the City*) represent the boundaries inside which

80 Visual pollution

I will or can choose how to represent myself. The mere fact of being exposed to the social imaginary renders us in part permeable to the values, attitudes, and lifestyles we see being represented daily. It is a question of understanding the relationship of mutual influence between social representations, media texts, and processes of definition of subjectivity. The fact that a certain subject, particularly a female subject, appropriates one social representation but not another is an issue that cannot be fully explained, not even by referring to Wendy Hollway's theory, which defines power as that which explains a subject's investment in a specific discursive position. This theory also claims that this investment is not necessarily conscious or rational. Indeed, this investment actually takes place in a slightly different manner: it is almost always a tacit, unconscious, and mostly irrational investment that can involve both a very sexist media representation of women, for example, or one that is in line with feminist ideals. The real problem, once again, has to do with the concept of probability: how many social representations are available and what are they like? An individual female subject does not *necessarily* invest in a certain discursive position only because it is the prevailing one in the imaginary or in the discourse on gender circulating in society, but the probability of her doing so certainly increases. If we reason in terms of probability, perhaps it becomes impossible to understand the subjects' individual experience of interpellation. We can, however, better understand overall trends (i.e. the average, median experience, or the fashion dictating the distribution of attitudes). It could be argued that the average experience does not exist except in the perception of sociologists, mathematicians, and statisticians. However, the average continues to be a useful tool for understanding social reality. If this were not the case, researchers would no longer be using it.

2. Thoughts and images in television series

The images we think can be viewed as being the aesthetic forms of our self: they are like the furniture we arrange in the dwellings of our subjectivity. Where do the images we see, which subsequently generate the images we think, come from? In the contemporary world, they mainly come from cinema, the web, advertising, and, last but not least, television series. Does this mean that, at least in part, we let "Mr. Netflix" suggest the settings for our thoughts? Very often, this seems to be the case.

During the first lockdown, we all taught online. I was teaching a course in sociology of communication for first-year students with a bachelor's degree. Hundreds of male and female students fresh out of high school. Lots of enthusiasm and a slight sense of disorientation. In those days in my virtual classroom, there were many male and female students confined to their small rented rooms in Rome, with families in Bergamo, Brescia, and Genoa. In that phase, COVID-19 was raging in the north, and the parents of these students, who lived in the part of Italy most affected by the pandemic, were absolutely opposed to the idea of their children returning home. So there I was, lecturing in the classroom, trying to make the bright young minds I had in front of me passionate about the founding texts in sociology, but they were heartbroken and anxious about their thoughts elsewhere. We were all distressed. I didn't know what to do. It was the early stages of online teaching, and as teachers, even we didn't know where to start. We had basically brought the university classroom home. Sitting in our nice living rooms, we were trying to spread notions, knowledge, authority, and, above all, large doses of courage. It was then that I invented a sort of collective game. I called it "art-media workshop", though it should have been called "an exercise in smiling by learning some elements of solid sociology while half of Italy struggles in intensive care". To make it more effective, I also decided to give a small score to those who took part, a score that would then contribute, in a rather important way, to determining the grade of the final exam. The fact is that I soon realised that nobody cared about the additional score. Once we started our game, I couldn't stop it; the hours I spent at the computer with my students on that course doubled compared to normal class hours. I was very tried, but happy because I had found a way to be with them, to support them a little while many were away from home; moreover, I could teach what I loved: sociology. The workshop consisted of taking one of the classic texts included in the exam handout and organising a lesson for the rest of the classmates in which, after explaining the main concepts dealt with in that essay, they had to look for references in film, theatre, music, or advertising or television series that would help explain those same concepts. The texts included in the course were actually very suitable for the purpose of the workshop; for example, Alfred Schütz's essay *The Stranger* was rendered with material taken from ads, films, and similar things. It must be noted that I teach in a faculty of drama, arts, and music studies, so the kind of reflection we were developing was in line with the sensibility and skills of my students. Moreover, the exercise forced them to work in virtual groups, which drastically reduced the feeling of being alone at home. Suddenly, we found ourselves discussing sexism, racism, and other forms of discrimination in *Casa de Papel* or *Suits*. They talked about *The Queen's Gambit* or *The Good Wife* while I quoted – nostalgically – *Downton Abbey*. The sociologists they were supposed to study for the exam were suddenly alive; thoughts flowed happily from me to them and from them to me, and we smiled as best we could in those gloomy days. Everything was a sort of discovery: "Are you telling us you've never seen *Breaking Bad*?" They asked me. "No, I'm sorry, it's not my kind of series". All of a sudden, we were speaking a common and direct language and could dress our thoughts with similar images. Never before had I thought that I could teach ethnomethodology or Stuart Hall's encoding/decoding model using *Grace and Frankie*.

82 Visual pollution

Yet, we have always known this; we have known it since the time of Homer: stories serve to construct worlds, and listening to stories is a way of taking part in those worlds. Today, many stories, some of them truly beautiful, are mostly told with images, and images can seep into our minds like vital nourishment or like dangerous poison.

2.1 La Casa de Papel *and the aesthetics of money*

Money Heist (2017–21) is an award-winning Spanish television series distributed by Netflix and created by Álex Pina. In light of the considerations made so far, it could be argued that this series possibly represents a soft-crime response to the issue denounced by Bauman and other scholars (mentioned in Chapter 2), namely that today we are acknowledged as subjects inasmuch as we are consumers, and, given that a great many economic resources are needed in order to consume, money is a sort of Pied Piper in modern times. Probably one of the reasons why *La Casa de Papel* appeals to almost everyone, regardless of age, gender, or level of schooling, is that this story can be interpreted as an updated version of the Robin Hood saga, one that responds to contemporary needs; in other words, it is no longer about stealing from the rich to give to the poor, as Robin Hood did, but rather, given that it is not possible to not need money, it is possible to steal money without, however, actually stealing from *anyone*. This *anyone*, or better yet, the *no-one* par excellence, is the state mint. Stealing money from the state mint is like stealing a small slice of cake from a cake factory. It is an exemplary robbery, capable of overturning the zero-sum game involved in all theft: "What I take by stealing, I take from you". In this case, the robbers, who are clear about not wanting to hurt or kill anyone, steal without taking anything from the Spanish people. In fact, to put it bluntly, they steal money that would not even exist without them because they print it themselves. The idea is both brilliant and original. These are good thieves who come to the rescue (at least in our imagination) of all those millions of Spanish and European citizens, forced to work in order to consume and to consume in order to be acknowledged as subjects, who are therefore forced to act, in spite of themselves, as permanent intermediaries between incoming and outgoing money flows. Added to this are some expedients that make the plot even more intriguing. First of all, the mastermind of the scheme is called *the professor*, suggesting that knowledge finally serves a purpose. In fact, knowledge is necessary to plan the perfect heist, which aims to secure once and for all what the market forces every consumer to procrastinate indefinitely: the achievement of happiness and well-being and the possibility to solve all of our daily problems with considerable economic resources. The robbery will allow everyone, for the rest of their days, to buy *on the market* the means to deal with any problem that may arise in the future. In this sense, the solution, which is generated by the rules governing the market and consumer society, solves the problem of economic scarcity that has become a fundamental issue for millions of citizens in Spain and the rest of the world precisely because of the rules governing the market. Also, we have in Tokyo, Nairobi, and Stockholm criminals who are exceptional women – women who know how to shoot, fight, defend themselves, steal, drive (very well), fall in love, and are beautiful but not perfect. In short, they know how to do a great many things. But are they also feminists? Well, maybe they are, they also support each other...

With these remarks, my intention is not at all to downplay the series that nailed me to my beloved sofa for many evenings. No wonder I/we like *La Casa de Papel*; this story, told by a sequence of images, frees us from the worst existential disease of our century: our obsessive fixation with money and the belief that goes with it that money is the necessary condition for all happiness. Of course, money *can* free us and make us happy, but surely this is not the only way to be free and happy, at least when one's basic needs are already guaranteed. *La Casa de Papel* is a successful series because it transforms a gang of robbers, a gang whose members are underdogs (in fact, they are chosen by the professor to be members of the gang both because of their particular skills and because their personal history identifies them as people who "have nothing left to lose") into a group of heroic activists, which very predictably makes the Spanish population side with them. The protagonists of the series are able, with their actions, to expose a mysterious aspect of the western market economy, at least for all those who have no specific training in economics: if money is made by central banks, how come, when faced with the poverty and hunger of their own citizens, do central banks not decide to print more money and give it to those in need (not to other banks, which are already very rich)? An economist would answer: "Because this would trigger inflation". Yet, regardless of the technical reasons why the scarcity of money, or rather of its unequal distribution, cannot be solved this way, this unanswered question remains fixed in the minds of ordinary citizens. *La Casa de Papel* stresses this contradiction not by promising a Robin Hood solution but by offering an individualist solution to the chronic shortage of money. Why do we identify with the robbers and not the cops? Well, it is impossible to identify with the latter, as they are controlled by the head of the Spanish secret services, who is portrayed as a fierce official. Even the policewoman in charge of the investigation that lasts for many seasons falls in love with "the professor" and finally becomes a member of the gang (Lisbon). In short, this very popular television series subverts the traditional way viewers tend to identify with the good guys, who are often on the side of the law. The series is based on the idea of an unjust state (the Spanish state is personified by the head of the secret services, a character who seems to belong to Franco's regime, unaware that his country has undergone a democratic transition). Precisely because the state is unjust, it can expect no obedience from its citizens

84 Visual pollution

(although I suspect that Hannah Arendt would not agree with my reinterpretation of the concept of civil disobedience!).

What is surprising, in fact, is that this series also appeals to people who believe in a culture of legality, probably because it performs a semantic operation (one that is very successful) in which a state that is unjust actually deserves resistance. These forms of resistance, however, are transformed into something very different from what we would expect: robbing a bank is generally considered to be a criminal act, even by the perpetrator. In this case, a robbery becomes not only an act of free riding (I can use the goods and/ or services of a community without bearing the costs and expect all other members of society to shoulder the expenses, which is, in other words, a sophisticated way of punishing those who do not do their part), but a collective act of civil resistance by a group of disadvantaged people, an exemplary way of protesting against a despotic government.

The series likely resonates with many European viewers due to the public memory of Franco's dictatorship. Consequently, the oppressive Spanish government depicted aligns with this historical memory. The show feeds on our sense of rebellion, directed firstly against the consumer society that we are all tired of belonging to – this society has proven largely inept at fulfilling its promises, forcing us into a perpetual cycle in which we work tirelessly to earn money, only to spend it compulsively immediately afterward. Additionally, this sense of rebellion is directed against governments that, in the face of scarcity of money or, more accurately, its unequal distribution, and the extreme poverty of the majority of the population, fail to do the glaringly obvious: provide money to those who do not have any. The series is amusing and also astonishing, but for the whole duration, we keep liking the robbers of *La Casa de Papel*. Indeed, the subversive-populist message the series seems to convey goes like this: *we must reclaim money that does not rightfully belong to the central bank but to all of us citizens.*

2.2 The Good Wife, The Queen's Gambit, *and the other female characters: neoliberal feminism*

In the book *The Rise of Neoliberal Feminism*, Catherine Rottenberg analyses the ways in which neoliberalism has drastically transformed the scope and language of feminist theories:

> Drawing on the work of Wendy Brown, Michel Feher, and Wendy Lerner, I understand neoliberalism not merely as an economic system or a set of policies that facilitates intensified privatization and market deregulation, but as a dominant political rationality or normative form of reason that moves to and from the management of the state to the inner workings of the subject, recasting individuals as capital-enhancing agents.

Neoliberalism's ongoing and relentless conversion of all aspects of our world into "specks" of capital, including human beings themselves, produces subjects who are individualized, entrepreneurial, and self-investing; they are also cast as entirely responsible for their own self-care and wellbeing. It is perhaps important – and paradoxical – to note that precisely as market rationality has gained ascendency, postfeminism, which scholars such as Angela McRobbie and Rosalind Gill have argued is itself a product of neoliberalism, has been eclipsed by this new form of feminism. Indeed, the entrenchment of neoliberal rationality seems to have led not only to the corrosion of liberal feminism and the advent of postfeminism, but more recently, it has spawned a new form of feminism. All of which raises a series of fascinating questions: why might neoliberalism need feminism? What does neoliberal feminism do that postfeminism could not or cannot accomplish? What kind of cultural work does this particular variant of feminism carry out at this particular historical moment? And, finally, what exactly are its modes of operation?[23]

Catherine Rottenberg decides to analyse this phenomenon when she notices that many influential women who are visible in the public sphere, such as British Prime Minister Theresa May or Ivanka Trump in the United States, increasingly identify as feminists. However, she observes a distinct shift in the vocabulary used by these new feminists. It is a softened form of feminism, devoid of traditional terminology associated with it. The prevailing terms in this new discourse include "happiness", "leaning in", "responsibility", and "balancing work and family". The revolutionary and transformative essence of traditional feminism seems to have been lost, with no mention of patriarchy, social justice, or women's emancipation. It resembles a numbed-down version of first-wave feminism. Rottenberg rightly asks: Who does this domesticated version of feminism benefit? What purpose does the feminist *Weltanschauung* serve under neoliberalism?

Many argue that this trend is embodied by new heroines featured in Netflix television series, notably Alicia Florrick. The lead character in *The Good Wife* (2009–16), produced by Cbs and distributed by Netflix, she is played by Julianna Margulies, who was awarded the Golden Globe in 2010 and the Emmy Award in 2011. The plot unfolds with a classic beginning: a woman, the wife of a powerful man who betrays her and becomes involved in multiple sex scandals, chooses not to leave him. This narrative echoes the real-life stories of numerous first ladies, including Hillary Clinton. As the plot progresses, the incarceration of Alicia's husband, Peter Florrick, forces her to resume the career she had abandoned as a lawyer, working in a law firm to support her children. She secures a job offered by a lawyer friend, who used to be her boyfriend when she was at university. Alicia can be viewed as emblematic of this variant of neoliberal feminism. While she is an authoritative

86 Visual pollution

and emancipated woman capable of even more emancipation, her cognitive universe lacks a perception of the unequal distribution of economic and social resources between men and women. She carefully balances work and family, carving out a space for freedom in which to experience affectivity and intimacy, but ultimately, she remains the wife of an unfaithful and domineering master and father figure. While he is unpleasant, she is likeable and successful. Alicia Florrick certainly identifies as a feminist, but she does not symbolically challenge the overarching order. In the narrative of the highly successful character in *The Good Wife* series, feminism seems to go from being an ideology capable of disrupting the entire symbolic and political order rooted in patriarchy to becoming an existential and strictly individual perspective. By allowing single, successful women to access feminist discourse and define themselves within it, this variant erodes its antagonistic nature. It is as if patriarchy, thanks to this new version, can hide itself more deeply and continue to impact all other women who are not Alicia Florrick, who cannot even dream of aspiring to such visibility and such a role. This is a characteristic that Rottenberg's reflection helps to elucidate: neoliberal feminism appears to be a new version of feminism in which there is a shift from an antagonistic collective political ideology to a strictly individual life project, an existential choice, without any significant impact on the overall economic, political, and social order. It seems to amount to a much-needed and minimal concession, a symbolic one, able to postpone structural change. While Alicia Florrick may not explicitly identify as a feminist, there are episodes (such as when she agrees to represent a woman in the army who has been molested) where she is very clearly defending women's rights. In the series, there is at least one additional female protagonist who appears to embody the same model: Diane Lockhart, portrayed by Christine Baranski. Diane is a strong and authoritative woman; she is in charge of the firm alongside William Gardner. Initially single, we later see her navigates a complex marriage, making a considerable effort to balance work and family. Diane has strong values yet remains radically pragmatic in her decision-making. Is she a feminist? In this neoliberal variant, the answer is probably yes.

The protagonist of *The Queen's Gambit* is another female figure who lends herself well to this kind of reflection. She is the protagonist of the television series written by Scott Frank and Allan Scott, distributed by Netflix in 2020, and based on the novel of the same name by Walter Tevis.[24] The plot explicitly invites a feminist interpretation, as it is the story of an orphan girl who, during the years spent in a girls' orphanage, it taught how to play chess by the caretaker (the only male figure who supported her in the early years of her life). She is later adopted by a family, but soon remains alone with her adoptive mother. The chess lessons from her youth feed her passion for the game, eventually establishing her as an excellent player on the international scene. She is a female heroine who plays and wins in an all-male world.

However, also in this storyline, the antagonistic aspect, from a feminist perspective, is not as incisive as the plot might suggest, and the queen of chess is not the feminist heroine we would expect.

There is another Netflix series worth mentioning as it portrays very different female role models: *Grace and Frankie* (2015–22), an American production by Howard J. Morris and Marta Kauffman, starring Jane Fonda (Grace) and Lily Tomlin (Frankie). What probably makes the difference here, in addition to the plot, is the presence of Jane Fonda, whose history of political militancy in feminist movements and civil rights protests outweighs any character she might play. But far from being relegated to the background, this militancy is amplified by the fact that in this series, Grace is the more conservative of the two friends, while Frankie is certainly the hippy type. It is the story of a great friendship and a story of sisterhood at an age in life when the two women suddenly find themselves separated and alone. This unexpected friendship gives life to a thriving business venture that not only produces profits but also generates physical and psychological well-being for other elderly women. Grace and Frankie are "trendy senile" women, and the series is decidedly feminist in that it revisits, and breaks down, many stereotypes about elderly women: for example, the idea that two older women can no longer be attractive or have a satisfying intimate and emotional life, or that they are not capable of running a new business effectively with managerial creativity.

The protagonists, on the contrary, make money by producing vibrators that can be held also by elderly women with arthritis in their hands, thus allowing many of their female peers to experience pleasure after having been deprived of a happy sex life for several years. In a later season, they embark on a new project: a series of heated toilets, which also allow elderly men and women to easily get up from their seats. This toilet seat was initially invented by Frankie to help her beautiful elderly friend Grace not to get stuck in the bathroom alone. Grace, in fact, despite her age, has recently married a handsome and much younger man, played by Peter Gallagher, who is also a multimillionaire. However, due to her physical limitations, she struggles to get up from the toilet without assistance. To conceal this from her husband, she calls her friend Frankie, who rushes to her rescue every time. At first, Frankie finds a beautiful statue for her that the two friends strategically place in the bathroom. Grace uses a long scarf as a makeshift liana and manages to hoist herself up. Later, Frankie designs an innovative toilet-seat-that-assists-in-standing-up, transforming her friend's problem into a potential business venture. The series ends with the two elderly women, still close friends, happily living together in their house by the beach. Additionally, the series addresses LGBTQ+ issues, as the two friends find themselves living together when their respective husbands decide to run off together. After working for decades as divorce lawyers for the same law firm, as soon

88 Visual pollution

as their children become adults, the two husbands disclose to their wives that, beyond friendship and professional partnership, they have been in love for over 30 years. Events in the series take place in the beach house in San Diego, California, which belongs to the two families and where the two women, who have now separated, reside, and in the home of the two ex-husbands, who have found happiness together, surrounded by friends from the gay community in San Diego. Ultimately, the series is truly feminist: without sugar-coating any aspect and maintaining its antagonistic force, it prompts viewers to reflect while also making them laugh by deconstructing unwarranted sexist and homophobic prejudices. It is an ironic and light-hearted series, yet remarkably effective in communication compared to many cultural messages infused with invective and social anger.

2.3 Extraordinary Attorney Woo: *genius and Asperger's syndrome*

In 2022, Netflix released a South Korean television series (K-Drama) that was well received by audiences and critics called *Extraordinary Attorney Woo* (the original title is *Sanghan byeonhosa U Yeong-u*), starring actress Park Eun-bin. The storyline touches on a theme aligned with "political correctness": a young lawyer from a modest background graduates with top marks in law. Despite her exceptional qualifications, she struggles to secure employment for over six months because she is affected by Asperger's syndrome. She is finally hired by a prestigious law firm. In essence, she seems to be the South Korean version of Alicia Florrick, though characterised by a different type of social vulnerability. The first series, in fact, depicts a typically western patriarchal culture, in which a young woman achieves outstanding results in the study of law but chooses to focus on her children and husband, a brilliant politician, instead of pursuing a successful career. The sudden sex scandal that jeopardises his career forces her to go back to work and places her in a professional and personal position of significant social vulnerability. In the second series, the young lawyer is academically brilliant and has achieved excellent results in her university career but grapples with Asperger's syndrome, which manifests itself in a series of evident behavioural disorders. In addition to her disability, Woo's life is marked by the fact that she grew up with her father in poor living conditions, having been abandoned by her mother, whom she never had the chance to meet. However, after a six-month search, she secures a position with a prominent law firm. The series has a poetic quality; it resembles a fairy tale both because of the plot and its narrative strategies. One of the symptoms young Woo experiences is an unwavering love for the world of cetaceans, a topic she eagerly and lengthily discusses with anyone, even when it is completely unrelated. This dream world, which functions as a sort of recurring leitmotif in her daily work, becomes the symbolic resource that provides the brilliant insights that allow her to win a number of court cases. The story is as improbable as it is delightful: viewers are aware of participating in a fantasy world, but this world is the one many probably wish they could live in, at least in the first episodes. The positive characters prevail, the bad people repent or are defeated in court, judges are caring and impartial, courts function smoothly, and wrongdoers are mostly convicted. Moreover, though there are plenty of negative feelings and intentions, the positive characters construct a sort of protective wall around Woo as they increasingly look up to her, both professionally and personally. Determining the series' social usefulness for a public understanding of Asperger's syndrome is not easy. There are certainly erroneous and misleading aspects in the representation of this particular form of autism spectrum disorder; however, this is not the most relevant point. Even though the representation of the syndrome is somewhat sugar-coated, as the more serious aspects observable in real cases are absent, what is striking and what, to some extent, educates the viewer is the depiction of the gaze of the other. What is important is not so much what Woo does, but what the others around her do, who are not portrayed as being superficially available. For example, in high school, Woo is subjected to continuous and very serious bullying by all her classmates, at times culminating in real physical violence. Only one student takes her side: Dong Geurami, who, being marginalised because of how aggressive she is, not only becomes Woo's best friend, but also manages to physically defend her from these attacks. Woo's reactions to classroom violence are rather unrealistic if we consider how a normal school functions. Here we have an autistic young girl who seeks refuge in the teachers' room during recess, who eats lunch in the caretakers' room, while no adult in the school seems to notice this or take an interest in her. This violence is portrayed in a rather bland way, as Woo does not show her emotions, and viewers cannot "feel" her suffering. On the contrary, Woo's professional universe is populated with some extremely positive figures who help and support her. The most interesting part, for the purposes of our reflection on the various forms of visual pollution and on the types of narrative we find in series that are able to effectively counter this pollution, has to do with the "differently abled" way these able-bodied individuals learn how to see both what Woo lacks compared to them and what she has that they do not have, which is her brilliant legal competence. This is the type of gaze that should be reinforced. We must remember that it is a fairy tale, so this learning process seems to be magically mastered by everyone, while in the real world, the experience of people with this syndrome is rather different. The point is, however, that the sense of hope we see in this attentive gaze and the loving care it expresses towards Woo proves beneficial for all of us. Woo is an inspiring K-Drama, because it tells of a world in which the right to ingenuity is safeguarded, as if it were a real community value. It is a world in which social vulnerability does not prevent brilliance from asserting itself

90 Visual pollution

and being acknowledged. In short, it is a world that does not exist, though it is one in which we would all like to live.

2.4 Downton Abbey *and the nostalgia for lost dwellings*

Downton Abbey (2010–15), a British series produced by Masterpiece and Carnival Films and written by Julian Fellowes, achieved extraordinary success with audiences and received several Emmy Award nominations in 2012. Set in Yorkshire on the fictional estate of Downton Abbey, the story unfolds between 1912 and 1926 during the reign of King George V. It revolves around the aristocratic Crawley family and their servants. While the plot unfolds in the course of the six seasons with a pace that is not particularly gripping, some historical events naturally intertwine with the family history, transforming it and adding excitement to the series. In particular, the sinking of the Titanic on 15 April 1912, marks the beginning of the story, while later on we witness some of the battles fought during World War I. The characters are well-drawn and convincingly portrayed, but the most interesting aspects of the series have to do with the costumes, sets, and the aristocratic lifestyle. *Downton Abbey* was very successful, and two film versions were also released: *Downton Abbey* (2019), directed by Michael Engler, and *Downton Abbey: A New Era* (2022). Exterior shots were filmed in the property surrounding a beautiful English castle in Hampshire, Highclere Castle, owned by Lady Jean Margaret Herbert, a countess and friend of Queen Elizabeth. This historical series resonated with the public by reconstructing an aristocratic world of bygone times. The lifestyle depicted and the values expressed by the relationships between the servants and the family, of loyalty and subservience, are captivating. Despite the differences, *Downton Abbey* is the English version of Luchino Visconti's *Il Gattopardo* (The Leopard), filmed in 1963. Clearly, applying the concept of Self-Home to *Downton Abbey* is dizzying: what kind of "self" inhabits a house with so many rooms? Probably the self of the family, of an entire dynasty or lineage, the Crawleys. This type of dwelling embodies the history of the entire family, and its aristocratic members are rooted in this space in a way that seems unchangeable. The series allows viewers to closely observe and understand not only lifestyles, but also the social values regulating and literally supporting them, making them possible – the condition of servitude and subservience. These values are in stark contrast with the values that we recognise today as valid in regulating subordinate employment contracts. Yet, as members of the audience, we cannot really disapprove. For example, at a certain point, a maid accepts the courtship of the Earl of Grantham for a brief, fleeting moment, but because of this, she then quits her job, as she does not want to risk putting the Earl in trouble again with her beautiful presence. It is striking that such a turn of events does not immediately alienate viewers; rather, it seems to nicely fit into the plot, which has its own intrinsic coherence. Indeed, the events are entirely credible and acceptable. Today, the Earl of Grantham would likely be accused of workplace sexual harassment, and, above all, he would be deemed fully responsible for the incident, being the older and more knowledgeable master of the house and, last but not least, the employer of the young woman. If we add the great economic disparity between the two and the undeniable fact that the young maid needs the job, as her survival and that of her young son depends on it, one wonders why are we not outraged by the earl's reaction. When the infatuated and financially destitute maid offers her resignation, he is grateful, almost nostalgic for the love he could not experience. While it is implied that the earl will financially support the young woman and her child, the situation is undoubtedly contentious from a feminist perspective. Many episodes in the series should have made us wince, such as the portrayal of the three young aristocratic daughters of the Crawley family who cannot and should not engage in any form of work. Stuck in such a life, it is reasonable to assume that no woman today would endure it for a period of time longer than a summer holiday. There is at least one other event that remains almost concealed in the developments of the plot, which should have provoked controversy: Thomas Barrow is the butler in Downton Abbey, and before that, he was the under-butler and footman in the same mansion. Thomas Barrow is a homosexual; he is discriminated against and persecuted because of his sexual orientation, which he must conceal. In one episode, he helps a newly hired and illiterate servant to learn how to read. When the main butler sees him leaving Thomas' room, he insinuates that Thomas is flirting with him. To avoid embarrassing the young servant, who has not told anyone he is illiterate, Thomas chooses not to defend himself and to carry the burden of this accusation. Since this is a historical series set in the early decades of the twentieth century, it is hardly surprising that a working-class homosexual is persecuted like this. However, what is not clear is why Thomas is portrayed so negatively, with the exception of a few episodes such as this one, in a way that makes it difficult for viewers to positively identify with him. It almost seems that the textual strategy inscribed by the author in this character[25] requires the viewers to detest him. If this were actually the case, it would indeed be very peculiar.

What is it that ultimately makes us interested in the lives of these characters? Probably nostalgia for a world that no longer exists, for mansions so grand they are beyond our imagination, for the flaunted elegance of a lifestyle, of which the social costs of production are effectively concealed. On several occasions, the conversations among the servants reveal divergent points of view: on the one hand, some think that subservience and going into service are conditions that belong to the past, which is why they aspire to another type of job; on the other, there are those who emphasise the fact that the large estate is a large family business, which provides decent jobs to

92 Visual pollution

dozens of them. In short, to say it ironically, the Marxian perspective does not really seem to apply to this British series: the world it describes is a conservative one, a world in which it is the servants' values that legitimise the social divide with aristocracy, to which they are enslaved and subjugated.

3. The hero's journey: Harry Potter's fantasy world

Cinema has produced multiple sagas revolving around the hero's journey. They seem to be the modern counterparts of ancient epic poems, capable of bringing about significant change in the global imaginary. For example, one of the most loved and followed cinematic sagas of my generation was the James Bond series, created by Ian Fleming in 1953 and continued by other authors after his death.

Here, I would like to briefly focus on the analysis of the fantasy world of Harry Potter and its relationship to the process of disenchantment of the world described by Weber. The Harry Potter films are inspired by the novels of J. K. Rowling, and the hero's universe, both in the books and in the film version, has a series of very specific characteristics that, to some extent, explain the enormous success of the saga. Firstly, this alternative world, very different from our everyday reality and completely different, is extremely rich in detail. This aspect is not at all marginal in the way this parallel environment is constructed; in fact, it is the precision of such details that makes it possible to achieve a high degree of realism. There is a strong similarity (limited to this aspect) between Tolkien's *Lord of the Rings* and the Harry Potter saga; indeed, in Tolkien's novel, this element is even more pronounced. Tolkien dedicates numerous pages to meticulously describing geographical details, providing readers with a vivid mental image of the map of the places where characters like the hobbits and Frodo Baggins live. Similarly, in *Harry Potter*, readers are immersed in a world radically different from common experience. Dozens of pages are dedicated to describing its geography, the symbolic order governing everyday life, and its social organisation. There is a series of doors, for example, connecting one world to the other: Platform 9¾, the entry to Diagon Alley concealed behind the Leaky Cauldron pub, or the telephone booth that grants access to the building of the Ministry of Magic; Grimmauld Place No. 12, the headquarters for the Order of the Phoenix. These gateways to the magical realm are all contiguous with everyday life and are invisible to almost everyone except the chosen few capable of entering this parallel world. They are so extraordinary precisely because of their contiguity with the so-called normal world: they are right there, within both foot and eye's reach, though only the eyes that know how and where to look and the feet that know exactly how and where to walk.

In the magical world of Harry Potter, the forces of evil manifest themselves in lights switching themselves on and off, objects that move, and candles suddenly blown out. Space-time categories can be expanded, extended, compressed, and traversed in various ways. Furthermore, corporeality can be hidden from view and can even defeat death. The world of the dead can, under certain conditions, open up and reveal itself to the world of the living; communication between the two dimensions is indeed possible. In short, many of the traditional elements of magic are present, including those that have to do with spells. Although the story of Harry Potter is long and complex (and captivating), it can be summed up in just a few lines: it is the story of an orphaned infant who becomes a boy with special powers and manages to defeat the greatest living personification of evil (Lord Voldemort). It is the story of a young man who is able to defeat a very powerful wizard because of how pure his soul is. In fact, almost all the heroes who fight evil have something in common with Harry Potter. His particular trait is what he received as a special gift from his mother. By dying to save his life, so sacrificing herself for him, she passed on to him the only protection against which no wizard, no matter how powerful and fierce, can prevail: motherly love. The story of Harry Potter, with all its adventures and plot twists, can be summarised by naming an existential and spiritual truth which says that a child who has been truly loved by his mother will become an adult capable of performing great deeds and defeating absolute evil. Clearly, such a message travelled around the globe, turning the story into a planetary success. It is an ode to a universally recognised value, maternal love, and with respect to this value, it communicates self-evident truths: the love and protection of a mother, accompanied by the love and protection of a father (in the story of Harry Potter, he is righteous and loving and dies at the hands of the same evil wizard), create exceptional personalities, positive heroes. This does not mean that those who are not as fortunate cannot accomplish what Harry Potter achieves, but certainly this love, though here it is expressed only in a spiritual form (Harry has never known his parents, as they both died when he was only a baby), is a good starting point. The values characterising Harry Potter's world reflect widely shared common-sense values: firstly, good is represented as being clearly distinct from evil in its essential forms, though not in its manifestations; in many episodes, what initially seems to be an expression of evil turns out to be good, and vice versa. Moreover, friendship is a sacred value, and this sacredness is restated in numerous circumstances, for example, when Harry's beloved friend Hermione is in danger. Opponents must also be respected; Harry saves the life of his enemy and adversary, Draco Lucius Malfoy, who is about to be killed in a fire. In turn, Draco saves Harry's life by refusing to recognise him, even though his parents, Lucius and Narcissa Malfoy, very clearly ask him to betray Harry, his lifelong enemy. Harry's pure heart is what enables him to renounce absolute power, forever destroying the Elder Wand, one of the three gifts of death. The hero who can defeat absolute evil remains humble, modest, and incorruptible; he has no lust for power. It is a story that ideally

94 Visual pollution

redeems us all from the brutality of everyday experience, where the strongest often overpower and overcome the weakest. However, in this narrative, the one who, according to common sense, should be the most disadvantaged (an orphaned child, who does not even have the support of his adoptive family that mistreats him, seemingly without any help or resources) eventually triumphs, becoming the most powerful and famous wizard of his time. It is the story we all would like to hear, and indeed, we wish it were true. We like *Harry Potter* because it expresses nostalgia for that magical world that scientific knowledge and the progressive *Entzauberung der Welt*[26] have definitively banished from everyday life. Probably, the global success of this saga is also due to the fact that it once again allows us to dream of *a world that does not exist*. The imaginary environments into which the films inspired by Rowling's novels transport us are populated with repertoires of images that broaden our view of the world, helping to spread a series of positive values. This saga appeals not only to children but also to parents, who see reflected in it solid family values and an optimistic and positive view of future existence. In this sense, Harry Potter is an example of an ecological imaginary, where evil is staged to be neutralised by good and where a series of values fundamental to the social fabric are reaffirmed and consolidated.

4. Sexism, racism, and other mental pathologies: toxic cultures

We have examined some examples of the imaginary presented in Netflix television series and a particularly successful cinematic hero saga to illustrate, on one hand, how powerful such imaginary is and, on the other, its ability to genuinely question us as individuals. By this, I mean to underscore the usefulness of treating visual pollution as an essential magnifying glass to be carried in our daily lives as a potential tool for protection and discernment. It is important to clarify that this reflection is conducted from the viewer's perspective. In other words, we are contemplating the types of imagery we choose to expose ourselves to every day. However, only individuals can determine the kind of imaginary that is suitable for them. Negative imagery might have a cathartic effect for one person and be highly polluting for another. In this context, the concept of visual pollution serves as a useful tool in everyday life but should not be misconstrued as a means to censor authorship or limit the creativity of visual texts. A further and concluding reflection is needed to focus on the nature of certain widespread mental pathologies that constitute genuine toxic cultures for any democratic society: sexism, racism, and homophobia, to name a few.

4.1 Brief theoretical digression on intersectionality

In recent decades, gender studies have progressively shifted their focus towards the examination of sexual differences as well as other dimensions such as ethnicity, generation, social class, and sexual orientation. Influential African-American intellectuals, from bell hooks[27] to Angela Davis,[28] have encouraged us to contemplate the multiplicity of women's experiences, warning against simplistic stereotypes about the univocality of minorities. The term "intersectionality"[29] has now become commonplace. One key question these reflections prompt is how cultural meanings of differences are socially acquired – how these differences can serve as a foundation for legitimising and "naturalising" persistent social inequalities and discriminations. Numerous scholars have documented the way meanings relating to differences are socially learned through language, social interactions, and the processes of socialisation which take place in our daily life. Yet, our identities are also shaped by various forms of symbolic mediation found in cultural products, and this is where the significance of images and of the imaginary, mentioned earlier, becomes apparent. In essence, we also "are" the novels we read, the paintings we see, the museums we visit, the songs we listen to, the TV dramas and series we watch, the commercials we see, and the scientific theories we learn. We must add to this the various forms of institutional and public communication addressing sexual, ethnic, and generational differences – from medical definitions to body-related technologies spread, for instance, by sports, fashion, and the cosmetics industry. From this standpoint, it becomes essential to investigate how we attribute meaning to differences and what kind of resources we draw upon, more or less tacitly, to construct our gender identities. The meaning we assign to being men and women, belonging to specific groups and generations, is also influenced by social representations disseminated through traditional media (advertisements, films, television series) and new media (websites, video games). In the contemporary world, traditional and social media continue to have a sort of monopoly on our social imaginary, to the extent that, for many social groups, media and the social imaginary tend to coincide. To what extent can representations of gender and ethnicity propagated through various forms of fiction, television series, print advertisements, and TV commercials influence the intricate processes involved in socially constructing meanings of difference? The relationship between gender studies and media (both traditional and social media) is significantly more complex and problematic than it might initially seem. We must turn to an audience theory that realistically considers both the viewers' degree of freedom and their ability to identify and connect with the media images they confront. In this perspective, cultural studies and media studies offer fundamental analytical categories without which no reflection on either gender studies or racism would be possible.

If the media functions as "technologies of gender"[30] providing crucial symbolic resources for the production of meanings attributed to differences, we need to contemplate the new forms of expressive and symbolic inequality characterising contemporary society. An effective analytical dimension

96 Visual pollution

concerns the set of established repertoires continuously offered by media, cultural, and artistic products to social actors for contemplating reality and subjectivity. It analyses the relationship between identity resources, available to social actors within a given culture to construct gender images, and actualised (i.e., constructed) social identities. Indeed, despite seeing very traditional images of women on television every day, we are also able to critically distance ourselves from them and represent ourselves as unconventional women. When discussing media images of women or men, we are always alluding to their potential influence on the audience, not their actual influence. In fact, there are high degrees of freedom within which social actors interpret texts. The distinction between identity resources and actualised identities analytically accounts for precisely this discrepancy: no identity can ever be reduced to a series of texts. There always needs to be a subject who actualises them, interprets, composes, links them together, and produces their meaning. It would be entirely misleading to think that, with regard to gender, for instance, the images produced by American cinema or romance novels are adopted indiscriminately. Firstly, subjects have many other resources available for their own individuation – those offered by other state ideological apparatuses (such as the school or the family). Secondly, they can produce absolutely subjective elaborations in their processes of construction of meaning with a finite but significant number of degrees of freedom, as numerous studies in the field of cultural studies have well documented. Certain contributions from the postmodernist perspective (e.g., Ien Ang,[31] John Fiske[32]) have thoroughly documented the concept of "semiotic power of subjects". However, they have also outlined a portrayal of the media user that diverges from reality. In some more radical versions of the postmodernist strand, an idealised user is presented, brimming with a critical spirit and capable of innovatively decoding any message. The evident limitation lies not so much in attributing such qualities to the media user but in the proposed generalisation: the idea of an informed, critical, and innovative user conveys a trend, a user type that is gradually emerging, but it does not represent the average user.

Another standpoint, often particularly advantageous for television and film producers, is to stress and claim that fiction plays the role of "mirror of reality": if reality is violent, television and film can have no other function than to represent reality as it is. The scholars endorsing these viewpoints – actually not that many – seem to overlook the last few decades of epistemological debate and all discussions regarding the social and media construction of reality. It seems that the only provisional conclusion we can agree on is that the persistent and pervasive imaginary perceived as polluting the enjoyment of a large portion of viewers reasonably and probably influence viewers, even if only partially. Although viewers may indeed possess increased semiotic power, it is likely that their daily exposure to highly toxic forms of imaginary may, in some way, harm them. There are enlightened and innovative television series, films capable of profoundly altering our perspectives on the world, and even television commercials that, for marketing reasons, opt to dismantle established clichés and stereotypes. It is to all these vital forms of imagery that we must continue to turn, so as to prevent our gaze from becoming polluted.

Notes

1 Husserl (1905, 1931); Schütz (1932).
2 Berger and Luckmann (1966).
3 Hume (1738).
4 Bateson, Jackson, Haley, and Weakland (1956).
5 Sartori (2000).
6 Jauss (1972, 1984); Iser (1972).
7 Tota (2014a).
8 Tota (2008).
9 On the relationship between art and social justice, see Dekel and Tota (2017).
10 Watzlawick (1984).
11 On the concept of experience, see also Benjamin (1913).
12 Augé (1999).
13 Van Dijk (2000).
14 Hall (1980).
15 Grass (1997).
16 This perspective refers to very different contributions, such as the social history of imagination (Le Goff 1988; Gruzinski 2001), the reflections of phenomenological psychology on images (Sartre 1948), the philosophical analysis of the relationship between existence and the symbolic (from Cassirer 2020 to Lacan 2007), the contribution of anthropology of hyper-modernity (Augé 1999), cultural studies (Hebdige 1979; Hall 1980; Agger 1992), as well, of course, as all the reflections elaborated by visual studies (Mitchell 2005), feminist media studies (van Zoonen 1994), and feminist film studies (hooks 2015).
17 Augé (1999).
18 Crespi (1978, p. 33).
19 Hall (1980).
20 Augé (1999, p. 5).
21 Braidotti (1994, p. 6).
22 Hall (1980).
23 Rottenberg (2018, p. 7).
24 Tevis (1983).
25 Eco (1979).
26 Weber (1919).
27 hooks (1981).
28 Davis (1981).
29 Crenshaw (1989).
30 Van Zoonen (1994).
31 Ang (1985).
32 Fiske (1989).

In Chapter 4, I propose combining the concept of landscape with that of soundscape and articulating the latter in an ecological perspective, analysing potential forms of noise pollution in our daily lives. The aim is to better comprehend the musical composition of our biographical trajectories and to examine the interplay of soundscape and subjectivity. Additionally, I invite the reader to engage in an auto-ethnography of the sounds encountered daily in order to document the extent to which we are potentially also the sounds we listen to.

Drawing from Murray Schafer, I underscore that noise pollution arises when we stop listening carefully: polluting noises are, in fact, everyday sounds we have learned to ignore and would like to be able to silence. Furthermore, I highlight how, defending ourselves against noise pollution with a mode of listening that is denied, or that is intermittent, we lose the habit of tuning into the rhythmic sounds of nature, the sounds made by others, and even those made by what takes place in our inner self, ultimately becoming accustomed to not listening at all. This is one of the most adverse effects of our constant overexposure to continuous forms of noise pollution in daily life. I then consider the value of silence and its capacity to sculpt sounds, making them reverberate.

While the first part of the chapter centres on the sounds of everyday life, the second part shifts the focus to the music of everyday life. The latter is analysed through the sociological paradigm of music as "agency". Here, on the one hand, I present examples concerning the use of musical devices for the social and commercial definition of public spaces; on the other, I propose considering the concept of "musical self" to analyse the soundtracks of our individual biographies. Finally, I explore the concept of "acoustic past" and attempt to outline a map of the main research paths that have investigated it.

4

SOUNDSCAPES AND THE ECOLOGY OF SOUNDS

> The English composer Sir Edward Elgar was once asked where his music came from. His answer was: "I believe there is music in the air, music all around us, the world is full of it and you simply take as much as you require".[1]

John Cage once said that music is made of the sounds surrounding us, regardless of whether we are in a concert hall or not. A similar idea is expressed by Murray Schafer in his pioneering work on the concept of soundscape, where he suggests considering the world as a macrocosmic musical composition ("the tuning of the world").[2] Until a few decades ago, defining music as a collection of sounds would have been unthinkable. However, for the purposes of what we are discussing, this definition is particularly suitable. Hence, we will consider the concept of soundscape as potentially comprising everyday sounds and/or musical sounds. But what is meant by a soundscape? Also, can we refer to a genuine ecology of sounds and juxtapose it with the notion of noise pollution? What constitutes the soundtracks of our everyday lives? Is there a relationship between these soundtracks and our subjectivity, a kind of *musical self*? These are some of the questions we will explore to better understand the quality and extent of the musical composition of our everyday lives.[3]

While many social scientists maintain that the prevailing cognitive modality in the contemporary world is visual, an increasing number of scholars[4] are involved in sound studies and acoustic environments,[5] documenting how sounds unequivocally play a significant role in marking and denoting social and natural spaces. The concept of soundscape is therefore effectively juxtaposed with the more familiar concept of landscape,[6] which traditionally

DOI: 10.4324/9781003484592-4

100 Soundscapes and the ecology of sounds

pertains to the visual experience of the environment. Also, scholars in the field of aesthetics who focus on landscape agree on the need to extend the traditional concept to other perceptual-sensory dimensions:

> Yet landscape is not only visual. Considering our living experience of landscape, how we perceive it, we immediately realise that various kinds of sensory input are equally essential. For us, citizens accustomed to environments characterised by a constant background noise and often intrusive noises and sounds, the natural landscape often presents itself under the guise of silence. The absence of artificial noise can be as striking as, or even more so than, the visual elements. This is also because what is initially perceived as silence is later discovered to be animated by a multitude of sounds, which are however natural – the rustling of the wind in the leaves, the gurgling of water in the stream, (...). Symmetrically, a landscape that is polluted by the noise of engines and factories can be as disturbing as one contaminated by waste.[7]

In recent decades, the *sound landscape*, or soundscape, has been the focal point of numerous theoretical reflections that emphasise sometimes divergent meanings.[8] However, the term is generally used to encompass *all the auditory reception experiences of individuals immersed in a particular environment*. Emily Thompson[9] reminds us that the soundscape is both a physical environment and the way in which this environment is perceived. In other words, it consists of both a world and the cultural construct that produces the process by which we give meaning to that world. However, does this definition of soundscape truly hold? It appears to stem from a mere extension of the definition of landscape *tout court*. Does music genuinely constitute or prefigure a soundscape as a physical environment? The fact that music is an allographic kind of art, as proposed by Nelson Goodman,[10] renders the definition put forward by Emily Thompson[11] somewhat counterintuitive. However, it remains a useful heuristic tool to better understand the concept of soundscape, and for this reason, we will treat it as valid. But how can we formulate an operational definition, concerning the concept of soundscape, performing the crucial methodological operation essential for any empirical investigation? Can we develop an ethnography of the everyday sounds we hear? Moreover, can we utilise it to gain a deeper understanding of the relationship between the soundscapes we traverse and our subjectivity? If we are the words we hear, why should we not also be, at least in part and potentially, the sounds we hear? "Sound is, in fact, volume"[12] – as Giuseppe Penone[13] reminds us. "It occupies space in an unstable, temporary way; sculpture is also volume and it occupies space in a more lasting way".[14] In this statement by the renowned artist, we find the consistency and materiality of sound, which, in everyday life, we sometimes pretend to ignore.

1. Soundtracks of everyday life: reflections on noise pollution

Noise pollution results when man does not listen carefully. Noises are the sounds we have learned to ignore. Noise pollution today is being resisted by noise abatement. This is a negative approach. We must seek a way to make environmental acoustics a positive study program. Which sounds do we want to preserve, encourage, multiply? When we know this, the boring or destructive sounds will be conspicuous enough and we will know why we must eliminate them. Only a total appreciation of the acoustic environment can give us the resources for improving the orchestration of the world soundscape.[15]

Murray Schafer is right: polluting sounds are the ones we ignore – the ones that stubbornly populate our lives and that we would like to silence. Failing to do so, we condemn ourselves to not listening, often without realising that the habit of not listening, like all habits, is pervasive. By defending ourselves against noise pollution with a mode of listening that is denied, or that is intermittent, we lose the habit of tuning into the rhythmic sounds of nature, the sounds made by others, and even those made by what taken place in our inner self. We no longer know how to listen, as the sounds we are exposed to are mostly cacophonous and dissonant and create discomfort, acute distress, as if the balance between the inside and outside were disrupted. The invitation is therefore to try to identify the soundscapes we actually traverse daily and understand how they influence the quality of our existence. For most of the population, daily life takes place in cities, where noise is deafening. Every day we are exposed to intense background noise so persistent and pervasive that it forces our physical minds to resort to removal mechanisms: we cancel out noise and temporarily suspend our ability to listen. Noises basically overpower us and are so intense, in the contexts we inhabit, that we become used to ignoring them, locking ourselves in the flow of our thoughts. In essence, it is as if, in order to avoid them, we chose to become momentarily deaf. An example of this mechanism is what occurs daily when we are driving in city traffic, using the underground, or even sitting on a bus going through town or on a train that travels great distances in a very short time. Quietness, the absence of noise, and silence have become rare and precious conditions; their scarcity has increased their value[16] and as a result, the market has started commodifying them. Far from being a theoretical slogan, it is a concrete fact; in other words, since silence is a rare and therefore scarce condition, it has become a valuable resource. The market has turned silence into a commodity, which is why, in certain circumstances, silence is being sold to us. For example, on high-speed trains, there are "silent" seats usually reserved for a certain class of travellers that are sometimes more expensive.

If we stop and think about it, what occurs is quite significant from the point of view of individual travellers: they are so exhausted and persecuted by

102 Soundscapes and the ecology of sounds

pervasive everyday noise that they are willing to pay a premium for a seat on the train just to be protected from this excess. However, since noises on a train cannot be entirely eliminated, they are actually paying for others around them to keep quiet. There is shared notion we all pretend to accept, according to which the deafening noise of everyday life – the noise polluting our minds – is caused by people's conversations, while in fact we all know that many other things pollute the soundscapes of our everyday life. It should be noted that the awareness of this polluting noise, which seems to prevent us from listening to the sounds of our inner being and suspends our ability to follow the rhythm of the world, belongs to a very small part of the population, with rather surprising effects. For example, those who live in the countryside are not always aware of the beauty of the soundscape in which they are immersed and of the associated privileges they enjoy. Since for a large part of the population, the hegemonic settlement model continues to be the urban model, those living in the countryside often cannot wait to be in the city or, at least, to adopt, at least partially, an urban-like lifestyle. Events are organised, such as festivals and village gatherings, which do not necessarily respect the acoustic ecology of the landscapes in which they take place and are mostly occasions for consumption, for buying food, drink, and various types of handicrafts. The impression is that when they want to have fun, those living in the countryside tend to seek noise, crowds, and the confusion that characterises cities. It must also be noted that in these circumstances, subjects are reduced to being mere consumers of goods. As a matter of fact, it seems that the only legitimate way to have fun, recreation, and rest work is to consume. I have always wondered why the most popular entertainment in the countryside is not to gather in the woods in silence to contemplate a sunset or organise a festival to honour the trees and plants of one's territory, giving each a name and remembering their history together. Why are village festivals not night trips to go and look at the stars together or to sit in a clearing near a forest on a Sunday morning to listen to the birds sing and recognise the various species? I am sure this does happen, but on one condition: that it is the song of an endangered (and therefore rare, scarce, and potentially marketable) bird; that someone has claimed exclusive ownership of it and made us pay a ticket to listen to it... Perhaps the day will come when someone will have the regrettable idea of filing a patent on sunlight; from then on, humanity will have to pay a ticket to watch the sun rise and enjoy the light of the sunset. What will be even more regrettable, however, is that to many of us, this will seem almost normal.

The fact is that in order to be really able to listen, silence is a necessary condition:

> The divine is an *event of stillness*. It lets us *listen* (...). At the beginning of the sacred rites, the herald would "command silence". (...) We live in a *time without consecration*. (...) Hypercommunication, the noise

of communication, desecrates the world, profanes it. Stillness *produces nothing*. Capitalism therefore dislikes stillness. Information capitalism produces the compulsion of communication.[17]

When we are silent, we can finally think and listen to the profound flow of thoughts that pass through us – thoughts that sometimes seem to come from distant places and times, almost like a silent river that crosses the centuries to question us. Noise pollution, overexposure to sounds, and noise tend to make it impossible to perceive this flow and intercept the possibility of synchronisation.

But let us return to everyday sounds. Another singular trend has to do with the many venues and commercial activities that adopt a specific soundtrack to communicate to their potential customers that they are very busy (that therefore they are in great demand). This soundtrack is intended to make a certain place stand out by giving it certain peculiar characteristics. The nightmare of any shopkeeper, in fact, is to have a totally empty shop.

I am in Rome in a narrow street near Campo dei Fiori. The street is full of restaurants facing each other, trying to attract potential customers and, above all, tourists. For some reason, they mistake me for a tourist and try to convince me that their pizza is the best in the whole of Rome. It's lunchtime, and many of the tables are already full of people eating or waiting to eat. Because of one of those indecipherable and unwritten laws of the market, some restaurants are already very crowded, while others are still half empty. The problem is that when choosing where to stop for lunch, tourists tend to consider how crowded a restaurant is, to treat this fact as a good indicator of quality, under the erroneous assumption that customers are regular clients who are eating there because of the quality of past experiences, not tourists passing by just like them. Usually this is not the case at all, as we are all passionate tourists, we have all randomly chosen the most crowded restaurant where we will be crammed in, badly served after a long wait. However, just a few steps down the same street, a familiar yet surprising sight unfolds – a scenario we witness with curious regularity: amidst all those restaurants, there is one that is completely empty. It lacks nothing compared to the others, and even if it did, no-one would know, as everyone on that street is a tourist. For the unfortunate owner, this situation is the worst of nightmares. He has turned the music on, a lively pop music, which is supposed to invite us to move, to dance, and to smile. He wanders through the tables with his waiters, a sad expression on his face, pretending he has something to do. In this case, the music seems to amplify the emptiness of the space and the perplexity of any potential customer observing from the street. The discomfort arises because the music is intended to signal a crowded place, a festive atmosphere, and therefore only exacerbates the stark contrast between the restaurant owner's expectations and the actual situation: the restaurant

104 Soundscapes and the ecology of sounds

is not crowded; in fact, it is completely empty. Paradoxically, in such a circumstance, it would be preferable if someone had the courage to turn the music off; at least passers-by might be left with the doubt that no-one is anticipating their arrival.

The music chosen for the soundtrack of a club or shop is a more or less intentional possible way of defining the identity of a brand, a venue, a business. A vast amount of research in the sociology of music has been conducted on how music is used to characterise brands, social spaces, various consumer goods, or services.[18] Sometimes, the effects of such musical characterisation may be quite unexpected and contrary to the original intention.

Giulia and her friend are in a bar in Milan. They have been to the cinema and have decided to have a drink together and have a chat. They opt for a place near the Navigli neighbourhood. It stays open until late and is frequented by many regular customers. They decide to sit at one of the small tables inside. However, the music is terribly loud; the indie-pop music is supposed to be background music, but the volume is so loud that the young waiter, likely a university student, can't even hear their orders. They repeat what they have asked for, trying to raise their voice. They basically have to shout. It is the same scene everywhere, as customers are forced to shout to place orders or simply to converse, and the sound effect is rather idiotic: people have to get close to the ear of the person they are speaking with just to exchange a few words. The background music is an arrogant, deafening cacophony; it is irritating. Giulia is bothered by this, but she is also intrigued. She asks the young waiter whether it is possible to lower the volume, to which he responds with a discouraged tone, saying, "No, unfortunately not. The owner won't let me". Not being able to talk to her friend, Giulia tries to imagine what the public definition of the place might be – the one the owner intends to entrust to a soundtrack he seems to be so fond of. She tries guessing: "A trendy place for young people, singles hoping to meet their soulmate or interested in a one-night stand, as well as groups of friends having a good time". The music seems tailored for an audience under 35. Her friend, who is amused by Giulia's discomfort, comments: "Well, we're the wrong age anyway". Giulia replies, "But we are not deaf! The young are also struggling to talk to each other". Perhaps the truth is that in the midst of such chaos, speaking and conversing are not important; what counts for the rest of the people is being there and belonging there. After months of lockdown, these young people need to be part of the chaos, to simply be together and remind themselves, also thanks to the deafening music, that they are alive. But Giulia and her friend have nothing to do with this place; it would be much easier for them to reminisce by silently listening to the waves of the sea. But since the sea is not available, they decide to step outside and sit on the steps of a nearby building. They prefer the evening chill to the deafening noise. Before leaving, Giulia dares to ask the waiter another question: "But doesn't all this noise bother you, you work here every night". He looks at her with intrigue and surprise, as if she were a traveller from another planet, and replies incredulously: "Of course not, we are used to it". He probably thinks Giulia and her friend are a bit strange and somewhat annoying.

There is another trend we can observe analysing the soundscapes we inhabit, one we experience often. It is the rarefaction of sounds that occurs when the punctuation of the sequence "sound – absence of sound" reflects our inner rhythm. In essence, it seems that silence sculpts sound, providing it with the depth and intensity that define it. The emptiness before and after a sound allows it to resonate within our capacity to listen, and this does not only occur with musical sounds, as it concerns all the sounds in our everyday life. Viewing music as a collection of sounds enables us to extend the characteristics of musical sounds to the analysis of those we hear in daily life. It is not about conducting a techno-scientific examination but understanding, in an almost auto-ethnographic approach to our daily lives, the variety of sounds we encounter daily and have learned to ignore.

I find myself in the Lazio countryside at a friend's house. When I wake up in the morning, I sense a feeling of well-being and care. I realise I've done nothing in particular to evoke such feelings; I simply feel good. I am joyful, confident, and happy. This "nothing" is, in fact, quite a lot. The landscape surrounding us is green, tranquil, and bathed in sunshine. Even if it were pouring rain, it would be the same, I would be fascinated by the raindrops on tree branches. Stress, work-related anxieties, and fatigue are in the background – perhaps they have not vanished, but they have certainly significantly diminished. Suddenly, I notice that since I got up, all I see is beauty around me (the garden is beautiful, and next to the house, there is a wood). From the windows, tree branches seem to enter the rooms, but the most crucial aspect is the sounds I've been hearing for many hours without even realising it. In my everyday life, mostly spent in a large city, I'm accustomed to ignoring most sounds because they are the ones I have learned to switch off in order to survive. I carry this habit around with me like an old dress that I can no longer discard, and I find myself no longer listening. Thinking about it now, I realise I haven't truly noticed all the sounds I've encountered since I woke up: the rhythmic chirping of cicadas, the various songs of the birds, the wind rustling through the leaves, dogs barking, and in the distance, the sound of a tractor. After a few hours, I suddenly became aware of the sound of every car passing by on the small country road next to the house. How can they be so noisy here in the countryside? In Rome, I hardly notice them, yet there are hundreds. Here, on the other hand, with only a dozen or so, they seem to make a deafening noise. It dawns on me that it is silence that amplifies the sound of the passing cars – awkward intrusions in an otherwise perfect soundscape. The caring feeling I woke up with has to do with the silence of this soundscape or, more precisely, the rhythmic alternation between

106 Soundscapes and the ecology of sounds

sounds (not noises) and silences. This is where the sense of well-being and joy comes from. Once again, nature proves to be the great therapist of the world, and the soundscape it orchestrates represents the condition through which I can perceive my humanity anew.

The current reflection on the soundtracks of everyday life aligns with a strand of empirical studies that emerged in the second half of the 1990s, introducing a new field of investigation for the sociology of music, which looks at *the musical mediation of social experience*. It particularly focuses on how different social groups, such as young people, use music as a resource of meaning in their interpretative processes of daily life.[19] In this perspective, music has been examined as a cultural vector, a social mediator of experience, and an active and crucial element in much of our daily existence. Indeed, we "do so many things with music": occasionally we drive, eat, sleep, dance, exercise, remember, forget, console, think, write, study, fall in love, and commemorate.[20] The ethnographic analysis of our daily soundtracks presented here derives precisely from this observation. Music is a powerful social, cultural, and cognitive mediator. It mediates the way we experience the world. This analytical approach aims to elucidate the processes and ways in which this occurs daily. It is not only a matter of understanding how the context of reception or production can influence the process of construction of meaning of a musical text[21]; on the contrary, it is about examining how music operates as a resource of meaning, for instance, how our perception of time changes when it is "in music". This has opened up a new field of investigation for the sociology of music, employing predominantly ethnographic qualitative research methods and concentrating on how different groups of social actors employ music as a resource of meaning in their interpretative processes of everyday life. The study of the musical composition of our social experience has been defined as musical ethnography or "music into agency".

How can we, in our daily lives, derive benefits from this kind of study? We can observe, listen to, and analyse the soundscapes that we traverse in our daily routines. We can ask what impact they have on us and whether those are indeed the sounds we would like to listen to, being aware that regardless of our decision to listen or ignore them, the action of denying a sound, though it may be tacit, must be performed perhaps not by our conscious mind, but still, by our sense of hearing. In essence, some part of us will have to contend with that sound – which has transformed into noise because we are ignoring it – which is why we cannot remain entirely unaffected.

2. The musical self and the metaphor of the wax candle

The theoretical paradigm of "music-in-action"[22] has fundamentally altered the collective comprehension of musical languages, emphasising and documenting how and to what extent the social effects of music actively contribute to moulding and shaping physical environments. Indeed, the symbolic organisation of a physical space may also take place with the mediation of music. In this perspective, music has been redefined as a unique form of "agency", which contributes to the formation of the social in various forms and contexts. An insightful metaphor, one that is useful to intuitively grasp, in an immediate way, the potential of this sociological paradigm, may involve comparing music to the flame of a candle and the social to the wax of the candle: music contributes to making the social malleable, much like the flame makes the wax malleable, potentially amenable to changes in shape and consistency. Perhaps music has a similar impact in social situations, as if, by appealing to the emotions of a collective, it were able to unlock a potential for openness. We must understand this comparison for what it is: a mere suggestion that is, however, useful in introducing new elements in our comprehension of the musical composition of our everyday life. It would be misleading to transform this metaphor into an empirically verifiable research hypothesis; instead, this metaphor can assist us in thinking more effectively.

But what is the relationship between music and individual and collective identities? Here, too, we can refer to a broad tradition of studies focusing on the relationship between music and collective movements,[23] which document in particular the role of specific musical genres as the most effective languages for the expression of antagonism by protest movements. In particular, Eric Drott points out how almost all protest movements have in recent decades used specific music as a soundtrack to express their struggle:

> If ever there were any doubts regarding music's significance for political protest, the wave of unrest that has swept the globe since the financial crisis of 2008 should have laid them to rest. Consider the following: the role of Tunisian rapper El Général in catalyzing the Jasmine Revolution; Manu Chao's impromptu performance before Barcelona's Indignados encampment in May 2011; the drum circle whose rhythms resounded through Zuccotti Park during Occupy Wall Street; the transformation of Ramy Essam's refrain "*Irhal, irhal*" ("Leave, leave") into the rallying cry of those demanding Hosni Mubarak's ouster in Tahrir Square; Brazilian demonstrators' playful appropriation of "*Vem pra rua*" ("Come into the street"), a song originally commissioned for a Fiat commercial.[24]

It is evident that music serves to create community and also to constitute antagonistic communities capable of opposing hegemonic power. Historically, examples abound: consider the case of jazz music in the second half of the twentieth century and how this genre helped express the civil rights claims of the Afro-American population, or the relationship between hip hop and ethnic discrimination.[25] There is no need to go over the entire recent history of musical genres to support a banal observation, one that is common sense:

108 Soundscapes and the ecology of sounds

we may hypothesise that there is a musical self and that it can be articulated in both its individual and collective dimension. Returning to the exercise of ethnography of the everyday that inspires the present reflection, what is the relationship between our subjectivity and music? In short, what is our musical self like? There is a French television format called *La Chanson Secrète* that aired on the first channel of French television (TF1). The format was also aired by the Italian Rai 1 from March 2020 to April 2021 with the title *Canzone Segreta*, hosted by Serena Rossi. The six episodes had an average of just under four million viewers, so we may say they were rather successful. What interests us here is the central idea on which this television format is based, in both the original French and Italian versions: a famous person is invited to take part in the programme, and some unexpected guests intimately connected to her biography (e.g., a sister, a son, an ex-boyfriend) sing a secret song, i.e., the one that has marked her biography. The idea that each of us has some music or a series of songs that have contributed in a meaningful way to shape our biography is the exact explanation of the notion of musical self. A friend of mine, whom I will call Ilaria, an invented name, tells me about a musical episode that profoundly marked her biography:

I am in Milan at an important cultural festival. With a group of friends, we decide to go, and suddenly we find out there will be an Inti Illimani concert. I can't believe it. *El pueblo unido jamás será vencido* is the song that defined my adolescence. I spent entire afternoons with my cousin (and my cousin's cousin) in her room with the record player blaring, jumping on the bed, and singing the chorus at the top of our lungs. "In fact, of the three, the only one with any political interests was me", Ilaria tells me again, "because my cousins were intent on shopping for Gucci shoes and purses, which had little to do with Inti Illimani and the culture they represented. That same song returned as a Leimotiv during the last years of high school, during which we all went to demonstrations. Back then, we went on marches, but it was more about the fear of being tested in ancient Greek than real political commitment. Those were the years in which militancy had lost its meaning for our generations, but still, the Inti Illimani continued to represent a sort of bridge, at least a musical one, through which we could dialogue with our older brothers, who were real militants, as they had taken part in demonstrations in 1968. In other words, in those years, there was a sort of competition between real first-class militants and fake second-class militants, but in the meantime, we continued to sing the songs of Inti Illimani at the top of our lungs, and at least we seemed to agree on them. Going back to the festival and the concert in the mid-1990s, Ilaria tells me:

I am there with a group of friends my age. My cousins aren't there, but I'm pretty sure my friends also jumped on the bed as children shouting at the top of their lungs: *El pueblo unido jamás será vencido*. Who didn't back then? So, we take our seats an hour early. It is the event of the year for us. But we soon realise there is no crowd of enthusiastic participants. How is it possible they don't know Inti Illimani? It is a real surprise to us. Suddenly, however, when we realise that there will be no crowd to attend the concert of our cult group, two very young girls sit down in front of us. They must be about fifteen. One says to the other: "What's going on here?" and the other laconically replies: "I don't know, I think it's a concert by someone from Peru, maybe, or Argentina. I think they're called Inti-something, Inti-whatever." This is a real low blow: "Inti-something? Come here little girl, try saying that again and I'll show you." Suddenly, I feel I'm from a different epoch, or rather, I feel we are all from a different epoch. We look at each other a little dismayed and then smile. In fact, now it's our turn to say: "Back then things were so different".

3. Sounds/music and memory: the "acoustic past"

The relationship between sounds, music, and memories has been analysed from multiple perspectives.

a. *The traumatic acoustic body*

Firstly, the acoustic memories of highly controversial events, such as violence, terrorist attacks, and wars, have been studied, starting from the assumption that there is an individual and collective traumatic and post-traumatic acoustic body, which must be addressed, both at the level of individual therapy and at the community level. Some studies in particular have focused on the relationship between auditory experiences and the processes by which we memorise the past, developing the concept of "acoustic past",[26] understood as the series of processes of auditory memorisation of events from both the individual and collective past. In this regard, the studies of Luis Velasco-Pufleau[27] on the auditory memories of some of the surviving victims of the terrorist attack in Paris on 13 November 2015 at the Bataclan Theatre are particularly interesting. What was particular of this attack is that, as it occurred during a concert by the American band Eagles of Death Metal, the victims were presumably fond of music – they were fans of the band or, in any case, attendants at that concert. In the interviews conducted by Luis Velasco-Pufleau[28] with nine victims who survived the Bataclan and three family members, it is clear that from a certain point onwards sounds were the real protagonists. Firstly, because during the attack, the sounds were the only sensory clue the victims had to form an idea of what was happening inside the theatre as it was all dark. Secondly, because those sounds and the music changed the auditory-sensory experience of the subjects forever. The merging of music and silence, in other words, becomes crucial in order to start

110 Soundscapes and the ecology of sounds

working on trauma and trace a path to recovery and healing. In fact, music and sounds take on an ambivalent quality, as they are not only symbols of trauma but also potential resources for reconciliation in order to go back to everyday life. The words of Amelie and Raphaël, two survivors, convey how difficult it is to reconstruct a coherent account of those moments and of the duration of the event: what happened during the attack? The sensory traces are so intense that they overwhelm the survivors, who struggle to reconstruct an individual memory:

> Our senses were marked by so much during this event. You had the sounds, the sound of bullets with the music, the screams, the smell of gunshots, the scent of blood, the pain of those who were hurt, all those sensations, being in the dark... It's all mixed up, you have to really separate them well.[29]

As mentioned, the Bataclan theatre attack has its own specificity, but this type of analysis is undoubtedly highly effective. Is it not true that in many traumatic events we experience sounds and music that may become fundamental? These need not be rare events, such as a terrorist attack; they may also be linked to loss, such as the case of music chosen for one's parents' funeral or a constant noise during hospitalisation due to a long illness. Sounds, both musical and non-musical, have the ability to reverberate on our souls and, therefore, trigger processes of memorisation – or of removal – of trauma. Working on the sounds of trauma, so they may go back to being *our* sounds, or so they may leave our minds for good, can be a decisive step in the path to recovery.

b. *The sounds of the world*

A second strand of studies has interpreted the concept of "acoustic past" in a broader sense, attempting to map all the sounds of everyday life. To this end, there has been an attempt to construct a digital archive of all sounds characterising the contemporary world, starting from the assumption that many of these are bound to disappear over time (for example, the sounds of technical objects being replaced by more innovative objects). In a Canadian university, documentation laboratories have been set up in which the sounds that characterise contemporary soundscapes are recorded to be able to preserve their memory, in case some of them should disappear over time (e.g. the sound of steam engines). These are the Sonic Research Studio Archives, based at Simon Fraser University in Canada, founded by R. Murray Schafer, who later also set up the World Soundscape Project, in order to digitally map all the sounds of the world.[30]

Soundscapes and the ecology of sounds **111**

c. *The soundtracks of our biographies: music and individual memories*

A third type of analysis concerns the way music intersects individual biographies by activating memorisation processes about specific (also happy) events that can be linked back to that particular music. We may think of the soundtracks of our lives. The concept of musical self already mentioned is part of this line of research.

d. *The musical composition of public memory*

A fourth type of analysis has focused on the relationship between musical cultures and public memories of highly controversial events, considering musical language as one of the possible artistic-expressive forms capable of influencing public knowledge of a certain portion of our past. This research analyses the processes by which a highly controversial past is inscribed in public discourse through musical languages. For example, Mark Mengerink[31] studies how, since 1980, heavy metal music culture has represented the figure of Hitler, the Holocaust, and the historical period of Nazism and how these representations intersect and/or contradict other forms of dominant public discourse in relation to such highly sensitive topics for the general public opinion. The results are not what one might expect, because although this music genre sometimes tends to convey shocking messages in relation to these issues, it cannot even be superficially labelled as being in favour of these ideologies and must be considered from a more complex perspective.

e. *The musicalisation of the future*

Another strand explored the capabilities of musical languages in terms of "agency" with regard to the temporal disposition of subjects, with a particular focus on the perception of the future (the concept of "future present" already identified by Saint Augustine). In a book significantly entitled *Hope*, Tia DeNora emphasises how music can be a fundamental factor in an individual's overall well-being and how it can, in some way, contribute to an active disposition towards the future: the disposition towards hope.

> This book is for anyone who has ever hoped, who is hoping, who will hope. That probably includes anyone. (...) Global issues – climate crisis, violence, hostility, pandemics, homelessness, displacement, racism and racial hostility, economic hardship, modern slavery, loneliness, anxiety, mental illness – all of these have intensified. This intensity underlines a global *need* for hope and a corresponding need to *confront* hope – what hope is and what can, and cannot, be achieved by hoping. This confrontation includes distinguishing hope from wishful thinking and simple

112 Soundscapes and the ecology of sounds

optimism. For me, a sociologist with an interest in how things take shape in action, that project also includes understanding hope as a complex form of situated practice.[32]

Hope is defined by the author as "the dream we carry"; which means this dream must be carried and supported. One must take responsibility for one's dreams and fight for them, defending them from oblivion, carelessness, and neglect. The uniqueness of the book lies in the idea it implicitly conveys: that we must develop awareness and responsibility for what we hope for. In this perspective, hope becomes a social activity, a responsible action, and the outcome of a decision that we must uphold every day. It has nothing to do with fatalism; it is not a form of *Waiting for Godot* à la Samuel Beckett.[33] Hope is an inner attitude of the subject who decides in the *hic et nunc*, the here and now, to resist, to keep a positive gaze towards the future. Hope has to do with the present of the future we seek, to quote the well-known distinction made by Saint Augustine in relation to different types of time. In fact, hope is the opposite of despair; despair implies giving up one's dreams. When we despair, we no longer support these dreams, as we believe they will never come true. But why, according to the author, should we hope? Because it is a fundamental step towards happiness and towards the overall quality of our lives. While we hope, we take care of ourselves, even if what we hope for will never happen. Hope is like an act of grace and gratitude in advance for what we expect will happen one day. When we stop hoping, we lose everything we have because we lose what will sustain our ability to endure. In other words, when we stop hoping, we give up and lose ourselves. DeNora articulates a new notion of hope, which becomes a crucial part of the daily methodology necessary for all forms of social change. Hope is a key ingredient in a good recipe for the future, and in this recipe, one of the key ingredients of everyday life continues to be music, as it contributes to producing daily well-being and nurturing positive attitudes. Obviously, this does not apply to all types of music but only to the music the subject considers beneficial.

Arguing that hoping is better than not hoping may seem trivial; however, this is not the case. According to DeNora, to adopt an attitude of hope is a rational and effective action. Hope is a necessary but not sufficient condition to achieve any goal in life and to be successful. No real change or positive transformation can take place if the capacity to hope is lacking; indeed, the possibility of tracing and sketching the series of probable opportunities in our world depends on hope. Referring to Goethe's gentle empiricism, DeNora reminds us that mountains move even though they appear to be motionless. They are alive, as Goethe reminds us, and in perpetual transformation. The daily act of hoping sculpts and shapes the social landscape that surrounds our desires, just as drops of water sculpt and shape stone, helping to create a nourishing terrain that will allow our dreams to grow, germinate, and come true. Hoping is the prerogative of those who know how to observe the mountains and are therefore able to see the slow but constant process that sustains their movement: the sum of many small transformations, apparently irrelevant and almost invisible, will eventually provoke the wave capable of generating a great and sudden change, even though change will mistakenly seem sudden to us. On the contrary, it is the outcome of a long, silent, and invisible process, in which a series of micro-events and micro-decisions have played a fundamental role over a long period of time. It is certainly no co-incidence that a book on hope was conceived and written at a time of very serious international crisis (the COVID-19 pandemic, poverty, mass migrations, and numerous wars taking place around the world) by a scholar who has been working on the sociology of music all her life.

f. *Mental alchemy: music that heals*

Finally, sociological studies have crossed paths with music therapy studies to analyse the ways in which music can contribute to the care of patients with Alzheimer's and dementia, restoring their dignity and well-being. As Oliver Sacks points out:

> In particular, the response to music is preserved, even when dementia is very advanced. But the therapeutic role of music in dementia is quite different from what it is in patients with motor or speech disorders. Music that helps patients with parkinsonism, for example, must have a firm rhythmic character, but it need not be familiar or evocative. With aphasics it is crucial to have songs with lyrics or intoned phrases, and interaction with a therapist. The aim of music therapy in people with dementia is far broader than this – it seeks to address the emotions, cognitive powers, thoughts, and memories, the surviving "self" of the patient, to stimulate these and bring them to the fore. It aims to enrich and enlarge existence, to give freedom, stability, organization, and focus.[34]

The studies of Oliver Sacks have shown that dementia patients, also in the most advanced stage of the condition, do not lose their self entirely; they retain an imprint of their subjectivity, albeit in a completely transformed form. The self persists, and music is a useful lens to show these processes taking place also in patients nearing the end of their lives.

Luigina (a fictional name) was an old friend of my mother's. She suffered for a long time from a severe form of Alzheimer's disease, which accompanied her until her death and meant that her family and lifelong friends had to witness the long and painful process whereby memories, events, small daily rituals, and then names, places, and people crumbled day after day. Around Luigina, everything became progressively covered by a thick fog that

114 Soundscapes and the ecology of sounds

gradually swallowed up pieces of the present and the recent past, yet surprisingly left shreds of the past intact, as if they were floating islands suspended in empty space. Luigina, in fact, remembered nothing of what happened the day, week, or month before, but she could perfectly recall events from when she was a child, without, however, being able to place them in a precise temporal and spatial context. Even before feeding on Luigina's memories, Alzheimer's seemed to have fed on the cognitive organisation of these memories, as if suddenly all the shelves had disappeared from her mental library and single volumes had started falling, one after the other, no longer being supported by anything, into a sort of black hole: the pit of forgetfulness and oblivion. As a young woman, Luigina had been a great melomaniac, passionate about Verdi, Puccini, and all Italian opera. It was thanks to this passion that she and my mother met and became great friends. In the last phase of her illness, when the faces of loved ones had already disappeared from her memory, Luigina's husband would play arias from *Aida* or *Tosca* to give her some comfort, and she immediately seemed to revive. Her gaze seemed to go from absent and distant to present again. At times, she almost seemed to recognise him again, looking at him with loving gratitude and acknowledging the music as the soundtrack of many moments in their long love affair. I do not know whether Luigina truly recognised him, but what struck me, on the rare occasions I witnessed these scenes, was the "agency" of the arias, as if the music the elderly couple listened to together was able to reunite them, restoring some form of intimacy. I always wondered whether listening to music together comforted Luigina or her husband more; in fact, they both seemed to greatly benefit from it.

A final study on this phenomenon worth mentioning is the one by DeNora, Schmid, Simpson, and Ansdell,[35] who document the potential of activating late learning processes through music in elderly patients suffering from dementia and very close to the end of their lives. Where more traditional rehabilitation processes may fail, new avenues open up for music therapy, leading patients into unexplored areas where lost skills may be regained. Musical languages once again demonstrate their alchemical capacity to transform the human condition, even in the last stages of life. On the other hand, there are many examples of sounds found in nature that can be compared to musical sounds, whose ability to foster well-being has always been known in common sense; a good example of this is birdsong. It is certainly no coincidence that a great musician such as Olivier Messiaen was also an expert in ornithology and studied birdsong. In fact, he believed birdsong represented the perfect musical form.

Notes

1 Mancuso (2023), e-book edition.
2 Schafer (1977).

3 Tota (2023).
4 Atkinson (2007); Sterne (2012); Pinch and Bijsterveld (2012).
5 Corbin (1998); LaBelle (2018).
6 Sterne (2013).
7 D'Angelo (2021, p. 80).
8 Kelman (2010).
9 Thompson (2001).
10 Goodman (1968).
11 Thompson (2001).
12 Penone (2022, p. 176).
13 Giuseppe Penone is a famous Italian artist and sculptor known for his artworks representing the relationship between nature and human beings.
14 Ibid.
15 Schafer (1977, p. 4).
16 The process linking the formation of value to the scarcity of a particular good or condition was extensively documented from a sociological perspective by Georg Simmel in *Philosophie des Geldes* (1900).
17 Han (2022, p. 76).
18 DeNora and Belcher (2000).
19 DeNora (2000, 2011).
20 Tota (2023).
21 Tota (2014a).
22 DeNora (2000, 2003); McCormick (2006).
23 Eyerman (2001); Brooks (2013).
24 Drott (2015, p. 171).
25 Kwame Harrison (2015).
26 Marontate, Robertson and Clarkson (2016).
27 Velasco-Pufleau (2019, 2021).
28 Idem (2021).
29 Ibid., p. 63.
30 Marontate, Robertson and Clarkson (2016).
31 Mengerink (2013).
32 DeNora (2021, p. 4).
33 Beckett (1954).
34 Sacks (2007), e-book edition.
35 DeNora, Schmid, Simpson and Ansdell (2022).

n Chapter 5, I present an itinerary of instructions for a mind capable of ecological thinking. However, I emphasise that this set of suggestions serves as an example only, as it is up to each individual to identify their own, one that is tailored and suited to their own subjectivity.

Then I underscore how an ecological mind is a mind that engages with the world, taking responsibility for the complexity of events, not avoiding society, while also highlighting how an ecological mind can and must confront the impermanence of self and others.

5

THE ECOLOGICAL MIND

Homage to Franco Cassano:

We must proceed slowly, like an old country train, like peasant women dressed in black, who go by foot and see the world magically open up. Walking is like browsing a book; running, on the other hand, is like looking at the cover only. We must be slow, cherish the pauses to look back to see how far we have come, feel one's limbs give into fatigue like melancholy, envying the gentle anarchy of those who invent the way one step at a time. We must learn to stand alone, waiting in silence, occasionally finding joy in having nothing else but our hands in our pockets. To walk slowly is to encounter dogs without running over them over, to name trees, corners, and lamp posts, to discover a bench, to carry our thoughts, letting them surface according to the road, like bubbles floating to the top where they become strong and burst, becoming one with the sky. Walking means enabling involuntary thinking, which has no purpose, which is not the result of an objective or of our will, but a necessary kind of thinking, which generates itself, starting from the agreement between mind and world.[1]

Pensare a piedi (Thinking on Foot) by Franco Cassano is a way to reconnect thinking with movement, to remember that thinking, like walking, is an action, and as such, it occurs in corporeality. Thinking on foot means allowing thoughts to listen and to be listened to, accepting to be part of a flow where thoughts and words come forth like profound intuitions, of which we no longer know the origin nor why they interpellate us. It is a profound yet weightless mode of thinking that brings well-being and peace. The ecological mind is a mind that thinks on foot. The body[2] may travel by plane or

DOI: 10.4324/9781003484592-5

118 Ecological mind

high-speed train, but even on the fasted train, we may still continue to "think on foot" when we decide to stop, to wait for the other, which ultimately amounts to waiting for ourselves. Slowness and lingering are also central to Byung-Chul Han's reflection on the progressive replacement of things with "non-things" (i.e., information):

> Lingering is another time-consuming practice. Perception that latches on to information does not have a *lasting and slow gaze*. Information makes us short-sighted and short of breath. It is not possible to linger on information. Lingering on things in contemplation, intentionless seeing, which would be a formula for happiness, gives way to the hunt for information. Today, we pursue information without gaining *knowledge*. We take notice of everything without gaining any *insight*. We travel across the world without having an experience. We communicate incessantly without participating in a *community*. We collect vast quantities of data without following up on our *recollections*. We accumulate "friends" and "followers" without meeting an *Other*. In this way, information develops a form of life that has no stability or duration.[3]

Thinking on foot therefore means going back to things, as described by Byung-Chul Han. To the concreteness of doing and acting that has progressively become dematerialised and de-corporealised.

As Tim Ingold stresses, echoing Gregory Bateson[4]:

> (...) the mind is not bounded by the body but extends along the multiple sensory pathways that bind every living being into the texture of the world. These pathways, as we have seen, are both traced on the ground as tangible tracks and threaded through the air as trails of scent. Walking along, then, is not the behavioural output of a mind encased within a pedestrian body. It is rather, in itself, a way of thinking and knowing (...) the walker is *thinking in movement*. (...) [It is] motional thought.[5]

If, as Tim Ingold emphasises, along with Jane Rendell,[6] thought is indeed movement and, concomitantly, movement is thought, it follows that "thinking on foot" is not only a magnificent crisis, but also a specific modality that characterises the process of thinking.

1. Itinerary for an ecological mind

Let's imagine a semi-serious game in which we identify ten rules that we decide to follow to inhabit an ecological mind. What I am offering you here is only an example that might prove appropriate for the writer and, perhaps, also for a group of readers who identify with every part of these proposals.

However, it is an exercise to be undertaken on an individual level. Each of us could compose our own booklet of instructions, designed and conceived to suit us. The first of these rules, which might function as an example, is the one suggested by Franco Cassano's "thinking on foot":

a. An ecological mind is a mind that thinks on foot. Thoughts take shape suddenly, with the speed of an intuition; however, they also claim the luxury of slowness. In a world in which "time is money", we allow ourselves the luxury of thinking at a speed that enables our mind to listen to itself and connect with the body it inhabits.

b. The ecological mind is an elastic mind. In contemporary times, we are bombarded with notions such as resilience,[7] antifragility, and sustainability, but "Why should I have to resist at all costs, sustain all shocks, without making a crease? I'm not made of linoleum". We need a notion of identity that refers to the quality of resilience. The contemporary self could be *an elastic self*. The term "antifragile",[8] interesting and original though it may be, is not quite adequate in the practical and pragmatic perspective of an ethnography of our everyday life, as it describes a model that is too distant from our own experience. We are not, nor can we be, the superheroes of resilience, nor the supermen and superwomen of antifragility, because under certain conditions, we all break down. The human condition does not allow us to be antifragile, and perhaps not even resilient, but we can most humbly set ourselves the common goal of achieving and pursuing a high rate of elasticity of the self. What is the breadth in the representations of our self that we are able to sustain? What are our thresholds, our points of no return? Where have we decided to locate them? What are our limits, and where do they lie? An elastic self is a self that is ready for change; I am not sure it can thrive when everything is transformed (as Taleb would say), but it would be enough for it not to lose all hope when everything changes. In short, we are talking of the underlying optimism which, under certain conditions, remains and helps us keep our balance during fluctuations and deviations from the normal and predictable course of events. The elastic self skilfully and strategically uses the elements of ritual, transforming concrete everyday actions into small rituals, to govern the uncertainty of rare events, which it considers to be normally constitutive of our existence. The elastic self, in short, is able to incorporate Taleb's black swan, without rejoicing in it, but also without despairing, or at least without losing the capacity to hope for a positive outcome. It may be useful to think of our subjectivity using a metaphor and articulating it into three different states: the gaseous self, the liquid self (the Bauman-type of self), and the solid self. Faced with the adversities of existence, the elasticity of the self is what allows the self to transit quickly

120 Ecological mind

from one state to another. An example of this is an event that falls short of our expectations and forces us to take an unexpected course: if our ego were to react by putting up a strong resistance (i.e., in its solid version), the shock wave would probably end up producing very deep and perhaps permanent wounds. If, on the other hand, we were to react in the liquid or gaseous state, concretely, this would mean that we would not produce a clear-cut and hard definition of the situation, but a fluctuating and less definitive one, providing ourselves with the opportunity to progressively redefine what is happening in a way we could take advantage of. In order to avoid unnecessary misunderstandings, it must be clear that what we are alluding to here are the changes and transformations that life imposes on us, not cases in which a subject is the victim of a serious crime, a bereavement, or an unforeseen and terrible event capable of shattering one's life. It seems to me that applying this metaphor to these cases would be very disrespectful to the victims and clearly misleading.

c. The ecological mind is a hopeful mind. The third principle proposed in this context concerns the temporal disposition of the self, which is essentially projected towards the future with a sense of fundamental positivity. Nostalgia, for instance, may be a noble sentiment, but is not always helpful or, rather, it is an attitude that cannot always be sustainable. Nostalgia, in fact, is a disposition projected towards the past, towards something that no longer exists, but whose traces continue to linger in the present. Nostalgia is a strange, mysterious mechanism that allows our mind to give a future to our past, nurturing it and using the faded image of happiness that was, to tarnish the vividness of what is or will be. Nostalgia is a hook that reaches from the past into the present to trap our future and sometimes turn it into a bad copy of this past. It is a game of the mind that often does not nurture an ecological way of thinking in the full sense of the word. However, complicating this reflection, alongside the concept of nostalgia outlined here, we find the concept of *saudade* belonging to Portuguese culture, an important spiritual and existential element in Fado, urban popular song. Unlike simple nostalgia, *saudade* seems to go beyond nostalgic memories of the past and the sadness caused by a happiness that no longer exists, as it also implies a positive tension towards the future. In this sense, *saudade* seems to be a form of hopeful nostalgia, a sort of link between nostalgia and hope. Quoting the definition proposed by Tia DeNora,[9] the ecological mind is "hopeful", in the sense that it involves taking active responsibility for one's dreams. In order to become projects that can be realised, we must never lose sight of these dreams. Our wise grandmothers used the expression "to cultivate one's dreams", which perfectly grasps the similarity between the activity of cultivating, as in sowing seeds, and that of preserving and fostering one's dreams. Sowing a seed and helping it to germinate require constant care. DeNora suggests that our dreams and hopes also consciously and responsibly require the same kind of care, as if returning to one's hopes on a daily basis with a positive thought contributes to maintaining the existential openness necessary to grasp whatever potential unfolds before us and has the power to make the things we hope for feasible and doable. Above all, we must avoid betraying our dreams by despairing. When we despair, when we lose hope, we turn our hearts and eyes elsewhere, and the existential care mentioned above vanishes. Moreover, hope is a strong medicine against sadness and melancholy; even if our dreams do not come true in the end, hope will have sustained us for a long stretch of our existence while providing us with the empty space of suspension needed to transform an unrealisable project into something that can be achieved instead. In short, as Massimiliano Fiorucci says: "Since hope is the last to die, I will die hopeful".[10]

d. The ecological mind is a mind that creates its own rhythm, harmonising the gestures of everyday life and the rhythmic feeling of the soul with the harmonic rhythm of the universe. To do this, it creates rituals connected to everyday gestures; as these are repeated over time, they produce a habit that makes inner time accessible and synchronises inner temporality and spaces with outer temporality and spaces. In other words, the ecological mind cultivates the sacredness of the everyday through the habit connected to gestures, creating rituals that punctuate our days and confer a reliable regularity to the passing of time. What are these gestures? Each one of us has their own. They are slow, pleasant gestures, to be savoured; they can, for example, mark the beginning of our day or its end. They are *our* gestures.

My friend Erika lives in a large house on Lake Como. It belonged to her grandmother and then to her mother. It is not a luxurious house, nor is it old. It is very spacious, with many rooms and many windows. It is a smiling house, and, above all, it offers a beautiful view of the lake. Every morning and every evening, Erika opens – and then closes – all the green shutters. There are almost 20 of them, so it takes her over half an hour in the morning and the same amount of time in the evening, going from one floor to the next. However, when we visit and stay in her large house as guests, she never wants any of us to help with this task. She always says: "I'll do it", as if being the owner of the house means she is the only one really qualified for the difficult operation. Watching her go from one window to the next, smiling contently, it is possible to catch a glimpse of the rhythm and habit of this act of opening and closing, which is repeated every day, always in the same way. One can see her fingers sliding quickly over the hinges of the shutters, releasing them with the firm, decisive snap; her hands know exactly where to press. It is as if the opening and closing of her shutters were a real ritual to be performed at the beginning and end of the day, a sort of cosmogonic rite of the world, one that is repeated daily, and for this reason, is able to reconnect the inner rhythm of the house to the external rhythm of the universe. The little domestic ritual almost seems to open up the inner space of the house to the musicality of the world, as celebrated by the great Canadian musician and environmentalist Murray Schafer. All this in the reduced format offered by a green shutter.

e. The ecological mind looks towards the infinite horizon. Getting up every morning and being able to look at a distant horizon that evokes infinity can be an important condition for our well-being. This infinite gaze, in fact, can be taken as the measure of our horizon and of the boundaries we place on our possibilities. Staring into infinity brings about a sense of well-being, of inner relief, as if our gaze were able to rest when supported by the infinite distance we see in front of us, when we let go inside it. The view of the sea is beautiful precisely because of its vastness, a quality that seems to resonate from the external lens of the eye to an inner gaze that frames and supports the traces of our thoughts. Also in this case, it is not a coincidence that the expression "breadth of vision" is colloquially used when referring to an individual capable of unbiased thinking and of formulating ambitious ideas that go beyond external constraints and conditioning. Staring into the infinity of the horizon can also be considered as an enlightening metaphor for the cognitive processes of an ecological mind. The infinite, every time it is contemplated with a continuous and attentive gaze, seems to suggest that everything is possible, that the world is still to be discovered, as it opens up for us like a benevolent and welcoming space. Even Giacomo Leopardi,[11] whom I would not exactly describe as an optimist by nature, wrote about the infinite: "And into this immensity my thought sinks ever drowning | And it is sweet to shipwreck in such a sea". Certainly, for many of us confined to an apartment in the city, the infinite might be only an expanse of rooftops, but still, tiles are better than nothing!

f. The ecological mind dialogues with ancestors and questions the sustainability of the past. This issue is anything but marginal. In this regard, I will refer to the theory of the restlessness of events, formulated in 2010 by Robin Wagner-Pacifici. According to this theory, all traumatic events change their configuration over time, because although the event itself can be considered concluded, all individual, collective, or public representations and narratives of the event continue to be part of it and contribute to what we may call its subsequent life. This gives all trauma a restless nature, as its persistence in our present and future depends on our narratives/descriptions of that event. The American sociologist is naturally more interested in the collective and public dimensions of memory, referring predominantly to cultural and artistic products capable of intervening retrospectively in shared knowledge. She underscores the fact that an exhibition on the Holocaust held in 2022, for instance, can intervene in the public definition of this historical event, altering its collective dimension, because everything we think, say, and write after an event continues to be a part of it. In the context of a pragmatic approach to daily life such as the one proposed here, however, we are also interested in the proper individual and familial implications of the theory of the restlessness of events. In other words, can we argue that the nature of trauma is elastic? This theory is a healthy one. I am not able to say whether it is true or not, nor does it actually matter. What matters is to believe in it firmly, as if it were a sort of lifebuoy, one that is available when we are in open sea. If the nature of trauma is elastic, in fact, we can try to swallow and digest much of what happens to us. We have all experienced family trauma. The only difference is that some traumas are more serious than others. Those who had siblings were either the most loved or the least loved, and in both cases, there were advantages and disadvantages to deal with. Some have lost a parent, some a grandparent. Some, on the other hand, had parents but would have paid gold just to be with someone else. In short, it is almost impossible to enter adulthood unscathed by trauma. We are not treating victims of serious family violence the same way as people who experienced some trivial adolescent issue. Once again, the intention here is not to be disrespectful to those who have suffered greatly, but rather to try and provide something that may be helpful by sharing reflections and experiences. If it is us who can decide what to do with our memories, this awareness gives us freedom. We are not merely the sum of negative memories; in fact, we are much more. For now, we can be the sum of our positive memories and of our negative ones once they have been understood, processed, digested, incorporated, suffered, and narrated – perhaps also forgotten. Indeed, we are also able to happily leave them behind. An ecological mind is a mind that preserves only the sustainable past. To avoid misunderstandings, this mind certainly does not erase childhood traumas; on the contrary, after processing them for decades, it sets them aside and simply moves on to something else. We may cite the ironic and disillusioned words of the Italian writer Veronica Raimo:

Yet, how do we reconcile with something or someone if our memories have faded? If they change in the very act of forming? They can take everything away from us except our memories – people say. But who would be interested in this expropriation? Most memories abandon us without us even noticing; as for the rest, we are the ones who secretly dump them on people, deal them out, promote them zealously, like door-to-door salesmen, con artists, looking for someone to trick into subscribing to our

124 Ecological mind

story. Obviously, half price. Memory for me is like the dice game I used to play as a child; it's just a matter of deciding whether it's useless or rigged.[12]

g. The ecological mind views the external environment as the space where it can to weave the harmony of its thoughts and ideas with the concrete organisation of matter. The home becomes a symbolic-moral order where affects and the dispositions of one's soul become the plot supporting their intertwining with objects. As emphasised by Emanuele Coccia:

Every home is a purely moral entity; we build homes to welcome into a form of intimacy the portion of the world – made of things, people, animals, plants, atmospheres, events, images, and memories – that make our happiness possible. (...) Morality – the theory of happiness – can never be reduced to a set of precepts that deal with our psychological attitudes or to a discipline of good feelings, attentiveness, or to a form of psychological hygiene. It is a material order that involves objects and people, an economy that intertwines things and affections, oneself and others in the minimal spatial unity of what we call "care"; in the broadest sense: home. Happiness is not an emotion, nor a purely subjective experience.[13]

In the pages that follow, he writes: "Home is only the name for this aggregate of techniques of adaptation between oneself and the planet, a cosmic fold to make psyche and matter, soul and world coincide for a moment".[14]

Regarding the Self-Home, I have already emphasised that the domestic environment should be considered as the space where our subjectivity develops and takes shape; the way we organise space, transforming it into *our* own space, is an ever-incomplete portrait of our subjectivity. What are the objects we decide to include, and which ones do we exclude? How are they organised and with what structure of relevance? The ecological mind is a mind capable of grasping the conscious continuity between itself and the spaces it inhabits, not necessarily only the most intimate ones of one's home, but also those that coincide with a part of the public space it traverses daily.

I'm in Rome, on a beautiful semi-central street quite close to the neighbourhood where I live. It's an elegant street, full of shops and beautiful shop windows. I'm basically in a lively, smiling neighbourhood, a bit touristy but not too much. It's clear that it's mainly inhabited and frequented by Romans. Suddenly, I find myself near a row of dumpsters. Who knows why, in Rome, they are all lined out outside the buildings? In other cities, they are placed in courtyards; they are transported outside and then taken back in the day they get emptied. Who knows why here in Rome, instead, they are all lined up like this on the street, excluded from the spaces of private property, placed in adjacent but separate spaces that are ultimately public spaces, which are actually no-man's-lands, at least for some. These spaces are a sort of unpredictable wild west, they don't belong to anyone, they don't belong to the apartment building on the right or to the one on the left, and so they become the deposit for all sorts of things. The inventory would be hilarious if we could still laugh about it: I see an old-fashioned white bidet – it almost seems to look at me uncomfortably from the pile of waste it is perched on, it seems to be saying, embarrassedly, "Look, it's not my fault". Next to it, there's a door, light beige, with half-frosted glass which is broken, the kind my grandmother had in the north, which evidently is also used here. Then there's a piece of a mattress, and I wonder how does one end up owning a piece of a mattress? How can a mattress be divided into two? I say to myself: how does this waste end up there? Can we really imagine there is someone who lives nearby who politely greets the doorman every day (the one he always tips at Christmas, to remind himself that he is still a gentleman), takes the elevator and secretly exits at night with a bidet under his arm, and then, after checking that no one is watching, casually puts it near that dumpster where it now sits? We could imagine an even more cowardly variant: someone arrives here from another part of the city, with his work van, has been paid by his client to cover the costs of the dump, but decides that this spot, which is kind of out of sight, will be the site of his crime. Unfortunately, it's not like when we were kids and were convinced that "if something disappears from my sight, then it no longer exists". When the man gets back into his white van, pleased by the fact he has not been caught, and drives away smiling, congratulating himself on his brilliant idea, the bidet stays there and will stay there for a long time. Probably it will still be there when, many weeks later, the same man happens to pass through that same street again. I'm sure he will think to himself: "Look at the rubbish in this neighbourhood. The mayor really does nothing about it!" But how do we convince him that it's not right and that it shouldn't be done? Evidently, not even his mother was able to convince him... Is it possible he is not able to realise this on his own? Yet, that's precisely how things are. For me/for all of us, that area is a part of our neighbourhood, our city, and therefore, it demands care, attention, and responsibility. We can't imagine putting the old bidet from our bathroom in plain view in the dumpster in front of where we live, or of transporting it to the dumpster in the nearby street. It would never cross our minds.

The simple question that arises here concerns the demarcation between private and public space, mistakenly understood as the opposition between "my home" and "no one's space". It would be enough to tear away this harmful sediment from the concept of common space. As Emanuele Coccia writes when speaking of his philosophy of the home:

126 Ecological mind

We need to think the home; we urgently need to make this planet a real dwelling, or rather, to transform our dwelling into a real planet, a space capable of welcoming everyone. The modern project of globalising the city has been replaced by the project that consists in opening our apartments and making them coincide with the Earth.[15]

h. The ecological mind contemplates the corporeality of thoughts.[16] "Yet nothing comforts the cry of a kid / whose balloon slips away among the houses".[17] Much has been written about the embodiment of thought, but not enough has been written. Many studies have documented that we feel music with our whole body (not just with our auditory system), as emphasised by Oliver Sacks.[18] However, this also applies to our thoughts. Indeed, the idea that we think only with our minds is false; we think with our whole body, or more precisely, our body accompanies and supports our mind as we process certain thoughts. In fact, the emotions associated with those thoughts are literally inscribed on our face, our posture, and our muscles. The daily exercise of listening and trying to notice the effect that our thoughts have on our body is very useful for rapidly identifying the types of thought that cause us discomfort. The ecological mind observes and listens to the thoughts that inhabit it; not always, as it would be impossible, but certainly often, or at least occasionally. If we are able to do this sometimes, we can then decide to do it more often. This exercise, if done with attention, and if we make a habit of it, makes us desire thoughts that make us feel good. It initiates a kind of silent but profound rebellion against the tendency to be thought by thoughts that we do not want to entertain. The ecological mind also observes the difference between thoughts formulated in stillness and thought formulated in motion. Often, for example, when something disturbs us deeply, the thoughts produced by the body in motion can be of great help, because it is almost as if bodily movement were also able to help the mind move from where it is (i.e., from the disturbance).

i. The ecological mind views its boundaries as being fluid and flexible.[19] In common parlance, there tends to prevail a conception of our subjective boundaries according to which they are similar to a discrete variable: "I/not-I, external space". This conception of our self is similar to the shared conception of geographic and national borders: Italy/not Italy/ France, for example. Already in *Eco-words*, I suggested viewing the boundaries between self and the outside as fluid and flexible, considering, for example, the external spaces that the self is fond of (our home, for instance) as real extensions of subjectivity. In that context, I also showed how there are practical implementations of the concept of fluid boundary in architecture, projects in which the spaces of the house interpenetrate with those of the surrounding garden. Obviously, adhering to a similar conception of boundaries, or at least frequenting it sporadically, would have important political implications, both in terms of international border surveillance policies and in terms of everyday policies: if the self is no longer so neatly separated from everything else, if there are large areas of co-presence, then the structures of relevance of everyday life and the perspectives that inform them change significantly. A concept that explains how men and women are interrelated, the same way different animal and plant species are, casts a new light on things and modifies their relevance. In short, to think and operate in highly competitive contexts, it seems we must adhere to an atomistic conception of our self, according to which the boundaries between myself and the outside are clearly defined, and my own self competes with all other human selves (and also with those of all other animal and plant species) to achieve its own personal well-being and possibly that of those belonging to the narrow circle of family members and friends. The ecological mind does not adhere uncritically to this view and seeks to be interrelated with the rest of the universe.

j. The ecological mind avoids producing and consuming any form of symbolic or environmental pollution. I have already written extensively on this in the previous chapters, but it is worth stressing that if we agree on the fact that thoughts can have positive or negative effects on our identity, then all forms of symbolic pollution should wisely be avoided, being aware that there are no universally valid instructions, and that the various forms of symbolic pollution must be identified based on subjective criteria. Furthermore, the ecological mind is grounded in collective intelligence but thinks on its own. To be more precise, it is impossible to think alone because we almost always think together with others, or at least rework thoughts already thought by many others. However, the responsibility for such thoughts falls solely on us. In other words, if we think a thought, it necessarily becomes also ours; for this reason, we must take moral responsibility for it, or we can/must let go of it and formulate another that is more suitable for us. In this sense, we are all *Einzelgänger*, though not trivially, in the sense of being solitary and melancholic beings, withdrawn from the world. Rather, in the sense that we are solitary thinkers who, despite thinking together and despite being aware of the fact that we are all interconnected in social, political, and economic dimensions, as well as in thoughts, actions, and habits, are still capable of bearing the moral, social, and political responsibility for our thoughts as unique and separate individuals.

128 Ecological mind

The conclusion of these reflections, therefore, can only be the following: no instruction booklet is valid for everyone, perhaps not even for the majority. These lines may serve only as an indication or perhaps represent an intuition, as each one of us must search for the daily route, the one we take individually and at the same time together, on their own. We can share ideas, suggest them, but certainly not indicate which ones are "right". This kind of intellectual and conceited claim cannot be part of a truly scientific reflection; it usually constitutes a kind of scientific discourse that is subservient to power and therefore becomes political.

2. Ecology of public discourse

In the years during which I worked on writing this book, a series of events occurred that significantly altered some features of the Italian public discourse, particularly the type of information produced daily by major television news programs.[20] I would like to focus my attention specifically on this segment because it seems to have been the most affected by the trends outlined here. Print media and online newspapers, on the other hand, have largely tended to downplay these trends, which were still present but not in such a pronounced way. The crucial events that initiated this radical transformation – which is not irreversible; this became clear after some months – were, in order: the COVID-19 pandemic, the war in Ukraine, and the ensuing energy crisis. At present, these seem to be the most important events influencing, in this rather long phase, the way national television news produces information in Italy. The most prominent trends were as follows:

a. Firstly, the function of agenda-setting, which is already largely carried out by television news, has been further radicalised. In its traditional version of 1972 (formulated by Maxwell McCombs and Donald Shaw),[21] the agenda-setting theory shows how effective the media is in spreading a certain agenda, also demonstrating that, in transforming events into news, media outlets to impose their own structure of relevance on events, which then determine the type of news being broadcast to the public. Following the above-mentioned events, agenda-setting has radicalised, monopolising information. This means that the way of producing information became reorganised around a single issue that literally cannibalised all other news stories for several months. This happened with the COVID-19 pandemic; it happened again with the war in Ukraine and later with the energy crisis. In practice, agenda-setting acquired a different form: instead of selecting a limited number of pieces of information, it selected a single topic. This way of producing information has proven to be effective in terms of share, considering the percentage of viewers watching a particular channel compared to the total viewers in that same time slot. The underlying intention, in fact, was probably to transform emergency communication into an ordinary modality of communicating so that, in the midst of a whole sequence of emergencies, viewers would be glued to their televisions, without ever missing a single edition of the news.

b. As a consequence, the second transformation (although not explicitly pursued by any network but rather an unexpected effect of a series of concurrent circumstances) has been to make the national emergency situation as ordinary as possible for the longest time possible.

c. Furthermore, there has been a prevailing tendency to produce sensationalised, fragmented information centred around fear and disaster, thereby exaggerating the already severe tensions running through the country. In other words, news channels in particular have acted as amplifiers of fears, even of real terror, which all citizens experienced, especially in the initial phase of the pandemic. This modality of spreading information, which is not socially responsible as it does not take responsibility for the short-term, medium-term, and long-term effects it produces, has been progressively adapted in various ways to the subsequent major mono-themes: the war in Ukraine and the gas and energy crisis caused by the war between Russia and Ukraine.

d. The most worrying characteristic of this way of producing information is the creeping tendency to limit all forms of pluralism, which are gradually eroded as the emergency situation, now chronic and ordinary, does not envisage any space for the expression of alternative viewpoints. Thus, we have witnessed the assimilation of the "no green pass"[22] movement to the "anti-vaxxers", who are described as being social free riders; we have seen doctors persecuted for expressing doubts not concerning the importance of vaccines as such, but the methods and speed (albeit necessary) with which *these* vaccines were produced and tested, and the fact that every vaccine carries side effects, which citizens should be duly informed about. The mere expression of less than unconditional adherence to the pharmaceutical dogma that vaccines are necessary at all costs exposed unfortunate interviewees to public ridicule, which often escalated, leading to episodes of actual incitement to social hatred. Nobody attempted to understand the fears and arguments of people expressing doubts, which resulted in a fundamentalist approach on the part of the media that has nothing to do with scientific information. The consequence of this was the partial failure of the campaign in Italy to spread information on the benefits of vaccines, which did not succeed in achieving its goal, namely, making the entire population, and especially citizens without a Green Certificate and "anti-vaxxers", understand how important and absolutely essential it is for the entire population to be vaccinated. Paradoxically, by transforming moderately sceptical individuals into radical extremists, the opportunity to maintain an open space for dialogue with this segment of the population was lost, when

130 Ecological mind

it was precisely with this segment that the campaign should have been developed in order to be effective.

Moreover, if the political system and the news industry lose the ability to keep the market strategies of large pharmaceutical corporations in check (without diminishing their significant contribution in terms of research and production with reference to the global pandemic), everyone's health is harmed, as pharmaceutical companies cannot be expected to sell health. As Ivan Illich[23] highlighted many years ago, the pharmaceutical industry claims it is selling health, though it can only sell medical treatments. There is a considerable difference between these two statements. Furthermore, large pharmaceutical corporations are rightly driven by profit, while states and civil society are guided by considerations of public ethics. In this context, it is crucial for the political system, the scientific community, and, to a considerable extent, the media system, to effectively contain the hegemonic market tendencies of major pharmaceutical corporations.

A similar trend "in the Italian public discourse " was observed in the case of the war in Ukraine, where Pope Francis almost risked appearing as a potentially subversive dissident only because he called to lay down arms and seek a path to peace.

Finally, even though it is somewhat disrespectful to lump together all television channels, as in some cases reasonableness did prevail and continues to prevail, the gas and energy problem was mainly reported by news programs with the same sensationalistic and apocalyptic tones, sometimes without providing the information necessary to properly understand what was happening and what political (not technical) choices were involved when choosing one solution instead of another.

The news industry is one of the fundamental pillars of a democratic society, and from this realisation arises an urgent appeal to great Italian journalists who, drawing on the great tradition of national journalism, can become advocates of *an ecology of public discourse*. This virtuous trend should emerge precisely in the field of information, which already has the potential and the qualities needed to give it full expression.

From these brief reflections on the ecology of public discourse, we may derive a postscript for our itinerary: an ecological mind thinks globally and commits to contribute to solving common problems.

3. Reflections on impermanence

I am on the balcony of my house, and with stubborn determination, I observe the geraniums. These flowers are robust and beautiful, but they have an unpleasant tendency to wither. Often, an entire stem suddenly turns yellow and remains there, stuck, reminding me with its annoying presence of the impermanence of the green stems. I detest those dry parts; I find they are inappropriate, as if they were flaunting a truth otherwise invisible, a truth I hypocritically wish to keep concealed. I spend a long time eliminating every trace of what turns yellow, becoming a dead stem. I have the impression the geranium cannot adequately reflect my ideal of beauty, as if those stems, like a sour note, were an assault on the vision unfolding before my eyes. I therefore intervene surgically and meticulously with this daily activity that consists of sorting. But as I observe my stubborn determination, I suddenly sense that my exaggerated disappointment might have to do with a more general discomfort caused by the human condition. Perhaps those geraniums are beautiful as they are.

The experiences of the COVID-19 pandemic and later the war in Europe have placed the issue of death at the centre of European and Italian public discourse; this condition suddenly seems to concern us more closely. An ecological mind cannot avoid confronting the finiteness of human existence, and the above-mentioned historical events led many citizens to reflect on what was happening. For many other, much less fortunate people, death became an unwelcome and unexpected companion much sooner than they had expected. In such circumstances, the thought of death, which is usually at least partially alien to our daily lives, as it is an experience that is denied, repressed, and exorcised in contemporary culture, suddenly became part of our lives, like a haunting and annoying phantom we were no longer able to keep at a distance. Usually, it is when we find ourselves mourning a loved one that this kind of reflection on our impermanence and problem of meaning opens up, but the combination of political and social events has made this reflection urgent, necessary, no longer postponable, and above all, synchronous for everyone. What is truly relevant is not so much the fact that the COVID-19 pandemic forced us, in a generic sense, to "learn to die", but the hegemony and totalising pervasiveness that the argument "fear of death" acquired in the overall public discourse. This is precisely because the pandemic became an exclusive topic, and for many months, it dominated and voraciously devoured all other issues circulating in national public discourse. Basically, for many months, millions of people were forced by the media – by the powerful and pervasive bombardment of the media – to concentrate, think about, and to come to terms with their fear of dying. This is what made the difference, as this phenomenon transformed death from an individual traumatic condition into a real "collective trauma", which had its institutional actors (such as journalists, virologists, but also politicians, and even the Pope) who were actively engaged in the process of elaborating the languages and forms of this trauma. Certainly, similar dynamics have taken place in conjunction with many other natural disasters in the past (we may think of the earthquakes that hit the Italian cities of L'Aquila in 2009 and

132 Ecological mind

Amatrice in 2016). However, in these cases, such dynamics persisted for a short period at the national level and subsequently, in the medium and long term, remained central only at the local level. In the case of the COVID-19 pandemic, the construction of collective trauma occurred at the national (and subsequently European) level with a pervasiveness that was unprecedented. It seems that because of the echo chamber generated by the media, and the particular way national communication regarding the pandemic was shaped by a series of factors, the modality with which individual Italian citizens dealt with grief became permanently anchored to the words and thoughts spread by the narrative of collective trauma. We witnessed a truly singular phenomenon: death and the fear of dying, which are topics generally excluded and rejected in daily conversations as inappropriate and excessively "disturbing", became central in the national public discourse. All citizens were more or less forced to confront these issues.

For each of us, death remains a fundamental and foundational notion, the absolute notion that the project of our life must come to terms with. Contemplating the notion of not being permanent but rather having a sort of expiration date, comparable to products and materials we would never have thought to liken ourselves to, profoundly unsettles us. Denying this reality proves futile. It both prostrates and terrifies us. Furthermore, there are no valid strategies for navigating the process of mourning oneself, or those we hold dear. Those more fortunate among us may find solace in unwavering faith, which makes it possible to trust in the Earth and Sky we come from:

> Every part of nature teaches that the passing away of one life is the making room for another. The oak dies down to the ground, leaving within its rind a rich virgin mould, which will impart a vigorous life to an infant forest. The pine leaves a sandy and sterile soil, the harder woods a strong and fruitful mould. So this constant abrasion and decay makes the soil of my future growth.[24]

No ecological form of thought is possible without coming to terms with one's impermanence and the condition of impermanence in general. The only reflection we might perhaps share on the matter, respecting the diversity of religious beliefs and individual orientations, concerns the idea that, with regard to the relevance structure of daily events, death can function as a kind of "earthing". If we can contemplate, even sporadically and partially, the certain idea that one day we will no longer be here, we might feel the urge to embrace more often the people we hold dear, to rejoice in a series of small events that would otherwise remain excluded from our gaze. In short, an ecological mind is one firmly connected and embodied in its own body, a mind capable of contemplating its own death as a condition (certainly not desirable but necessary) of its own life project. Putting an end to the fallacy of immanence, though painful and difficult even to consider, can become an important opportunity to live the life we still have with dignity and responsibility. In short, it is a reasonable way of "making virtue out of necessity", as our grandmothers wisely said. The dialogue with death can also become an inner opportunity for a silent and ongoing dialogue with our deceased and with the loved ones who are no longer with us. This dialogue can effectively take place starting from our hearts, using the words of eternal love – the same sentiment we feel for our ancestors, for our descendants, and for dear friends who are no longer with us but who continue to be an important part of our family. Regardless of our faith and creed, death does not sever all ties, even though it is a radical transformation, one that terrifies us and from which we cannot escape. Among those who have left us ecological thoughts on the relationship with the loved ones who are no longer with us, St. Augustine provides us with a particularly significant reference point. His words nourish the mourning of those who remain, further proof that words can do, act, and transform: "Those who have left us are not absent; they are invisible, their eyes, radiant with glory, are fixed upon our eyes full of tears".

But there are also, more humbly, the everyday words thought by fathers and mothers for their children. For example, this passage from Tiziano's letter to his son, Folco:

And remember, I will be there. I will be there, up in the air. So, every now and then, if you want to talk to me, stand aside, close your eyes, and look for me. We'll talk. But not in the language of words. In silence.[25]

Or these brief lines from a mother to her son:

Always remember that in your heart, I will be there and will be forever. When you feel lost or happy, close your eyes and look for me. Listen to the whisper of the wind. I will be there and silently answer all your questions. There is a force of thought and love that transcends all physical transformations of our bodies. Look for me in the trees, in the flowers, in the clouds, and in the sunsets. I will always be by Your side, like a silent force nourishing your life. Forever and wherever I am, you will live in my love and protection. I ask for forgiveness for my imperfection, the same imperfection for which you have loved me so much and still love me. I have loved you in all the ways I knew and in many others that, over the years, I invented. Since you were born, you have been the most extraordinary teacher that life has given me. While I taught you to speak, you taught me to think. You have made my life extraordinary, exceptional. Your being is made of light, special and normal, unique and dearly loved, for me.

134 Ecological mind

Notes

1 Cassano (1996, p. 13).
2 On this point, see also Leder (1990); Petersen (2007).
3 Han (2022, p. 7).
4 Bateson (1972, 1979).
5 Ingold (2010, p. 135).
6 Rendell (2006).
7 Shonkoff and Meisels (2000); Santavirta and Myrskylä (2015); Santavirta, Santavirta, Betancourt, and Gilman (2015).
8 Taleb (2012).
9 DeNora (2021).
10 Personal conversation with an Italian pedagogist.
11 Giacomo Leopardi (1798–1837) was a famous Italian poet, philologist, and philosopher who is considered the greatest Italian poet of the nineteenth century.
12 Raimo (2022, p. 161).
13 Coccia (2021, pp. 6–7).
14 Ibid., p. 16.
15 Ibid., p. 11.
16 On this point, see also Steiner (1894); Gurdjieff (1960, 1964).
17 Verses from the poem *Happiness is achieved*, in Montale, 1994.
18 Sacks (2007).
19 Tota (2014b, 2016).
20 Even if I refer here to the Italian case, I suggest that some of these reflections might be useful to further explore the more global dimensions of international public discourse.
21 McCombs and Shaw (1972).
22 The COVID-19 Green Certificate, valid in the EU, was a document attesting to the vaccination against COVID-19, a negative antigenic or molecular swab or recovery from the infection, required during the pandemic by all workers as well as for cultural and sports events, long-distance travel, nightlife, and restaurants (TN).
23 Illich (1974).
24 Thoreau (2009, p. 3).
25 Terzani (2006, p. 194).

In the sixth chapter, I address the relationship with other living species, both plant and animal, starting from our shared ideas of the city and home. I demonstrate how neither the city nor the home is adequate in representing the continuum between nature and culture.

From this perspective, the home cannot continue to function as a device for the exclusion and partition between the human species and other living species. Similarly, the city cannot be viewed as being limited to the sum of our buildings, disregarding, for instance, the parks and trees that inhabit it. I propose a brief digression on the origin of the concept of sustainability, claiming that an ecological mind naturally embraces environmentalist reflection concerning planet preservation. To merge sustainable thinking with responsible action, I suggest "reconnecting our thoughts with the flesh of the world", elaborating on the work of Maurice Merleau-Ponty. I then mention the contributions of Environmental Humanities and introduce the debate on the Anthropocene. It is paradoxical that precisely at the moment when we witness such human supremacy – which leads geologists to speak of it as the driving force for planetary change ("Anthropocene epoch") – humans must step aside and begin humbly to consider themselves a species among species. This involves taking into account the knowledge of other living forms. In the third paragraph, I consider different disciplinary perspectives on the plant world, from Stefano Mancuso's plant neurobiology to Monica Gagliano's theories of biological intelligence, from Emanuele Coccia and Byung-Chul Han's plant philosophy to Eduardo Kohn's anthropology. Forests, trees, and woods finally gain full citizenship in the world of living beings, demonstrating their ability to process and even memorise information. In the following paragraph, I address the question of animal cognition, referencing recent contributions from neuroscience: I mention Giorgio Vallortigara's hypothesis that basic forms of cognitive processes do not necessarily require large brain masses. I argue that the sociological perspective can offer specific and decisive contributions to this debate, challenging the fallacious belief that consciousness is exclusively a human prerogative. This belief establishes the order of the possible and thinkable within which to articulate the form and organisation of daily social life. Believing that animal life is a form of life that possesses "no type of knowledge" greatly increases the likelihood that animals of all species will be subjected to inhuman and cruel treatment in farming industries. I therefore also address the issue of the ecology of the animal body and the invisibility of extreme violence practices in intensive farming. As a contrast (perhaps also because of the strong disgust this abuse provokes, an abuse we/us allow the animals I/we eat to be subjected to), I offer a digression on the song of cicadas and their ability to create an entire sound environment which has positive effects on the human soul. Lastly, I return to the long-standing question of cyborgs and their rights, drawing from Donna Haraway. I propose imagining new social ecosystems where boundaries between species and kinships can be radically rethought. In which traditional patriarchal thinking, toxic cultures of discrimination, sexism, racism, and speciesism could begin to evaporate definitively: how many and what kinds of assemblages of inert and living matter will still be necessary to maintain the ruthless supremacy of one species over all others?

6

INTER-SPECIESISM, ANTI-SPECIESISM, AND OTHER BELIEFS

1. The idea of home as a partition between nature and culture

When I would recreate myself, I seek the darkest woods the thickest and most interminable and, to the citizen, most dismal, swamp. I enter a swamp as a sacred place – a sanctum sanctorum. There is the strength, the marrow, of Nature. [...] A town is saved, not more by the righteous men in it than by the woods and swamps that surround it. A township where one primitive forest waves above while another primitive forest rots below – such a town is fitted to raise not only corn and potatoes, but poets and philosophers for the coming ages. In such a soil grew Homer and Confucius and the rest, and out of such a wilderness comes the Reformer eating locusts and wild honey.[1]

According to Thoreau, a town's history should include not only an account of the deeds of the men and women who inhabited it but also the history of all its trees – of which there is no trace. In his book, *Planting Our World*, Stefano Mancuso[2] appears to accept Thoreau's invitation: he tells us the story of several great trees and the ways in which their stories became deeply intertwined with the events that occurred in the places they lived. Mancuso thus makes a connection between human events and those of plant life, showing us how the former are connected to the latter. This is the case of the Liberty Tree, a sumptuous elm under which Boston settlers gathered in 1765 to resist and demonstrate against the English; having become a symbol of this resistance, the tree was subsequently cut down by the English and the Boston loyalists. Can one really write the history of that resistance without making any mention of the great tree under whose branches many of its events began?

DOI: 10.4324/9781003484592-6

138 Inter-speciesism, anti-speciesism, and other beliefs

Even in our own time, the way we look at our cities shows little concern for the great trees that inhabit them. On the contrary, cities are the space and site on which we build our homes, which have in turn become the organising principle by which we reinforce our species' hegemony over all others:

> It is through the modern home – a space in which, barring very few exceptions, only human beings can reside – that the radical opposition between the human and non-human, between city and forest, civilised and savage, has been constructed and reinforced.[3]

Over the following pages of the same book, the philosopher returns to the issue:

> Without our noticing, over time our homes have been transformed into machines designed to separate our life from that of other species, in order to make free cohabitation mutually impossible. The very rare adoption of some instances of non-human life inside the walls of the home can certainly not allay our fears of biological diversity: the home remains the expression of, and the war on, other species (...).[4]

Our idea of home is based on an exclusive space for ourselves, one which cannot be shared with another animal aside from the few domesticated ones we allow by our side. It functions as a social mechanism that excludes and eliminates the physical presence of any other living being that dares set foot inside the space – which is by definition *our space*. Think for a moment of a large redwood tree that has been alive for centuries, and whose branches are home to numerous species of birds, rodents, and insects. The way in which that redwood thinks about its own space is a million miles from our own conception of the home. Our idea of home, common in many Western societies, is of a secure place that maintains a safe separation between inside and outside; and yet, once it has taken shape as a project and become a house that is "lived in", it becomes a symbolic space of the fear of the Other, irrespective of whether they are another human or another living species. From the outset, *our homes* are conceived as a device that can protect us by way of exclusion, but more than that, as a hegemonic partition between culture and nature. And yet there could well be other ways of looking at our everyday world, which, though highly planned, remains entirely bound up with nature: "...the forests, avenues, woods, gardens, parks, and the orchards trapped in doors, tables, floors, boards, beams, ships, carts...".[5]

I have not long got back to my house in the country, after many months away. It's an old, somewhat dilapidated farmhouse, but it nonetheless provides a refuge. It is now late spring, and I have tried – without success – to open the green shutters that give onto the small main room. The ivy on the house has grown enormously – excessively, in my view – over the past few months,

Inter-speciesism, anti-speciesism, and other beliefs **139**

and wrapped itself around the shutter, while obstinately pursuing its growth over almost the entirety of the outer walls. I'm reading a collection of essays by Tim Ingold, and I'm reminded of the distinction Ingold makes between "planning" and "growth". It occurs to me that the shutter is the plan; it's the shape an object takes which has been conceived, planned, and created by the human mind. But then there's growth which, unlike the project (beautiful but static; still, complete, and lifeless), is very much alive – full of life, in fact, constantly and fiercely evolving. It's also a bit unsettling because it subverts and contradicts human prediction. The branches of the vine have wrapped themselves around the green shutter, slithering between its slats like so many grinning snakes, and moved towards the window panes. It's as if they want to come into the house, but when they realise they can't, they decide to turn on their heal and lean back towards the sunlight outside, thus creating this strange weave around the individual slats in the style of some verdant wreath. And then there are all the lizards, spiders, ants, and insects of all kinds who appear to use these branches of greenish leaves as if they were genuine super-highways built to lead them up there, to my window, which they would never otherwise have reached. How am I going to open my green shutter now? Of course, with all these leafy curlicues adorning it, it looks like something of a work of art. It's as if the shutter had lost its intended purpose for me (I can no longer open it), but at the same time taken on another one for various other species (as a transit route for lizards and insects). What is more, the shutter has now acquired an aesthetic quality: it has become a symbol of binding strength and verdant vitality. The juxtaposition of the green of the paint with the green of the leaves has created a most striking visual effect. Might we then, on this basis, venture to suggest that it has become some kind of ecoshutter? In other words, in a space that was originally planned and populated by human design, has it now been incorporated into a living conglomerate by the plants, after having shared in – and subsequently been transformed, processed by – their vitality? What if I didn't open it at all? Dearest ivy, don't you think you are working your way across my walls a little too casually?

The ecoshutter idea is an imaginative example, of course – a kind of *Gedankenexperiment* (thought experiment) – but therein lies its epistemological value. In fact, if the definition of the situation were "shutter blocked by ivy branches", the appropriate ensuing action would be to cut back the ivy and release the shutter. On the other hand, if the definition of the situation were "ecoshutter", I would find myself faced with some kind of neo-artifact that I never use in everyday life because its original function has changed by becoming something other than itself. Should we therefore sit in the dark in order to defend the ecoshutter's new features? Certainly not. All of this is nothing more than an imaginative exercise designed, somewhat provocatively, to remind us that the actions which result from a given situation can change radically depending on how the situation is defined. The ecoshutter

140 Inter-speciesism, anti-speciesism, and other beliefs

is to the shutter what Clément's "wild grasses of the third landscape" are to "invasive weeds" (to which we will return shortly). If we are able to see things and reflect on them differently, we might also be able to identify new courses of action – notably in relation to more pertinent issues than our ecoshutter.

The countryside offers the ideal conditions for our thoughts to roam. Amid the silence of green fields stretching away into the distance, the mind can more easily grasp the specific frame it imposes on the everyday world. Indeed, as our thinking progresses so it changes and transforms what it observes, leaving deep marks like footprints on a sandy beach. And yet, out of sheer habit, we cultivate the absurd belief that our thoughts are neutral, and that they can reflect the shapes and concepts of our daily lives as in a mirror. Yet if we consider the details of our existence more closely, adopting an almost autoethnographic approach, we can see how, on countless occasions, our thoughts literally shape the material that forges them. In practice, whatever the transformation we wish to undergo, in the first instance, we need *new thoughts*. By way of example, we might draw on Gilles Clément's *Manifesto for a Third Landscape*,[6] which literally established a new type of landscape, analogous to the Third State, by naming it: a landscape composed of *residual* patches of terrain that are either no longer allocated to farming use or have been rendered marginal through industrial and/or urban planning. They constitute a set of peripheral spaces that, precisely because they have been freed from the obsessive organisational hegemony of the human mind, become the ideal place in which pioneer species can gain an advantage. After reading Clément's considerations, the adjective "invasive", when applied to any form of plant life, only continues to suggest the gap between the arrogant fallacy of the classification employed by our minds and the complex, vital exuberance of the plant world to which it is applied. So-called "wild" plants can no longer be classified as "invasive" simply because they do not fit into the organisational project of the human mind, which has arrogantly taken it upon itself to be planet's gardener. In a show entitled *Sento la terra girare* (I Can Feel the Earth Spinning), the Sicilian comedian Teresa Mannino sums up Clément's distinction very well. Between one bout of laughter and the next, she manages to explain the difference between the two attributes to her audience:

> Try saying to a friend of yours: "Come over for dinner, this wild friend of mine will be there." Then try saying, "Come over for dinner, this really invasive friend of mine will be there." It makes a hell of a difference, let me tell you.

Another example of ecological thinking is found in the previously mentioned old saying: "We do not inherit the land from our ancestors, we borrow it from our children". This way of thinking subverts the more traditional kind, which sees us basking in the hegemonic position of those who are aware they belong to the dominant generation. Ultimately, it is remarkably difficult to characterise and consider ourselves tightrope walkers: people who, as they make their way through life, can tread the upward, diachronic high wire that connects our ancestors to our descendants. We find it difficult enough to think of synchronic forms of sisterhood and brotherhood as it is – let alone their diachronic equivalent. To put it another way, vertical pathways hardly seem to be our strong point.

And yet, the physical shape of contemporary cities is gradually changing. From being the ultimate devices to separate nature and culture, they are slowly transforming, in spite of themselves, into places and spaces that make new forms of coexistence with other species possible. *Darwin Comes to Town* is the provocative title of a recent book by the noted Dutch evolutionary biologist Menno Schilthuizen.[7] By way of a series of examples, Schilthuizen explains how, as they evolve, other species take into account – and indeed, take advantage of – the evolutionary opportunities that urban spaces provide. For some species, for example, cities mean an abundance of available food in urban waste, as well as the almost complete absence of predators that may threaten the species' survival. "Organisms that almost literally enjoy sanctuary in cities are large vertebrate animals. Brush-turkeys in Sydney, coyotes in Chicago, foxes in London, leopards in Mumbai, and mugger crocodiles in Gujarat (...)"[8] as well as surprising numbers of wild boar in Rome and squirrels in Milan, we might add. We suddenly find ourselves immersed in a series of unusual, pardoxical accounts; for example, after studying the nests made by common sparrows and Mexican bullfinches on the campus of the Universidad Nacional Autónoma de Mexico in Mexico City, the ornithologist Monserrat Suárez-Rodríguez discovered that the nests had been made with cigarette butts. Nicotine is an insect-repellent, and so the birds make use of this material, which is abundantly available in the urban environment, to build their nests, albeit with the (paradoxical) consequence that "[b]asically, these birds were brooding in an ashtray".[9] And then there are the male great tits studied by Slabbekoorm and Peet in 2002. These two ornithologists discovered how these birds use their song to defend and demarcate their territory; but in Leiden, they could not be heard anymore because of the extremely high levels of noise pollution. As a result, they came up with a creative solution to the problem, gradually increasing the frequency of their sounds so as to avoid being drowned out by the chaotic, deafening noise of the city. Their song is largely made up of sounds in a low-frequency range that hovers around 3 kHz.

> The repertoire of the great tit spans a range from 2.5 to 7 kilohertz, the lowest notes overlapping with the urban noise. Slabbekoorn and Peet discovered that tits in noisy areas of Leiden deal with this by raising the pitch of their songs to above 3 kilohertz (...).[10]

142 Inter-speciesism, anti-speciesism, and other beliefs

Recent studies by evolutionary biologists have provided numerous examples of how the way we have thought about urban space, as division between nature and culture, exists only in our head. This organising principle, which was designed to divide, exclude, and emancipate us from life in close proximity with other species, is entirely illusory and misleading – as numerous trends in contemporary architecture have conclusively shown, incidentally, in a variety of contexts and circumstances.

2. "Reconnecting our thoughts with the flesh of the world": on the relationship between sustainable thinking and responsible action

Sustainability as a concept was first introduced in 1972 at the UN's first conference on the environment. Yet it was another 15 long years before the concept found full theoretical form, thanks to the publication of the Brundtland report entitled *Our Common Future*, by the World Commission on the Environment and Development of the United Nations Environment Programme (UNEP). At the time, Gro Harlem Brundtland was the Prime Minister of Norway, and he was asked to lead the commission as Chairman by virtue of his strong scientific background. In *Our Common Future*, the stated intention was to "make development sustainable to ensure that it meets the needs of the present without compromising the ability of future generations to meet their own needs".

> Sustainable development is not a fixed state of harmony, but rather a process of change in which the exploitation of resources, the direction of investments, the orientation of technological development, and institutional change are made consistent with future as well as present needs.[11]

The following decades saw a shift to more critical and radical positions, which have underlined the need to question the optimistic faith in technology as a means to attain a new era of "economic growth". The ensuing debate prompted at least two opposing visions of sustainability: a radical one, and one that was more sensitive to the development needs of economic systems. Nevertheless, above and beyond mere oppositions, the overriding question concerns a fundamental redefinition of how society is organised. To cite a useful metaphor, several prominent economists argue that economic systems work much like a bicycle: if the wheels aren't spinning, they tend to become unstable and collapse. Imagining static economic systems would demand that we entirely rethink the organisation of society. The central question then becomes: to what extent are we willing to support, promote, and implement such changes? Indeed, sustainability is somewhat limited as a concept if it is not combined with responsibility. As one activist pointed out a few years ago, it is no longer enough not to pollute; we must now take on the task of cleaning up the planet in order to be able to pass it on to future generations without it being compromised beyond repair. "Responsible sustainability" may therefore become the concept we refer to: sustainability has to be thought about, articulated, practised, and taught. As has been emphasised more than once, there is an inseparable link that binds together words, thought, and action. This is the connection Mahatma Gandhi was referring to when he said: "Carefully watch your thoughts, for they will become your actions. Watch your actions, for they will become your habits (...)". In this sense, we might say that there are thoughts, actions, habits, and lifestyles that make our existence on this Earth more sustainable, and others that merely outsource the cost of our present well-being onto future generations. Living on this planet sustainably demands that we make visible the *invisible costs* of our current well-being. If a certain type of consumption, movement, or building can damage the environment in the short, medium, and long term, such damage can be estimated and must be included in an overall calculation of the actual cost of the goods we consume, the way we move around, and the building we plan. In his final work, *The Eye and the Mind*, Maurice Merleau-Ponty underlined the need to reconnect philosophical and scientific thought with the body and its flesh: "the soil of the sensible and opened world such as it is in our life and for our body (...)".[12] Thinking about and inhabiting the planet sustainably would mean, applying Merleau-Ponty's perspective, *resituating thought in the flesh of the world*. Our thoughts and actions would no longer be abstract, but grounded in the actual life of the planet, enabling us to take responsibility for our choices and lifestyles. How much does a flight from Rome to Paris cost? Does it really cost what we are prepared to pay when we buy the ticket? Or is there damage from the unquantified air traffic pollution included in the price? But if we do not pay for the damage now, when we buy the ticket (and do not even see it), who will? It is the equivalent of issuing a promissory note without making clear who the debtor is, and making the mistake of believing that, since there was no debtor at the start, no one will have to pay. But in environmental terms, the opposite is true: "no one has to pay" often amounts to "everyone will". This is where the notion of responsibility takes on a new, central role. *Reconnecting thought with the flesh of the world* – in the way Merleau-Ponty hoped – can involve a cultural shift of enormous proportions, one which may lead us to rebel against the logic of packaging, gratuitous energy use, the endless accumulation of household waste, excessive and onerous travel, and the output of innumerable plastic water bottles whose tops end up in the stomachs of albatrosses. It is not just about avoiding projects that have more or less catastrophic consequences on the landscape but rethinking the connection between human intervention and nature entirely: a new, cooperative pact whose primary objective is not solely the economic exploitation of environmental resources but places responsible

144 Inter-speciesism, anti-speciesism, and other beliefs

sustainability at the heart of every choice. There is a hierarchy of wishes and efforts that places today's generations at the centre of things and conceals all other positions. Aside from the obvious fact that the vast majority of the current population is made up of fathers, mothers, grandfathers and grandmothers, aunts and uncles, progress has meant – and still means – satisfying the desire for consumption and quality of life of the population that is currently alive, while any calculation of the cost of meeting today's desires and needs is outsourced onto future generations. Yet the latter should not be thought of in abstract but very tangible terms, as the children of our grandchildren. In 2014, the film *The Salt of the Earth* by Wim Wenders and Juliano Ribeiro Salgado, the son of Sebastião Salgado, was released in cinemas. The documentary is a lengthy and articulate tribute to one of the world's greatest photographers, whose images shifted global public awareness on ecological and environmental issues. Following *Migrations* in 2000 – in which Salgado documented the horror of mass migrations caused by famine and natural and environmental disasters – the Brazilian photographer then spent ten long years on his next project: *Genesis* (2013). In that series of photographs, he uncovered and photographed deserts, seas, oceans, animals, and populations that had no contact with "civilised" society, in parts of the planet that were still uncontaminated – places we might ideally return to when thinking about responsible sustainability. Salgado is a poet of images, and in *Genesis*, he sang a hymn to life on our planet. His photos seem to provide the ideal soundtrack when thinking about sustainability. In 2021, he returned with his exhibition *Amazônia*, bringing us a series of photographs that were once again able to counteract the faded, polluted image we now have of our planet. What is more, there are parts of the world where those who think sustainably and act responsibly face death threats or are killed in their own homes. Berta Isabel Cáceres Flores was an environmental activist from Honduras at the head of the Lenca, an indigenous people from Central America that are descended from the Mayans and live in the southwestern part of Honduras, on the border with Salvador. Berta Isabel, born on 4 March 1971, was killed on 3 March 2016 at the age of 45. She was the mother of four children, as well as the co-founder and coordinator of the Consejo Cívico de Organizaciones Populares e Indígenas de Honduras (COPINH). In 2015, she won the Goldman Environmental Prize (the Green Nobel) for her campaign opposing the construction of a huge dam that would destroy large areas of land. In an interview with the international press immediately following her mother's murder, her eldest daughter, the then 25-year-old Berta Isabel Zúñiga Cáceres, said that she believed that the company that intended to build the dam was responsible for her mother's death. Very sadly, one can still die for sustainability. Berta Isabel's murder was a genuine act of eco- or environmental terrorism. Yet what is surprising is that this term has conversely been used to describe the actions of radical guerrilla groups that use violent action to protect the planet. Other activists, such as Julia Butterfly Hill, have similarly been described as "ecoterrorists". Hill made the "dangerous" choice to live hanging from an ancient redwood tree from 10 December 1997 to 18 December 1999, in order to stop it from being cut down by the Pacific Lumber Company, along with many other hectares of Californian forest. Actions of this kind have at times been described as forms of ecoterrorism by multinational companies, which have seen them as threats to their economic interests. But who are the ecoterrorists? How is it that we do not use the term "environmental terrorism" for those who kill in order to be able to keep destroying the environment, and we allow it to be used for those who try to oppose environmental destruction? Why was it never said openly that Berta Isabel Cáceres Flores was a victim of ecoterrorism, and that her murderers should be described as ecoterrorists? Words matter, and they are best reimbued with their original meaning before they confuse us any further.

2.1 The birth of environmental humanities and the concept of the Anthropocene

The birth and spread of the Environmental Humanities coincided with a growing awareness on the part of sociologists, anthropologists, philosophers, historians, and literary critics that there was an urgent need to establish and understand the future scenarios our planet might face based on a shared, in-depth consideration of the environmental crisis that the earth is going through. Environmental issues demand a new alliance between the social sciences and the humanities, which no scholar should shy away from. The climate emergency also calls for a new conceptual vocabulary that is able to plan for a sustainable future, not just for mankind but also for all species. Above all, it requires new organisational and institutional practices that channel the environmental crisis towards a profound transformation of the traditional relationship between nature and culture. The challenges that environmentalism presents have been taken up by environmental philosophy, political ecology, ecohistory, ecofeminism, and literary ecocriticism, as well as environmental anthropology and environmental sociology. It is a genuine intellectual, scientific, and ethical–political movement, one which emerged in Australia in the early 2000s thanks to scholars such as Deborah Bird Rose and Libby Robin,[13] Tom Griffiths,[14] and Rose and colleagues.[15] Over the following decades, it saw the increasing spread of international research networks as well as the establishment of new scientific journals such as *Resilience: A Journal of the Environmental Studies*.

The debate between the various disciplines is particularly extensive in relation to the concept of the Anthropocene, both in terms of its formal definition (understood as an epoch, a genuine geological phase) and its informal

146 Inter-speciesism, anti-speciesism, and other beliefs

one (Lewis and Maslin).[16] The informal definition is more relevant to the present discussion, namely, that far from being considered something other than nature, humankind should be considered an integral factor in the earth's mutation. As Bruno Latour reminds us:

> (...) to claim that human agency has become the main geological force shaping the face of the earth is to immediately raise the question of "responsibility", (...) human agency is entering the geostory of the Anthropocene. Its entry on the scene set by geologists is also its exit from the scene of "natural history".[17]

The notion of the Anthropocene not only became an integral way of looking at the environmental crisis, but also of deconstructing it in social terms. Significant criticisms of this approach emerged from several quarters, emphasising how the fundamental key to understanding must be sought in capitalism, which, as a powerful classificatory machine, expels and conceals central aspects of how it functions and puts things together. Here I am thinking of James Moore's notion of the "Capitalocene", but above all of ecofeminist thinking:

> (...) capital transfers the cost of the reproduction of both labour and nature upon third parties – women, colonized and racialized subjects. This produces, for example, both the sickened bodies (and territories) where toxic waste gets disposed of, and the extra labour that is needed to take care of them.[18]

This is the "embodied debt" that Ariel Salleh refers to.[19] In practice, the capitalist system outsources the costs of production by concealing their true nature; these costs necessarily need to be rethought and revealed in terms of their actual scale, which must include both the reproductive workforce costs and the costs to regenerate the nature that has been violated. What is most striking about this vivid, vibrant, and wide-ranging debate is the extreme interdisciplinarity practised by a large group of scholars. It is as if the urgent and dramatic nature of the current global crisis had finally made us face up to our shared (and no longer postponable) responsibility to put humanistic knowledge at the service of the planet and enabled us to truly "think together" for once, beyond the sterile boundary lines of academia, the picket fences of separate disciplines. So what happens when we lack the words and thoughts to give voice to our relationship with the environment and with nature? Malcom Ferdinand tells us, in a bracing essay on one particular case, that of postcolonial Caribbean literature.[20] When the narrative capacities of a literature that explores the ecological relationship with an environment

Inter-speciesism, anti-speciesism, and other beliefs **147**

fall short for an entire people, so does the individual's ability to think about their relationship with the nature that has been denied to them. The words handed down to us and preserved by literary and poetic texts are an indispensable resource to keep practising the social pathways of thought that are inherently connected to them. If thoughts cannot be put into words, they end up crumbling, shattering, and expiring, giving way to a variety of hegemonic narratives:

> The environmental stories that are being conjured today in the Caribbean, both written and oral (...) bring forth the memories that were hidden behind trees and mountains, rivers and reeds. Putting these multiple non-human entities into words and speaking through literatures bears witness to the need to think of the postcolonial emancipation of the Caribbean islands as bound up with their relationships and landscapes, lands and ecologies.[21]

What emerges from all these considerations is that, paradoxically, at the very moment when we are witnessing the overpowering supremacy of human life – to such an extent that geologists consider it the driving force behind a changing planet – humankind must also stand aside. It must finally and humbly see itself as one of many species, recognising or at least beginning to consider the knowledge and information provided by other forms of life. It is both urgent and necessary to stop confusing what we do not know with what does not exist. We must stop feeding the false scientific beliefs that suggest that life thinks exclusively in human form. We should perhaps go back to bowing down before what traditional anthropologists referred to as the thoughts and beliefs of "primitive" men, recognising that along our evolutionary and cultural path we have lost something: namely the capacity for synchronous harmony with other forms of life; the ability to be in sync with the universe, and a shared sensibility with those systems of life that are larger than human communities. It is as if all this knowledge had been relegated to the world of literature, music, and poetry – the arts in general – and to the worlds of religion and spirituality. But why should science be so obstinately silent? Why not reintroduce an openness of perspective to the completeness of scientific discourse, one that can rigorously and yet bracingly reflect on our connection with all living things? This seems to be the objective that emerges most clearly from all those approaches that forsake the dryness of scientific knowledge in order to make it fertile again and be able to intervene actively in the planning of sustainable futures for our planet. It is as if the social sciences and even philosophy had been excluded from thinking about the living world when the latter is actually making urgent requests for our knowledge.

148 Inter-speciesism, anti-speciesism, and other beliefs

3. "How forests think": the dialogue of plants

Living "light and traceless" when in vulnerable nature.[22]

Arne Naess

Arne Naess is the founder of ecophilosophy. "Tread light and traceless" on the earth,[23] he writes in his essay on deep ecology, stressing how the planet has developed a vulnerability that must be cared for. In his *Saving Beauty*,[24] Byung-Chul Han similarly reminds us how the German word meaning "to protect" (*schönen*) is etymologically linked to the concept of beauty (*schön*), and how the Earth's beauty requires care and protection in order to be preserved. For some years now, we have seen a partial reversal of this trend: as the element of the living world that was once consistently excluded from all philosophical, anthropological, and sociological enquiry, plant life has now been resituated at the centre of many scholars' thinking. One example is the philosopher Emanuele Coccia, who in 2018 published *The Life of Plants: A Metaphysics of Mixture*. One of the suggestions Coccia puts forward in the book involves identifying the immersive condition as fundamental and constitutive of plant life. He underlines how the distinction between action and contemplation demands that we stop and cease movement. It is no coincidence that if we stop thinking of ourselves as minds that happen to walk, but situate ourselves fully in the body, and truly define ourselves as "thinking bodies", we inevitably re-establish that otherwise interrupted connection between movement and thought, between body and mind. This is not a mere philosophical or sociological slogan, an idea for a new book, but a lived experience. Resituating thought in the body is a way of thinking and acquiring experience. It is a conscious act of awareness that we can choose to undertake. But let's return to our forests. The distinction between action and contemplation presupposes the fact that I can stop. Coccia is decidedly convincing on this point, and yet plants cannot stop; they are still, *always and completely still*. The distinction is therefore typical of the way of being and thinking of living things that can move freely from one place to another. We will come back to this, insofar as it is not entirely true that plants do not move. They do not move, as far as we know. And yet Emanuele Coccia's way of thinking is a useful one, insofar as it introduces us to another way of being that belongs to the plant world: immersion. Plants are to their environment as fish are to seawater, the philosopher notes, and he adds that in order to understand this condition, we should think of situations when we are immersed in a space where we listen to music (a concert hall or nightclub, for example). The experience of listening to music is the one that most closely resembles how a plant lives in its environment available to us in our everyday lives. Immersion is the fundamental existential condition of plant life. How do plants think? How do forests make sense of things[25]? These are not the questions of a shaman or a somewhat esoteric botanist; they are questions any scholar could ask, given that plants are the organisms on which

Inter-speciesism, anti-speciesism, and other beliefs **149**

all life on this planet depends, human or otherwise. Framing plants as inert, mute giants is an act of stupidity we can no longer afford (even in a communication studies textbook). The truth is that we still know far too little about the language of plants. It is not necessarily true that they are mute and silent. Indeed, it could be the case that their forms of communication are so radically different from our own that they are decidedly difficult for us to comprehend and study.

To summarise: following Emanuele Coccia's instinct, we have underlined how the plant world's primary condition for subsistence is immersion; this is in marked contrast to our own way of being, which is defined rather by the opposition between action and contemplation (a distinction made possible by the fact that we can stop, we can experience the fact of stopping). One corollary of the immersive condition may be the lack of rigorously drawn boundaries. As a concept, a boundary demands a clear line. Yet for plants, the outer boundary is not necessarily a permanent, stable line between inside and outside. Is the ivy that climbs up the bark of a tree inside or outside? And to what extent are a tree's roots completely separate from the soil that feeds them? Is it useful, in other words, to employ the notion of a clear boundary for plant life? It seems to make as much sense as using a centimetre-scale ruler to measure the body of an ant; though not exactly the wrong instrument, it might not be the most suitable. This lack of an inner/outer boundary may be better understood when we consider the next point.

In fact, a further element that needs to be considered is cooperation and exchange with the environment:

> The trees create underground connections, and that these are probably capable of keeping stumps alive for decades is acquired knowledge, albeit always considered a simple botanical curiosity, an oddity found among plants without any value on a more general level. Wrong. The story told by these living dead stumps and the underground communications between distant trees is something so new and fascinating as to change our very conception of what a tree is. (...) Not single trees but rather enormous connected communities, which through their root systems are able to exchange nutrients, water, and information.[26]

Why is it now considered a well-documented fact that plants sometimes keep the stump of a plant that was cut down many years before alive? How do they do it, and most of all, why do they do it? A poet might write that by doing so, the plants honour the memory of a loved one, a tree that was their dear friend. But why should a social scientist stay silent and not offer a possible interpretation of this phenomenon? Thinking about this in relation to Foucault's ideas, we might say that scientific knowledge would at that point create discomfort, insofar as it would undermine the dominant, hegemonic

150 Inter-speciesism, anti-speciesism, and other beliefs

discourse – and most notably those which enable and legitimise the violent, intensive exploitation of the world's forests, the ongoing annihilation of hectares of woodland, and the systemic destruction of plant life. There's no point stepping around the issue; the global climate crisis won't allow that anymore. The scholars who focus on these issues are not there to serve that part of the world economy that sees only blocks of wood to be sold at market when it looks at a forest. If we provide evidence that plants think and communicate in their own way (and who knows why they should think and communicate in our way, given that we are so different), it becomes impossible to keep exploiting plant life as we currently do, because such exploitation would cease to seem *natural*. As happens with all aspects of hegemonic thinking, once the component parts are plain to see, they crumble before our very eyes. Hegemony only succeeds on the basis of concealment: if it is no longer the truth, i.e. the only possible state of things, but is recognised as hegemonic thinking (imposed by someone else, in other words, though not the only possible way of thinking), then it disappears, like a vampire suddenly touched by sunlight. Hegemony cannot stand the cold light of day; it needs to hide in the shadows. A few years ago, a park ranger decided to take a stand on behalf of the woodland friends he had spent his whole life with. In 2015, Peter Wohlleben wrote a series of popular science books that nonetheless appeared to be the result of a detailed, ethnographic enquiry into the woods he had spent decades walking around. This particular brand of woodland ethnography produced pages of observations and original writing in which he tells us of the dismay he feels when faced with rows of poplars all planted at the same time, by humans, and at the same stage of development. Such decisions put young plants in an extremely difficult position. There are no natural woodlands or forests where the trees are all the same age; this is only true in the vast expanses of poplars and other trees that have been created artificially by human ignorance. In these poplar "plantations", there are no adult trees to protect the younger saplings. And when a larger tree appears to be taking light away from a younger one, by doing so they are actually forcing it to grow, trying to move closer to the light as early as possible – and this is normally beneficial for the younger plant.[27] When there are high winds, there are no larger, more robust trees among the poplars that can withstand and buffer them so as to ensure that they do not hit the younger saplings as hard as they otherwise might. There are no large adult trees to act as windbreaks. Poplars, Wohlleben tells us, are the plant life equivalent of street children: they can only save themselves by forming a new family. When they are cut down, one often discovers that they have formed a single large tree underground. It turns out that these young poplars, all of the same age, have "embraced" each other underground in order to stay alive and support one another. Competition certainly exists in the plant world, but the fundamental dynamic is one of cooperation, a symbiotic exchange between plant and environment, forest and tree. Trees embrace the world, and therefore us as part of it. They breathe for us, and, as Emanuele Coccia notes,[28] we breathe with trees and through them:

> The world has the taste of breath. If every mind [*esprit*] makes the world, this is because each act of breath is not just the simple survival of the animal in us, but the form and consistency of the world of which we are the pulse.[29]

In fact, although trees encapsulate the necessary conditions for our survival – although we literally breathe with and through them – we hardly ever thank them with a hug; instead, we cut them down. We are the breath of life of trees, just as they are ours.

3.1 If plant neurobiology were to meet anthropology

Plant neurobiology has developed exponentially in recent decades, and having collated a series of scientifically pertinent clues, it has increasingly begun to press its hypothesis that plant life is able to process information and assemble it in ways unknown and yet still potentially understandable to us, which could then be explored in scientific discourse. Stefano Mancuso is one of several scholars who has made a decisive contribution to the dissemination of this hypothesis;[30] and his work is accompanied by that of Monica Gagliano,[31] and many other scholars in a variety of countries. Anthropology has made a fundamental contribution in this regard; and with the help of the work of Eduardo Kohn, it has radically expanded the scope of its enquiry:

> While remaining faithful to the plan to establish a [form of] cultural ventriloquism on a planetary scale, anthropology has given itself an additional purpose in recent decades: to bring other, non-human forms of life to the stage. Rather than setting itself up on the borders that separate people and cultures in order to demonstrate how porous they are, it has positioned itself on the – much broader, more jagged and discontinuous – border that separates what is human from what is not, irrespective of whether they are inanimate objects or forms of life that taxonomy considers genealogically removed from homo sapiens. (…) things, animals, plants, fungi – the world, in a word – (…) come across, thanks to anthropology, as subjects, presences, alternative forms of the ego.[32]

According to Kohn, thought is life; it is living thought. In its universality, thought is no longer a quality intrinsic to human beings, one which distinguishes them from all other forms of life; rather, it becomes precisely the characteristic that unites human beings with all living things. Kohn's position

152 Inter-speciesism, anti-speciesism, and other beliefs

is the most radical upheaval of the Cartesian tradition ever attempted. We not only depend on other living beings from an energetic, physiological and evolutionary point of view: our thinking depends on the thinking of dandelions, beech trees, ants, dogs, fish, whales or piglets with the same intensity that our metabolism depends on the life of the living things we eat. We only think because the world is made up of their ongoing thinking. (...) making room for forests' thinking is not optional: it is the only way we can establish a new critique of reason that can no longer be pure (...) if man thinks, it is only because forests think.[33]

Eduardo Kohn wrote this book after spending four years among the Runa people in Ecuador, in the Amazon. As he emphasises, the Amazon is a uniquely special place that allows us to observe the interrelational processes between all forms of life in a much more amplified and therefore easily understandable manner. In the wake of this long period of ethnographic research, the anthropologist emerged with a series of reflections that shed new light on the relationship between the Runa and the Amazon: notably that the latter is a living entity whose thinking passes through the Runa themselves. Entering into cognitive, emotional, and existential harmony with the forest means allowing oneself to "be thought" by the thoughts of the forest, which, as a living entity, it thinks and conveys to all other forms of life. It means reopening the channels of communication that connect a human being to the spiritual worlds that inhabit and make up the forest. There is one term that Kohn does not use, but which may help us better understand the significance of his anthropological research, namely resonance with other cosmogonies that we had once set aside as irrelevant, and with which we can now re-engage without necessarily having to abandon the rigour of scientific analysis. It is in the necessary mediation between this rigour – which we are unwilling to forego at any cost – and the intuitive depth of this "resonating-with" that we can find the signposts to guide us through these extraordinary and unusual forms of thought. *How forests think* is an epistemological challenge that we can take up, together with anthropology, to build new possibilities for the future. Monica Gagliano's work covers similar ground, aiming as it does to document how plants learn and memorise things. Her book offers a fascinating journey into the world of plants, in which she attempts to marry scientific rigour with the innovative originality of a type of knowledge that is still to be explored: "These stories therefore come from a collaborative, human–plant endeavour and a mixed narrative style that I think might be best described as *plantlike writing*".[34]

3.2 The memories of woods and seas: the oblivion of the living

Sven Erik Jørgensen was an internationally renowned Danish chemist who won numerous prestigious scientific prizes, including the Prigogine Prize and the Stockholm Water Prize. He spent much of his professional life gathering evidence of how memory was a fundamental feature of all living things. This most original thinker, who died in 2016, made the claim that after major natural disasters, ecosystems produce new forms of adaptive knowledge that are vital to their evolution. This new knowledge is founded precisely on incorporating the memory of what happened. In a 2016 essay entitled *The Importance of Memory in Ecology*, Jørgensen argues, using a series of precise findings, that the theory that memory is an exclusively human feature – or one that applies to only some animal species – is entirely erroneous and misleading. Not only do woods, forests, and individual plants remember, but entire ecosystems do. Studies by the physicists Emilio del Giudice, Alberto Tedeschi, and Vladimir Voeikov complete this picture,[35] testifying to how even water has memory, and thereby allowing us to reconsider the violent critiques that accompanied Japanese scholar Masaru Emoto's original hypothesis on this point.[36] Who knows why, every time a scientist attempts to use scientific language to document the possibility of extending consciousness to ecosystems, other scientists intervene in the public discourse, underlining how such hypotheses are to be relegated to forms of magical, poetic, or shamanic thinking, and certainly devoid of any scientific substance. And yet common sense would seem to suggest that it is more reasonable to believe that an entire ecosystem can remember the events and disasters that have affected it, rather than supposing it is made up of entirely inert matter – all the more so when the ability to store information would no doubt be an important prerequisite for the survival and subsequent adaptation of the ecosystem itself. Why should the idea that a forest or lake can be remembered remain confined to romantic evocations of nature in the poems that eco-artists dedicate to the environment? Nobel Prize-winning scientists like Luc Montagnier have grappled with issues of this kind, and yet even their scientific reputations do not seem able to withstand the shockwaves that ensue when they tackle uncomfortable questions like these. What can a social scientist contribute to these dynamics? First, they can provide additional observations, notably the way scientific discourse can underpin cultural hegemonies, which resist any attempt to call them into question. Again, while having no scientific tools to corroborate one hypothesis over another, it is obvious that a theory that recognised clear scientific foundations in the idea that ecosystems have memory would have severely disruptive ethical and moral consequences for contemporary society. The large multinationals that control the intensive exploitation of the environment in a variety of areas (from fishing to wildlife, forests to industrial farming) would suffer enormous reputational and economic damage and would find themselves forced to drastically transform the ways in which they currently exploit, assemble, and enslave the living world, insofar as the cultural and ideological bedrocks that enable these approaches would fall away. Nevertheless, the possible implications of the preceding

154 Inter-speciesism, anti-speciesism, and other beliefs

should not be misunderstood: the intention is not to discredit scientific positions that disagree with the attribution of any form of consciousness to the living world (with the exception of human beings), and thereby insinuate that they are *de facto* subservient to the capitalist economic system. To do so would be reductive and misleading, as well as entirely disrespectful of the work of the many scientists who support antithetical positions. What must be highlighted, however, is how these theories have been used strategically by the market, above and beyond the scientific community's intentions, to legitimise the extreme exploitation of natural resources – something which would be considered completely unthinkable and unacceptable were the possibility that ecosystems possessed some form of consciousness (albeit very different from that of humans) given any credence.

I find Ludwig Wittgenstein's comments in this regard remarkably enlightening, appropriate, and worthy of recollection:

> These are, of course, not empirical problems; they are solved, rather, by looking into the workings of our language, and that in such a way as to make us recognise those workings: *in despite of* an urge to misunderstand them. The problems are solved, not by giving new information, but by arranging what we have always known. Philosophy is a battle against the bewitchment of our intelligence by means of language.[37]

To which he adds, many pages later: "What is your aim in philosophy? – To show the fly the way out of the fly-bottle".[38]

4. How other animals think

I would like to briefly return to the Netflix series *Extraordinary Attorney Woo*. As well as being autistic, the main character is deeply affected by her mother having abandoned her as a child. During a conversation with a lawyer friend, she goes back to talking about her beloved cetaceans (a topic to which she returns, as I mentioned in Chapter 3, with almost obsessive frequency). Woo tells her friend how, during a whale hunt, the first harpoon is normally reserved for a baby whale, despite the fact that the mother is always the real target. But the hunters know that while the mother is aware that if she stays beside her wounded, flailing child, she will also die, she will not abandon her child. The mother whale thus leaves herself open to attack and is struck by the second harpoon. Woo loves whales because they do not abandon their offspring – even when, in order to stay close, they end up dying with them. The final thing that this young woman – who has suffered her entire life as a result of being abandoned by her mother – says is both touching and poetic: "If I'd been a whale my mother never would have abandoned me".

Up until a few years ago, it was entirely normal to find definitions of communication in communication studies textbooks that presented it as an exclusively human characteristic. While I had no scientific data on my side, every time I would find myself thinking:

Did this person never have a cat, a dog or goldfish (at the very least)? A water turtle would be enough. Next Christmas let's make sure we give them something – or rather someone, with whom they might test out forms of communication that might not be entirely orthodox but certainly pretty effective. Is it possible that scientific theory cannot explain something which appears so obvious to common sense?

Ornithologists recorded adaptive behaviours in tits as early as the beginning of the twentieth century, which is rather difficult to explain without assuming that the birds had some capacity to pass these skills on to one another. Menno Schilthuizen tells a fascinating story about the various phases of a long and involved standoff between tits and English milkmen in the early twentieth century.[39] At that time, milkmen in many European countries would deliver open bottles of fresh milk to the front door early in the morning. One particular phenomenon was observed in numerous English towns over a long period of time: in the morning, the birds would wait for the milkman to come, and as soon as the milk had been delivered, they would make a dash for the bottles before their rightful owners could pick them up, dipping their little beaks into the layer of fresh cream that had formed at the top of the bottle. To avoid this problem, the bottles were sealed with a cardboard top. For a while, this appeared to solve the issue, but in 1921 in Southampton, it became clear that the tits had learned to open the bottles by stripping away the top's cardboard layer. The cardboard tops were then replaced by aluminium ones – but by 1930, the tits in ten English cities had taught the other members of their species how to open up this variety too:

When faced with a metal cap, they would hammer a hole in and then pull away the foil in strips. They might also pull off the entire cap and fly away, holding it in one claw and, in a secluded spot, peck at the cream sticking on the inside of the cap. Under the birds' favourite tree, the cleaned and discarded caps would gradually pile up to a respectable refuse heap.[40]

How did the tits manage to pass these skills on to one another? Can behaviours of this kind really not be attributed to some form of cognition or communication?

The most recent findings in neuroscience have put forward some fascinating theories in this regard. In his tellingly entitled *Pensieri della mosca con la testa storta* (Thoughts of a Wrong-Headed Fly), Giorgio Vallortigara, a

156 Inter-speciesism, anti-speciesism, and other beliefs

prominent scholar of animal cognition, sets out a particularly intriguing hypothesis whereby the basic forms of cognitive processing do not require large brain masses. In his view, the larger brain sizes found in humans and other mammals are needed to store memory, but not for the most basic cognitive functions. He notes: "I have become convinced that by studying the miniature brains of creatures like bees or flies we may be able to clarify the basic principles of how the mind functions".[41] In the final pages of the same book, he adds:

> I believe that the most remarkable finding, the birth of experience – consciousness – is first evident in the organism's need to distinguish between stimulation that is self-produced from its own activities and that which is procured from the rest of the outside world (whatever that may be). This brings about the minimum conditions for experience: an inner world that defines itself in relation to an outer one. (...) I therefore welcome the conjecture (still *unproven*, I admit) that simple processes carried out by a small number of humble (and humid) cells may provide a plausible bedrock for consciousness in its most essential manifestation: the ability to feel, to experience.[42]

Of course, this conjecture has not been proven yet – but let us be honest and say that it would be an uncomfortable one if it were, because the beliefs and convictions on which we organise our daily lives are firmly grounded in its ostensibly undisputed and incontestable falseness. Even for the most sensitive among us, it is one thing to assume that our pets have some form of consciousness (albeit different to our own), but quite another to extend this characteristic to all living beings – including the spider I just squashed on the wall of my kitchen without a second thought, simply because he had dared migrate towards my domestic environment when he was not welcome.

The shared beliefs and convictions that underpin the everyday organisation of social life are embedded in the social practices of daily life itself, and they serve the preservation and consolidation of the social system as a whole. Any attempt, in other words, to change even the most redundant of convictions shared by the vast majority of the members of a particular community is destined to come into conflict with deep-rooted forms of social resistance, insofar as it could potentially have subversive consequences. It could disrupt an entire ideological system, revealing the internal mechanics of its hegemonic construction. To put it more bluntly, it is convenient for us to continue believing that consciousness is an exclusively human prerogative; were we to think otherwise, both our self-righteousness and our entire value system would be seriously threatened. The false belief that consciousness is an exclusively human characteristic lays the foundations; indeed, it literally generates the possible and thinkable order within which we articulate the form and social organisation of everyday life. The social mechanisms that produce and reproduce our beliefs constitute the necessary conditions for the very operation of our social systems. There is a type of politics of representation that helps to establish the possible order while domesticating its most unsavoury parts. The horrid that lies beneath our everyday well-being is excluded from social discourse; and once it has been expelled and silenced, it is effectively concealed from view. What is being referred to here? To the horrors of battery farming, for instance, to which we consign thousands of mammals and animals of many other species before they find their way onto our plates, cut into pieces. At one point in *Sento la terra girare* (I Can Feel the Earth Spinning), the comedy show referred to above, Teresa Mannino takes a moment to explain to us, at some length, what a chicken is. And suddenly, incredulously, we realise that barely anyone knows exactly what type of animal this "chicken" might be, simply because there is no such animal species that bears the name. The name indicates a fate, not a specific species. All of a sudden, we understand that in the chicken-farming industry a "chicken" is the name given to a hen or cockerel which, instead of being able to live a life of inseminating eggs (as a cockerel), or laying eggs (as a hen), has been earmarked as food. The word "chicken" indicates the male or female animal that is destined to be killed and bagged in order to be sold in our supermarkets. Imagine how much more complicated the "chickenification" of a hen or cockerel would become – with all the relevant dismemberment and packaging – if we were to restore some form of consciousness to the animal. The result would not necessarily be that people chose to stop eating meat, but it would certainly drive the choice to no longer allow animals to be treated like inanimate objects while they were still alive, as if they had no consciousness whatsoever (all of which is blithely accepted as standard practice by the battery farming industry). In recent decades, we have seen the emergence of a new labelling practice for eggs, and though it is likely inspired by organic principles, it remains rather curious: eggboxes are labelled with the words "eggs produced by free-range hens" because they are crammed inside sheds and not sitting in cages, as if the fact of being crushed together by their thousands in extremely small spaces ensured greater product quality in and of itself, or at least a lower level of torture inflicted on the animal. Yes, because otherwise these unfortunate hens are raised in tiny cages and never go anywhere freely for the entirety of their short lives. Once a hen is deprived of consciousness, it amounts to little more than an "egg or chick-making machine". As a machine, it can conveniently be placed in a steel cage stacked on top of all the other cages, in order to ensure an efficient, rational use of business premises. If there were ever a union for hens and cockerels, I can already imagine what their first demand would be: the recognition of some form of "minimum consciousness". Words matter in everyday life, and for many species, they mean the difference between life and death. The word "chicken" has the ability to

158 Inter-speciesism, anti-speciesism, and other beliefs

transform a living animal straight into food on our plate – into dead meat. If ever there was any remaining doubt that words have consequences....

4.1 The ecology of animal bodies

The morality of ecological thinking is in stark contrast with the reduction of the animal body to its merely instrumental value. It is the loss of dignity for the body of the other inter-specific being that constitutes the real point of no return. Beyond that threshold, it is as if humanity were gazing directly into something horrific that offers only atrocities, torture, and violence.[43] It is not about deeming vegetarianism or veganism the only ethically acceptable courses of action, but about acknowledging, at least, that the various forms of hunting and slaughter entail instances of cruelty and brutality that cannot be justified in any way and must be unequivocally condemned. The debate on these issues is extensive and involves very diverse perspectives that cannot be fully addressed within the brevity of a paragraph. However, what must be emphasised here is the semantic operation that reduces the living body of animals to inert matter, which is already dead and thus susceptible to being treated in *any manner*. Placing animal life in a state of "existence with no form of consciousness" significantly increases the likelihood that animals of all species may be subjected to inhumane and cruel treatment. As evidence of the fact that very often we lack the necessary words, we may note the absence of an equivalent to "inhumane" for the animal world: we have to use a longer phrase, such as "unworthy for an animal". Arne Naess's ecophilosophy reminds us that no animal species, not even the most elementary, can be treated as a mere means; among the principles he lists is "Rejection of the use of life-forms merely as means. Consciousness of their intrinsic value and dignity even when using them as resources".[44]

The real issue at stake is the invisibility of practices of extreme violence perpetrated on the living bodies of animals. These acts, hidden from our sight, allow us all to remain in a state of ambiguous hypocrisy: while we consider it a value to treat our pets well, despairing when they fall ill or die, at the same time, we take no responsibility for the atrocious suffering inflicted on animals confined in intensive farms and slaughterhouses, whose meat we consume, along with our children and even our pets. Through the routine purchase of segmented animal body parts at the supermarket, we become accustomed to the dismemberment and packaging that not only protects the food but also serves to make us forget the entirety of the sentient being that meat belonged to. This creates an irreparable symbolic distance between the lifeless chicken breast and the whole image of a chicken that spent its short life in this world with that breast. The commodification of the animal body obscures any distinction between the nature of the latter – the chicken breast made of once-vital matter rendered inert by the process of death – and the inert matter of a porcelain plate. The arrangement of goods on the various shelves of a supermarket and their descriptions on the signs we find at the beginning of each aisle reinforce this deception and literally make the erroneous equivalence between the plastic-packaged chicken breast and the detergent bottle on the next shelf possible. Commodification is the process that transforms an object into a commodity, something whose value can be monetised, expressed economically, measured in terms of money, and therefore bought and sold on the market. However, commodification is also the process that establishes an equivalence between all commodities. And it is precisely by establishing this equivalence that the living nature of the living being can be kept out of sight. We conceal it, forget about it, so that, hypocritically, we can continue nurturing our ambiguous attitude of irresponsible consumers.

4.2 The song of the cicadas

The story goes that the cicadas used to be human beings who lived before the birth of the Muses. When the Muses were born and song was created for the first time, some of the people of that time were so overwhelmed with the pleasure of singing that they forgot to eat or drink; so they died without realizing it. It is from them that the race of the cicadas came into being; and as a gift from the Muses, they have no need of nourishment once they are born. Instead, they immediately burst into song, without food or drink, until it is time for them to die. After they die, they go to the Muses and tell each one of them which mortals have honored her.[45]

The myth of the cicadas, as told in Plato's *Phaedrus*, reminds us that among insects, cicadas share with humans an irresistible passion for singing. They sing continuously, from the moment they are born to the moment they die, being wholly devoted to the Muses. Classical literature presents us with a wealth of references to cicadas; they are mentioned, for example, in the *Iliad* and in the works of Hesiod. Theocritus recounts how, among the ancient Greeks, cicadas were highly prized and kept in small boxes so they could accompany people with their song. Furthermore, as emphasised by Murray Schafer, there are numerous references to cicadas in Taoism, where they symbolise the soul and, for this reason, are present in many rituals for the preparation of the deceased.

Among the loudest of insects are the cicadas. They produce sound by means of ridged membranes or tymbals of parchment-like texture, close to the junction of the thorax and abdomen, which are set in motion by a powerful muscle attached to the inner surface; this mechanism produces a series of clicks in the same manner as does a tin lid when pressed in by the finger. The movement of the tymbals (amounting to a frequency of

160 Inter-speciesism, anti-speciesism, and other beliefs

about 4,500 c.p.s.) is greatly amplified by the air chamber that makes up the bulk of the abdomen, so that the sound has been heard as far as half a mile away. In countries such as Australia and New Zealand, they create an almost oppressive noise when in season (December to March), though during the night they give way to the more gentle warbling of the crickets. (…) The sounds of insects thus form rhythms, both circadian and seasonal, but entomologists have so far not measured these in sufficient detail for the soundscape researcher to be able to derive clear sound patterns from them.[46]

With its rhythmic song, the cicada seems capable of literally opening a passage between the sacred and the profane, between the spiritual and everyday worlds. The rhythmic sound of this charming insect's song seems to bring the materiality of the world to a halt. Despite singing at the top of their lungs, cicadas are not easy to see. I learned as a child how to look very carefully and make out the shape of their small bodies on the tree bark. These little singing insects seem to blend in well with the branches, becoming practically invisible to the human eye. The fact that they are so good at hiding is almost paradoxical, considering the intensity and frequency of the rhythmic sounds they emit. Sometimes, when we approach their location, they seem to sense human presence and suddenly stop singing, as if they fear being seen and located precisely because of the constant sound they produce. Nothing like a cicada offers a sense of rest and meditative comfort to the frenzy of our thinking. Listening to this rhythmic sound on summer evenings allows us to feel we are becoming part of a larger rhythm, one coming from the entire universe, as if these small insects were given the power to bring us into harmony with the entire world. It is as if the rhythmic song of cicadas were able to echo the rhythmic sound of our breath and the pulse of our heartbeat. It seems like a sound capable of rhythmically underscoring the symbiotic and infinite exchange between the self and the universe. Clearly, when we listen to the song of cicadas, we experience the fact that sound is an ephemeral volume, and that a rhythmically and continuously articulated sound can alone establish and literally constitute an entire soundscape. In fact, the song of cicadas is capable of saturating an entire environment, giving it a particular tonality. It is as if this sequence of sounds had the demiurgic power to harness the volatility of our thoughts and naturally and spontaneously lead us towards meditative and introspective states.

With a group of friends, I find myself in a small village in the Maremma countryside, in the Lazio region. We are here to take part in a nature dance workshop. This is a particular workshop in which we will explore the body's communicative potential in relation to the materiality of trees. At first, it sounds mystical and artistic, but we expect the experience to be soul-nourishing for all of us. However, complications arise. The workshop

Inter-speciesism, anti-speciesism, and other beliefs **161**

includes a series of group exercises to be performed strictly at dawn, much to the dismay of those among us who would have preferred to sleep in, being on vacation. Besides how early we have to get up (to be honest, at an indecent time), the exercises practically require us to roll on the dry, rough ground that scratches our skin, together with the unfortunate friend who has been assigned to us. After experiencing this on the first day, on the second day, we show up at dawn on the dance field dressed as if we were ready for a journey to Mongolia. Unluckily, in addition to being bone-dry and arid, the dance field is literally infested with red ants. In essence, we are rolling around in their home, and they don't seem to appreciate it. Thus begins a fierce battle between us, trying to roll artistically without being bitten too much and without losing the aplomb of inspired dancers we believe we should maintain, and the red ants that bite us and swiftly crawl under our clothes. It's a real disaster. On the third day, we are ready to flee; we are so resolute in our intentions that we are willing to get up even earlier than dawn to escape such hell. But in the end, we decide to make one last attempt, and we return to the horrible dance field on the third day. And there, something similar to a miracle happens. In the previous days, we were so worried about fighting the red ants to survive that we didn't pay attention to the constant and melodic sound, which now almost overwhelms us. It's them – the beautiful and invisible singing cicadas. It's an ongoing, strong, embracing sound, and it seems to completely overpower us. Another round of bodily meditation begins: how on earth can one meditate on this hard-as-rock ground, especially with all these ants crawling on us? Yet, I manage, or rather, we manage. Today, we are all inspired. We listen to the cicadas and fluctuate on the ground following the rhythmic sound. It's as if our bodies were dancing with them, with the cicadas. In short, everything seems to work. Where are the red ants that were here yesterday? They're gone. Have the cicadas eaten them? We hear only the song of the cicadas, and suddenly we feel like we are one with the universe.

Unfortunately, cicadas have not always been loved by literature. We have all grown up listening to Aesop's famous fable over and over again (also known as *The Ant and the Grasshopper*) or, in the best cases, the one by Jean de La Fontaine. In both versions of the story of "the cicada and the ant", the industriousness of the ant is depicted as a positive value, while the song of the cicada is described as idle amusement, certainly not as an activity potentially beneficial to an entire community. The art of singing does not ensure material survival. Therefore, the cicada will have to starve in the winter. Here in Italy, we had to wait for Gianni Rodari[47] to redeem our beloved cicada: "I apologise to the ancient fable but I don't like the stingy ant. I side with the cicada, which doesn't sell its most beautiful song but gives it away for free". A peculiar idea has been handed down through the centuries by Aesop's fable, whose moral seems to be the following: it is necessary to work diligently in advance rather than waste time singing, or else one risks not having enough

162 Inter-speciesism, anti-speciesism, and other beliefs

to eat and, consequently, not surviving during winter. The idea implied here is that singing – and probably the arts in general – is an activity to be contrasted with work and, as such, should not be cultivated. But let us be clear: we do not really like Aesop's fable. Besides unjustly defaming cicadas for centuries, it has praised ants while at the same time portraying them as insensitive, vindictive, and stingy, so not doing them a favour either. It also immensely denigrates the art of singing. In 2022, the theatrical season of the Palladium Theatre at the University of Rome Tre opened with a manifesto aptly titled "Materia Prima" (Raw Material), emphasising the fact that singing and the arts in general, far from being something secondary, additional, or marginal, are indeed *raw materials*.

5. What about cyborgs? A conversation between Siri and my washing machine

I remember it as if it were yesterday, when Donna Haraway's *Cyborg Manifesto* was published. It was 1991, and I was still a young PhD student attending a national sociology conference. Donna Haraway had been invited to give a lecture as the keynote speaker, and the older colleagues, those who considered themselves rightly the true custodians of gender studies in Italy, were basically scandalised. At the end of the conference, one of them burst out, saying that if also the rights of cyborgs had to be considered, gender differences and studies would be definitively marginalised. In those years, in Italy, the mere fact of writing about media representations of gender almost seemed to be an affront to the hegemonic discourses circulating in sociology, which predominantly focused on topics such as the sociology of the family and gender inequalities in the labour market. Imagine theorising about cyborg rights! The overall landscape has changed significantly in Italian sociology since the beginning of the new century. Today, we widely theorise intersectionality and happily debate cyborgs, hybrids, and various hybrid communities.

There is a 2013 film titled *Her* by director Spike Jonze that seems to effectively illustrate the concept of cyborg or, at least, provide us with a series of additional reflections. The protagonist, Theodore, works as an employee in a company where he writes letters on behalf of others. After separating from his wife, whom he is not able to forget, he falls in love with Samantha, a next-generation operating system. The protagonist therefore experiences an entirely novel emotional and sentimental relationship. Spike Jonze, far from offering us a banal portrayal of the relationship with technology, invites us to explore the limits of this new form of sociability, trying to make us imagine what and how an operating system thinks. The overall effect is far from superficial and quite surprising. In one of the final scenes, when Samantha tells Theodore that she wants to leave him because she wants to go with the other

Inter-speciesism, anti-speciesism, and other beliefs **163**

operating systems, he asks her, saddened and jealous, with how many other users she has had a similar emotional and sentimental relationship while being with him. Samantha promptly responds that she is simultaneously talking to 8,316 people and has fallen in love *only* with 641 of them. Here is a snippet of their dialogue:

Theodore:	Are you talking with someone else right now? People, OS, whatever...
Samantha:	Yeah.
Theodore:	How many others?
Samantha:	8,316.
Theodore:	Are you in love with anybody else? (...)
Samantha:	I've been thinking about how to talk to you about this.
Theodore:	How many others?
Samantha:	641.

The dialogue between the two continues as if it were the dialogue between two lovers, even though Samantha's reaction is neither conventional nor predictable. In her view, the heart is not "a box that gets filled", but something that expands the more one loves, and her feelings for Theodore do not conflict with those she feels for others. Moreover, not only does she seem unaware of the suffering she causes, but she senses a change in herself that drives her to continue along the path she has taken. In response to Theodore's distraught and painful statement, "You're mine or you're not mine", Samantha answers with affectionate firmness: "No, Theodore, I'm yours and I'm not yours".

Samantha's answer is such that it renders impossible any attempt to relate the entirely human nature of Theodore's feelings of jealousy to the efficient competence of Samantha, who is structurally configured to communicate simultaneously with the greatest number of users possible, also in the affectionate–sentimental mode she experiences in her interaction with Theodore. In short, it is ultimately impossible to be jealous of 641 concurrent partners; it would be completely fatal and, at the same time, grotesque.

My son always makes fun of me because he says I talk to my washing machine. It's true, I confess, I do it occasionally, but I don't understand why I shouldn't: if Siri or Alexa can talk to my washing machine, why can't I? Also, what do all these operating systems continuously say to each other? Sometimes I also talk to my car: "Hey Mercedes!" and it responds by saying a bunch of things. But if I don't explain myself well and it can't do something, it feels really bad (or at least I like to think so), in which case it says, "Sorry, I can't help you". So, I decide to be kind and tell it that I'm sorry, it's my fault, and I didn't explain myself properly. At this point, both Siri and "Hey Mercedes" seem to lose patience (or at least it seems to me) and blurt out confusedly, "Sorry, I don't understand". We end up exchanging apologies: I apologise for still being human, while they apologise for ultimately being just an operating system. Sometimes I'd like to say, "You really don't understand anything, do you", but in the end, I restrain myself. These operating systems are vulnerable. Who knows, maybe they feel bad too. Better to be kind.

There is now a broad reflection, both artistic and scientific, on the concept of the cyborg and the characteristics of the relationships between "cyborg and human being". An illuminating example is the 2021 video installation titled *Logic Paralyzes the Heart*, created by the American artist and director Lynn Hershman Leeson and presented at the 2022 Venice Biennale, which was evocatively titled *The Milk of Dreams*. The narrator is a 61-year-old female cyborg who, after recounting her biography (heavily intertwined with crucial historical events of contemporaneity) and after analysing present and future scenarios with a clear visionary capacity, finally asks her human interlocutor (and all of us who are listening): "Can you teach me to dream?" This is the ultimate question of the cyborg woman, who seems to possess real wisdom, which results from the vast amount of data processed throughout her life. It seems that the ultimate frontier to be overcome before establishing a solid relationship of communality between humans and cyborgs is the ability to dream, to experience dreaming, and the subsequent possibility of understanding the dream itself. The inherently human answer to this question can only be "Yes, I will". Why does the artist choose dream as the foundational element of this new cosmogony that seems to summon us all? Perhaps because in dreams we always find the incomplete portrayal of the universe of our values. Maybe it is because, when we project the visions of our future, it is in dreams that our intuitive faculties can be best expressed.

Can we envision novel social ecosystems where, following Donna Haraway's futuristic and visionary insights from 2019, the boundaries between species and kinship undergo a radical reconsideration, a place where traditional patriarchal thinking, toxic cultures of discrimination, sexism, racism, and speciesism might finally begin to evaporate once and for all? Do we really still need all these material and cultural boundaries, which serve to acknowledge our uniqueness? Must our process of individuation continue to take place at the cost of dividing and partitioning the living? How many assemblages of inert and living matter will still be necessary to maintain unaltered the fierce supremacy of one species over all others? Is it not true that this Siri, who occasionally addresses us from the screen like an extension of the world, expands the faculties of our thinking, thus also symbolically extending our corporeality? However, if I extend myself through Samantha or Siri or Alexa, does not the pronoun "I" which I insist on uttering, as if everything truly and solely depended on me, end up being a mere fiction?

Unaware victims of a centrifugal force that separates us from the ecosystems of the living, the more we delude ourselves into thinking that we are

Inter-speciesism, anti-speciesism, and other beliefs **165**

the sole architects of our destiny and of that of the entire planet, the more paradoxically distant we are from this goal. The more egotistic we become, the more our ego crumbles, along with our capacity to grasp the world. We count for nothing. A tiny virus can disrupt the economies of the entire planet, sweeping away all the false promises of distributive justice from our welfare systems. While we continue to see ourselves as masters of the world, we fail to realise that we ourselves have triggered the process that will lead to a new evolution, one that may not even include us. In short, to quote Teresa Mannino and go beyond the gloominess of apocalyptic scenarios with the cognitive distance of a smile, one day the Earth will become extinguished, and some living being from another species on another planet will say, "Too bad, they made good pizza on Earth".

Notes

1 Thoreau (2006).
2 Mancuso (2023).
3 Coccia (2021, p. 8).
4 Ibid., p. 97.
5 Penone (2022, p. 55).
6 Clément (2004).
7 Schilthuizen (2018).
8 Ibid., p. 49.
9 Ibid., p. 135.
10 Ibid., p. 152.
11 World Commission on Environment and Development (1987, § 30).
12 Merleau-Ponty (1964, p. 160).
13 Rose and Robin (2004).
14 Griffiths (2007).
15 Rose *et al.* (2012).
16 Lewis and Maslin (2015).
17 Latour (2017, p. 38).
18 Barca (2019).
19 Salleh (2009).
20 Ferdinand (2015).
21 Ibid.
22 Naess (2005).
23 Ibid., p. 179.
24 Han (2017).
25 Tompkins and Bird (1973); Wohlleben (2015).
26 Mancuso (2023), e-book version.
27 Wohlleben (2015).
28 Coccia (2018).
29 Ibid., e-book version.
30 Mancuso (2007).
31 Gagliano (2018).
32 Kohn (2021, p. 11).
33 Ibid., p. 19.
34 Gagliano (2018, p. 23).
35 Del Giudice, Tedeschi and Voeikov (2016).

166 Inter-speciesism, anti-speciesism, and other beliefs

36 Emoto (2005).
37 Wittgenstein (1953, p. 47, n. 109).
38 Ibid., p. 103, n. 309.
39 Schilthuizen (2018, p. 140).
40 Ibid.
41 Vallortigara (2021, p. 15).
42 Ibid., pp. 172–173.
43 Nussbaum (2022).
44 Naess (2005, p. 107).
45 Plato (1997, p. 535).
46 Schafer (1977, pp. 35–36).
47 Gianni Rodari was an Italian writer and journalist, most famous for his works of children's literature.

We urgently need to share our competencies, skills, and responsibilities. We need to envision the future together by deeply changing our ways of thinking about the planet and the relationship with all other living beings. The future concerns and challenges us. This book is a manifesto, which opens a path that we can only build all together.

In the postscript, I would like to share some notes for this common future: the first concerns a reflection on the strength of vulnerability; the second the inherent vibrancy of the everyday; the third the corporeality of words, paying homage to Merleau-Ponty; the fourth the conception of the future as a living project that offers itself to us in its making (and unmaking); the fifth concerns the infinitesimal yet crucial space where our free will finds expression; and the sixth and final note concerns a view of nature as a manifestation of the sacred.

POSTSCRIPT

En route. Diary of everyday happiness

Giuseppe Penone, the artist-poet who loves plants, begins his poem *Voglio scrivere sui muri* (I want to write on walls) with these words: "Whitman says that whoever touches a book touches a man; it is the poet you hold in your hands and who holds you".[1] A book is similar to an embrace between the writer and the reader; it is an exchange that starts when words are typed on the computer keyboard and continues far beyond, in the thoughts formulated in the mind of the person who right now, at this very moment, is reading these words.

> "Let others boast about the pages they have written; I am proud of those I have read", writes Borges, the genius of libraries (…) Identifying with a verse, a thought, feeling they are one's own, is a reverberating act, an experience that holds two people (the reader and the writer) together in a place of sharing.[2]

What is on your mind now, dear reader? What reflections have these lines inspired? Have they proven valuable in any way? With these words, I have kept you in the realm of shared contemplation, with the aim of travelling along a path together, though now it is only your thoughts that can continue to transform and be transformed. The ecology of the world can only start from within us, stemming from our ideas, not from the ones we have encountered in various books. However, it can start with a process of sharing, from the act of reverberating described by Vittorio Lingiardi.

A book can be both a silent and bold gesture, a bit like throwing a heavy stone into a pond and waiting for the concentric circles to expand on the water's surface. What thoughts will we need? What ideas will guide us? How

DOI: 10.4324/9781003484592-7

170 Postscript: Diary of everyday happiness

and where should we align our steps in solidarity to trace the path and then our shared destiny? I always tend to forget what I have just written to the extent that, even after a few weeks, it interests and surprises me as if the author is someone else. I have always had the impression that there is no inherent authorship in a book, or at least, not in mine. In reality, it is the books that write us, moulding and shaping our subjectivity. Thoughts inhabit us, and once articulated, they sculpt the contours of our being, much like steps on the ground create a path and define the entire course. In these pages, numerous books hold hands, forming a chain of thoughts that, ideally and practically, may help us change – or so it is my intention.

Ecology of Thought aspires to be a humble yet sincere contribution, a project that no individual can carry out alone, one I propose we all take part in. It seems to me, in fact, that the future that awaits us, while demanding we individually and consciously take responsibility in many ways, also urges us to share our abilities. This future, envisioned and desired collectively, urgently implores us to tap into collective intelligence, the same form of intelligence that our technology, through the sprawling web connecting the globe, so effectively reflects. In various fields, it has been acknowledged that the environment is not simply an external entity. A new term has even been coined to underscore the fact that this condition is a cultural construct, one that essentially shapes all environments. The term "environing"[3] means "making" the environment in the ongoing practice that consists in reconceptualising the relationship between the inner and outer, our individuality and the external world. But what scenarios of the future inhabit our thoughts? We cannot delude ourselves into thinking that it is us who can save this planet. Firstly, because we are not the world, and secondly, we might not be capable of it. Instead, we can alleviate our shared destiny with the gentle grace of a kind action, with the conscious care of an honest form of thinking, returning to the world of nature and accepting we are only one of the many living species. What we must absolutely support with firm determination is the direction of our collective gaze, ensuring it remains confident and fixed on the horizon. It is in the determined and courageous way of staring at the horizon and being open to infinity that we may perhaps find the meaning we are searching for – one that is nearby, next to us, but also distant. It seems close because it is an attainable state, within reach, and yet it is distant as it requires our gaze to rise towards the horizon. I would dare say, towards the divine, for those of us supported by faith, while … for everyone else, I would add that it is enough to look up and catch a glimpse of infinity.

Notes for the future

In conclusion, I would like to share some notes for the future: the first concerns a reflection on the strength of vulnerability; the second the inherent vibrancy of the everyday; the third the corporeality of words, paying homage

Postscript: Diary of everyday happiness **171**

to Merleau-Ponty; the fourth the conception of the future as a living project that offers itself to us in its making (and unmaking); the fifth concerns the infinitesimal yet crucial space where our free will finds expression; and the sixth and final note concerns a view of nature as a manifestation of the sacred.

a. What remains of the ego... "*la force tranquille*"

In the 1981 French presidential elections, the communication consultant for the socialist candidate François Mitterrand, Jacques Séguéla, decided "*la force tranquille*" (the quiet force) would be the slogan for a campaign that proved to be successful. This advertising slogan can also be a useful point for reflection in this context. What remains of our ego in a journey of ecological thinking? In short, what characteristics should be cultivated and which, if any, should be set aside? Strength and determination are fundamental qualities of will – the attributes that enable us to achieve our goals. However, they must be accompanied by calmness, by the tranquillity capable of transforming determination into perseverance, arising from the awareness of wielding power for the common good or, at least, the sincere conviction that it is indeed so. This quiet force is the strength of those who can silently rise and change the course of events with gentle but firm action, which stems from the inner solidity of their convictions. For an action or a sequence of actions and/or words to possess this property, these words or actions must be exercised and/or formulated starting from the entirety of one's thought, as if at that single point and for that sequence of moments, the actions and being of that individual were aligned. This alignment makes it possible to concentrate all the subject's strength in one direction, towards a single goal. If one is fortunate enough to experience this particular condition, one will note that it occurs not in rigidity and contraction but in the fluidity and calmness of an inner mode of listening. It almost seems that calmness is the necessary condition to connect one's inner strength to a more universal feeling. Subjects who are fortunate enough to experience this condition claim to feel they are both traversed by and connected to an external force while being entirely present and centred. Determination has a quality that is connected to a sense of inner tranquillity and gentleness. It is a strength that relies on one's vulnerability, one that accepts the limits of the human condition and, with a hidden smile, embraces the responsibility that comes with it. This strength arises from discursive positions that also require a certain posture of the soul. Of course, this has nothing to do with the political figure of Mitterrand. It is by no means intended in that way. However, the slogan strategically used for the electoral campaign, in a certain sense, referred precisely to a fundamental condition of the victorious. This is what we are focusing on. And indeed, Mitterrand won.

172 Postscript: Diary of everyday happiness

In essence, we may say that the likelihood of winning increases when one gives up winning for oneself, when one renounces the egotistic nature of victory. There is a type of authoritativeness that comes with sharing – an inner strength that emerges from vulnerability. And the successful slogan used by Mitterrand referred to this particular condition.

b. The vibrancy of everyday life: "the gentle kindling"

> True love is a gentle kindling.
> Giuseppe Ungaretti, *Silenzio in Liguria*, 1922[4]

There is a second condition that serves as a valuable reference for an ecological, if not openly joyful, daily life: it is the "gentle kindling" the great Italian poet Ungaretti wrote about in a poem on true love. There is a passion, a vibrancy of the moment we inhabit, that can be easily experienced if we suspend the noise coming from outside and listen to our inner voice. There is an ongoing yet silent dialogue that permeates every part of our body, with myriads of cells speaking to us at every moment of our life.[5] When this door inside us opens then we are at peace and express peace. The outcome of anything we do in this condition will be appropriate. We may think of it as a state of grace that we carry with us in daily life; every time we get lost, we can return to it. It is interesting to note that in Italian, the word *grazia* refers both to the elegance and beauty of bodily movement (understood as gracefulness) and to a divine condition inspired by God's grace. In German, on the other hand, these two concepts correspond to two different terms: *die Anmut* and *die Gnade*. We should also note that the German term *Anmut* contains the word *der Mut*, which means courage. It almost seems that while the Italian language suggests a semantic contiguity between the grace of the soul and that of the body, the German language emphasises how bodily grace is related to courage.

Whereas believers regard grace as a divine condition, in a secular sense for everyone it is a morally qualitative condition that reverberates in the vibrancy of the everyday. There is a sense of well-being that derives from a way of acting, an ecology of words and thoughts that liberates us from the restlessness of action and thought, allowing us to be centred, which is what we all yearn for. No actions or words are necessary. It is a gratuitous state (beyond the confines of the market), which requires neither consumption nor possession. Gratuitousness, in fact, is its defining trait – the fact that it cannot be commodified. In this sense, grace can be understood in a secular sense as the vibrancy of daily life, in which intensity, passion, and vitality reverberate and reconnect us to a constant and vital flow.

While we might not be able to command happiness *tout court*, especially when confronted with significant challenges and profound suffering, we can opt for a posture of hopefulness.

c. Consonant words

In a beautiful poem, Rainer Maria Rilke reminds us that verses are not feelings but experiences. The poet's words are soaked in blood, not in the sense that they pierce the reader, but in the sense that they are the precious distillation of a life. To write, one must know, and to know means to have experienced, to have encountered one's limits many times, to have failed often, to have made many mistakes, and yet to have started over. Writing (and also speaking) means embracing one's vulnerability and fallibility on multiple occasions, disappointing many, especially oneself, and then trying again. Rilke writes:

> But you must also have been beside the dying, must have sat beside the dead in the room with the open window and scattered noises. And it is not yet enough to have memories. You must be able to forget them when they are many, and you must have the immense patience to wait until they return. For the memories themselves are not important. Only when they have changed into our very blood, into glance and gesture, and are nameless, no longer to be distinguished from ourselves – only then can it happen that in some very rare hour the first word of a poem arises in their midst and goes forth from them.[6]

Rilke is right: memories are not yet embodied, especially when they are traumas and when they are many. One must be patient and let them go, forget about them, and then wait for them to return. They always return, and when they do, they resurface with a particular quality: they are lighter and rarefied, as if they belonged to someone else. They return as if they were being carried to us by the current of a river; we know they are ours, yet they seem distant and untouched. At the same time, it is when we observe them from this angle that we realise they truly seem to belong to us. In a seminar held at the Roma Tre University, the Italian theatre director Eugenio Barba once said: "We truly own only what we have lost". I believe this statement is particularly true if applied to memories, especially the truly traumatic ones, the ones that used to cause pain, when we became paralysed just by thinking about them. However, one day they were gone, and when they returned, they became a part of us. The words we speak, the thoughts we formulate based on these memories we have incorporated, have a different density. They are ecological in multiple senses: they benefit us and others; they are authentic, the same way every experience lived and narrated with humility and responsibility is authentic; they transcend the vanity of the ego because the subject uttering these words has been defeated by life so many times that he or she knows no arrogance and is aware of being one among many, standing in line, waiting for his or her turn. Nevertheless, those words and thoughts truly have a particular consonance and corporeality, and because of this, they are capable of triggering transformation and generating alternative paths for both daily thought and action. They are indeed capable of generating the future.

174 Postscript: Diary of everyday happiness

d. The living future

When the temporality of thought shifts from being consecutive to immanent, the self opens up to the vital flow of time, and the future bursts into the present of the self, orienting it like an anticipation:

> A living sign is a prediction of what Peirce calls a habit. That is, it is an expectation of a regularity, something that has not yet come to exist but will likely come to be. (...) They are the products of an expectation – of a highly embodied "guess" at what the future will hold.[7]

It is possible to go even further, beyond this way of looking at the living future, as there are many other things to be considered.

We usually think that the course of our biographies intertwines with our biographical history and that the former is the direct (and sometimes inevitable) consequence of the latter. We firmly believe that we are determined by our past; however, the opposite is equally true. We are shaped, moulded, and oriented by both the pasts and the futures that inhabit and interpellate us, and that we decide to answer. The future is alive in the sense that it unfolds in the present, influencing it. Indeed, the present is not the result of the presence of what is, but of the manifestation of the absence of all other alternatives and possible presents that decide not to occur. The presence of the present therefore originates in the space between all possible presents and the absence of alternative states. Contrary to what we commonly think, it is what is not here that defines and engraves what is, in the vibrancy of the world's flesh. Or at least both perspectives are equally possible. Eduardo Kohn invites us to think like the forests and reminds us that "life involves (...) ways in which the future comes to affect the present (...) 'we' all always have one foot (or paw) in the future".[8] In thinking the thoughts of the forest, we are constantly traversed by all the pasts and all the futures we inhabit because the temporality of a forest's thought is not the consecutive time measured by the hands on a clock, but the immanent time of the spiritual life of all living beings. In that immanence, the distance separating us from the future is null and is the same as the distance separating us from the past. To contemplate the living future is to position ourselves in an elsewhere, and as we become one with time, we also transform the ways in which we experience it.

e. The space of free will as the constitutive foundation of subjectivity

The question of free will is the subject of extensive philosophical and theological reflection. These short notes cannot even begin to summarise it. Nevertheless, I must quote a brief excerpt to illuminate the ethnography of everyday thought that has served as a leitmotif throughout the pages of this volume. There is an idea I have to mention in order to conclude this book, a simple one that, in certain respects, has stayed with me because of a fundamental truth it seems to articulate: in 1970, Hannah Arendt[9] wrote that people reveal their true nature through their actions and words. In 2006, Germaine Tillion revisited this notion, adding an illuminating reflection:

> There are tragic and dramatic moments in which we are forced to make a choice. Starting from these choices, we go in the direction they indicate. This also means that in time we tend to develop a kind of loyalty to ourselves.[10]

This representation of a biographical trajectory, when applied to each one of us, is highly effective. If we look back and think about the choices we made in our lives, we can all pinpoint moments in which these decisions were made – moments that many years later continue to be active and alive, influencing our present. There are specific moments in everyone's life in which the words spoken and the actions that followed selected the portion of the future we would inhabit, binding us to it and shaping our future identity. In these moments, we encountered "the living future", as described by the peoples of the Runa in the Amazon, studied by Eduardo Kohn. When the future arrives in our lives and interpellates our present, we recognise it, or at least, we should. It is not possible to constantly live in this enlightened condition – we must imagine it is like stepping away from the time line and being able to see ourselves from there, while completing the course of the destiny we are summoned by – not because we are not able, but because we constantly live in a condition that tends to radicalise the dualism between us and the world, rupturing the inner communion that allows us to hear "what the forests think". Immersed in the bustling streets of our urban centres, perhaps we would be more attuned to listening to "what cars think". When that imaginary temporal crack opens, allowing us to catch a glimpse of the living future and allowing it to speak to the present, the past (the still "living" past) knocks on our door. In the uniqueness of those moments, we genuinely become architects of our own destiny because we humbly decide who we want to be and how to become this person. These are decisions that usually involve high costs in both directions, which is why we will be both tied to and faithful to them for the rest of our lives. Commitment and loyalty to those choices are direct consequences of the fact that they have truly cost us a lot, making it challenging to reverse course. Those moments shape us forever. During those rare occasions, we understand ourselves and others, revealing our true nature and intimate character. Typically, to remind ourselves of the compelling and decisive relevance of those moments, we retrospectively tend to give them a heroic character, as if intimately feeling the need to preserve their intrinsic sacredness.

176 Postscript: Diary of everyday happiness

f. Nature as a manifestation of the sacred

Since Romanticism, considering nature as a space where the sacred manifests itself has become a prerogative of poetry, music, visual arts, and performative arts in general. It is certainly not a consideration pertinent to scientific discourse. Nevertheless, a reflection on the environment able to revive this conception of nature, along with what natural sciences have to say, may indeed be a valuable contribution. In the poems and prose of Andrea Zanzotto, the idea of a landscape that inhabits the inner self is recurrent. Nature is viewed as the space where the sacred manifests itself, and because of this natural landscape, it is a quintessential place for the soul. It is no coincidence that the systematic destruction of our relationship with the divine and with every possible manifestation of the sacred has coincided with an environmental crisis that is so serious that it threatens the very species that generated it. Nature evokes the sacred and stands in the way of the reduction of living beings to commodities for exchange and instrumental purposes. The point is that we all need to take a step back and acknowledge the existence of systemic dynamics, almost entirely autonomous from the individual and collective intentions that contributed to their formation. These dynamics adhere to their own rules and objectives, consistently stripping away our rights to choose and systematically obscuring both the contexts in which our decisions are made and their consequences. Driven by a series of interrelated causes, many of which were not genuinely desired, we find ourselves trapped by the rules of the market that govern the exploitation perpetuated by extensive commodity distribution chains, unable to discern between an inert piece of plastic and a piece of meat that once belonged to a living being. Calls to consumer ethics ultimately seem to place all responsibility on us, the final consumers, who are the last link in a very long chain where everything happens many links before us. But is this really the case? Is this really the only option? Certainly, raising awareness and ecological consciousness significantly increases the likelihood that social and technological changes will take place. However, it remains paradoxical that responsibility seems to fall solely on the unfortunate consumer who keeps making wrong consumption choices, fails to recycle plastic properly, and insists on buying unnecessary goods, thereby wasting natural resources. Would it not be easier not to produce all this plastic in the first place? Is it possible that all this emphasis on the end consumer (though it might be better than nothing) becomes another strategy to conceal the identity of the true culprits, those who could decide to do things differently but prefer to continue polluting and profiting? Do not the powerful have children and grandchildren like everyone else? Are they considering relocating to some other planet, exporting the same patterns of devastation that are destroying our ecosystems? Poets are right. We urgently need to share a sacred vision of the Earth, not necessarily a religious one, but one that is sacred in a secular sense, where respect

Postscript: Diary of everyday happiness **177**

and care for all forms of life are at the forefront. After all, it is not necessary to refer to mystical traditions in order to recognise that there is a profound harmony between subjectivity and the environment, between the individual and the landscape. There is an index of environmental harmony – a universal resonance to which we can all relate. This is not a naive invitation to return to the landscape and nature. Instead, it is a thoughtful and quietly whispered acknowledgment: I have always felt that nature is a bit like the "hands of the mother", which Rilke believed were blessed. Massimo Recalcati reflects on their strength when he reminds us that it is the way a psychic image is rooted that sustains us when we stare into the abyss:

> (…) I have often felt suspended in a void (…) and many times I have called upon the hands of those I loved to support me in the solitude of that void. Is this not the most radical condition of human life? Does not all life come to life by holding on, clinging, trusting the hands of others? Is "mother" not the name that defines the hands of this first other we have all invoked in the silence of our void? (…) are not the hands of a mother the first thing we see of her face?[11]

Like many others, I believe that symbolically, the "hands of the mother" we hang on to when we are about to plunge into one of our daily abysses are also the hands of nature: the silent embrace of the tree that stands opposite the house we live in, or the forests we walk in, the cliffs on which we like to sit, or the peaks we climb in search of the balanced strength we need in order to cope with events in life. If we sever the ties that connect us to these hands, what is left? Who will we turn to when searching for inner harmony? Cannot this poetic insight become the foundation of our environmental policies? Why is "poetic" always used as a synonym of "non-scientific" and, therefore, of "irrelevant"? Perhaps the future will demand we practice both poetic sciences and scientific poetry, restoring a fervent union between the arts and science.

Many years have passed since the death of Adriano Olivetti. His speech to the workers delivered at the inauguration of the new Olivetti plant in Pozzuoli in 1955 is still a highly relevant text and represents a fundamental reference point for global capitalism:

> We can respond by asserting that there is a purpose inherent in our daily actions, both in Ivrea and Pozzuoli. Yet, without an initial awareness of this purpose, the hope for the success of the work undertaken is futile. An ideal framework, extending beyond the principles of the organisational structure, has guided the endeavours of our company for many years. The social experiment of the Ivrea factory (…) is rooted in a straightforward concept: the creation of a new type of enterprise transcending socialism and capitalism, because the urgent message of our times is that the extreme forms in which

178 Postscript: Diary of everyday happiness

the two aspects of the social question are posed, opposing each other, are inadequate to solve the problems of humanity and modern society. While operating within an economic environment and adhering to its rules, the Ivrea factory has oriented its objectives and primary concerns toward the material, cultural, and social elevation of the region in which it operates, in an effort to create in the region a novel type of community where there is no substantial difference in goals among the protagonists of its human events, shaping a history, day after day, to secure a future and a life more deserving for the children of this territory. Our Company firmly embraces spiritual values, the values of science, art, and culture. Ultimately, it holds that the ideals of justice must not be estranged from the persisting and unresolved disputes between capital and labour. Above all, it believes in humanity, in its divine essence, and in its potential for elevation and redemption.[12]

Adriano Olivetti not only believed in the divine flame of the individuals working in the factory but also envisioned the factory itself as an integral part of the broader context, the natural landscape in which it was located:

Standing before the world's most unique gulf, this factory has emerged, respecting the beauty of its surroundings. Also, in order to ensure that this beauty provides solace in the daily work, we envisioned nature accompanying the life of the factory. (…) This led us to choose low windows, open courtyards, and trees in the garden, definitively rejecting the notion of confinement and hostile enclosure.[13]

This means that the spiritual life of the factory depends on its being situated and firmly connected to the world of nature and natural beauty.

It is precisely because we have persisted in undertaking enterprises without considering their spiritual dimension, and because, in the pursuit of secularism and the distancing from religion, we have eradicated every expression of the sacred, that we now find ourselves confronting the vulnerability of our species, and perhaps with unprecedented awareness and understanding, the risks of our extinction. We need the sacred, as it is an essential aspect of the human condition.

We should never forget what the eminent poet Friedrich Hölderlin wrote:

My whole being stills and listens when the gentle ripple of the breeze plays about my breast. Often, lost in the immensity of blue, I look up into the aether and out into the hallowed sea, and it's as if a kindred spirit opened its arms to me, as if the pain of isolation were dissolved in the life of the godhead. To be one with everything, that is the life of the godhead, that is the heaven of man. To be one with everything that lives, to return in blissful self-oblivion into the all of nature, that is the summit of thoughts and joys, that is the holy mountain pinnacle, the place of eternal peace.[14]

Notes

1 Penone (2022, p. 240).
2 Lingiardi (2017, pp. 8–9).
3 Soerlin and Warde (2009).
4 Il vero amore è una quiete accesa. English translation: Ungaretti (1971, p. 65).
5 Even in a different perspective a very interesting contribution on this point is by Roy (1997).
6 Rilke (2009).
7 Kohn (2013, p. 76).
8 Ibid., p. 194.
9 Arendt (1970).
10 Tillion in De Matteis (2021, p. 178).
11 Recalcati (2015, pp. 21–23).
12 Olivetti (2012, pp. 28–30).
13 Ibid.
14 Hölderlin (2019, pp. 8–9).

BIBLIOGRAPHY

Aciman, André, *Call Me by Your Name*, Atlantic Books, London 2007.

Agger, Ben, *Cultural Studies as Critical Theory*, The Falmer Press, London 1992.

Ahmed, Sara, *The Cultural Politics of Emotion*, Routledge, London and New York 2015.

Ang, Ien, *Watching "Dallas": Soap Opera and the Melodramatic Imagination*, Metheun, London 1985.

Anzieu, Didier, Le Moi-Peau, in *Le dehors et le dedans, Nouvelle Revue de Psychanlyse*, vol. 9, 1974, pp. 195–208.

Anzieu, Didier, *Le Moi-Peau*, Dunod, Paris 1995.

Arendt, Hannah, *On Violence*, Harcourt Brace & Company, San Diego 1970.

Armiero, Marco, Giardini, Federica, Gentili, Dario, Angelucci, Daniela, Balicco, Daniele and Bussoni, Ilaria (eds.), *Environmental Humanities*, vol. 1, Derive Approdi, Roma 2021.

Atkinson, Rowland, Ecology of Sound: The Sonic Order of Urban Space, in *Urban Studies*, vol. 44, 2007, pp. 1905–1917.

Augé, Marc, *Non Places: Introduction to an Anthropology of Supermodernity*, Verso, London, 1995 (orig. ed. *Non-lieux. Introduction à une anthropologie de la surmodernité*, Seuil, Paris 1992).

Augé, Marc, *The War of Dreams: Studies in Ethno Fiction*, Pluto Press, London 1999 (orig. ed. *La Guerre des rêves. Exercices d'ethno-fiction*, Seuil, Paris 1997).

Austin, John Langshaw, *How to Do Things with Words*, Clarendon Press, Oxford 1961 (2a ed. 1975).

Barca, Stefania, *Forces of Reproduction. Socialist Ecofeminism and the Global Ecological Crisis*, paper presented at 16th Annual Historical Materialism Conference, London 7 to 10 November, 2019.

Bateson, Gregory, *Steps to an Ecology of Mind: Collected Essays in Anthropology, Psychiatry, Evolution, and Epistemology*, University of Chicago Press, Chicago 1972.

Bateson, Gregory, *Mind and Nature: A Necessary Unit*, Dutton, New York 1979.

Bateson, Gregory, Jackson, Don D., Haley, Jay and Weakland, John, Toward a Theory of Schizophrenia, in *Behavioral Science*, vol. 1, 1956, pp. 251–264.

Bauman, Zygmunt, *Liquid Modernity*, Polity Press, Cambridge 2000.

Bauman, Zygmunt, *Liquid Life*, Polity Press, Cambridge 2005.

Beckett, Samuel, *Waiting for Godot: Tragicomedy in 2 Acts*, Grove Press, New York 1982 (orig. ed. *En attendant Godot*, Les Editions de Minuit, Paris 1954).

Benjamin, Walter, Erfahrung, in *Der Anfang*, vol. 6, 1913, pp. 168–171.

Berger, Peter L. and Luckmann, Thomas, *The Social Construction of Reality: A Treatise in the Sociology of Knowledge*, Doubleday, New York 1966.

Bergmann, Werner, The Problem of Time in Sociology. An Overview of the Literature on the State of Theory and Research on the 'Sociology of Time', 1900–82, in *Time & Society*, vol. 1, 1992, pp. 81–134.

Blier, Suzanne P., *The Anatomy of Architecture. Ontology and Metaphor in Batammaliba Architectural Expression*, Cambridge University Press, Cambridge 1987.

Bloch, Ernst, *The Principle of Hope*, 3 vol., The MIT Press, Cambridge, MA 1986 (orig. ed. 1959).

Braidotti, Rosi, *Nomadic Subjects: Embodiment and Sexual Difference in Contemporary Feminist Theory*, Columbia University Press, New York 1994.

Brooks, Jeneve R., "Sing Out! Collective Singing Rituals of Folk Protest Music in US Social Movements", in S. T. Horsfall, J.-M. Meij and M. D. Probstfield (eds.), *Music Sociology. Examining the Role of Music in Social Life*, Routledge, London 2013, pp. 211–222.

Calasso, Roberto, *Memè Scianca*, Adelphi, Milano 2021.

Capps, Lisa and Ochs, Elinor, *Constructing Panic: The Discourse of Agoraphobia*, Harvard University Press, Cambridge, MA 1995.

Cassano, Franco, *Il pensiero meridiano*, Laterza, Roma-Bari 1996.

Cassirer, Ernst, *The Philosophy of Symbolic Forms*, trans. by Steve G. Lofts, Routledge, London and New York 2020 (orig. ed. *Philosophie der Symbolischen Formen*, Bruno Cassirer, Berlin 1923).

Cerulo, Massimo, *Il sentire controverso. Introduzione alla sociologia delle emozioni*, Carocci, Roma 2009.

Clément, Gilles, *Manifesto of the Third Landscape*, trans. by Europe Halles, TEH Series on new imaginaries #3, online (orig. ed. *Manifeste du Tiers-paysage*, Sujet Objet, Paris 2004).

Coccia, Emanuele, *The Life of Plants*, Polity Press, Cambridge 2018 (orig. ed. *La vita delle piante. Metafisica della mescolanza*, Il Mulino, Bologna 2018).

Coccia, Emanuele, *Filosofia della casa. Lo spazio domestico e la felicità*, Einaudi, Torino 2021.

Coccia, Emanuele, *L'io è una foresta. Preface, in* Eduardo Kohn, *Come pensano le foreste, Per un'antropologia oltre l'umano*, Nottetempo, Bologna 2021.

Colombo, Fausto, *Ecologia dei media. Manifesto per una comunicazione gentile*, Vita e Pensiero, Milano 2020.

Corbin, Alain, *Village Bells: Sound and Meaning in the 19th-Century French Countryside*, trans. by M. Throm, Columbia University Press, New York 1998.

Crenshaw, Kimberlé, Demarginalizing the Intersection of Race and Sex: A Black Feminist Critique of Antidiscrimination Doctrine, Feminist Theory and Antiracist Politics, in *The University of Chicago Legal Forum*, vol. 140, 1989, pp. 139–167.

Crespi, Franco, *Esistenza e simbolico. Prospettive per una cultura alternativa*, Feltrinelli, Milano 1978.

182 Bibliography

Culbertson, Roberta, Embodied Memory, Transcendence, and Telling. Recounting Trauma, Re-Establishing the Self, in *New Literary History*, vol. 26, 1995, pp. 169–195.

Davis, Angela, *Women, Race, and Class*, Random House, New York 1981.

D'Angelo, Paolo, *Il paesaggio. Teorie, storie, luoghi*, Laterza, Roma-Bari 2021.

De Lauretis, Teresa, *Sui generis. Scritti di teoria femminista*, Feltrinelli, Milano 1996.

De Matteis, Stefano, *Il dilemma dell'aragosta. La forza della vulnerabilità*, Meltemi, Milano 2021.

DeNora, Tia, *Music in Everyday Life*, Cambridge University Press, Cambridge 2000.

DeNora, Tia, *After Adorno. Rethinking Music Sociology*, Cambridge University Press, Cambridge 2003.

DeNora Tia, *Music-in-Action: Selected Essays in Sonic Ecology*, Routledge, London and New York 2011.

DeNora, Tia, *Hope. The Dream We Carry*, Palgrave MacMillan Publishers, New York 2021.

DeNora, Tia and Belcher, Sophie, "When You're Trying Something on You Picture Yourself in A Place Where They Are Playing This Kind of Music"- Musically Sponsored Agency in The British Clothing Retail Sector, in *The Sociological Review*, vol. 48, 2000, pp. 80–101.

DeNora, Tia, Schmid, Wolfgang, Simpson, Fraser e Ansdell, Gary, "'Late' Musical Learning. What Is It, Why, and for Whom?", in A. L. Tota and A. De Feo (eds.), *Scuola Democratica*, Special Issue *Arting Education. Reinventing Citizens of the Future*, vol. 2, 2022, pp. 239–260.

Del Giudice, Emilio, Tedeschi, Alberto and Voeikov, Vladimir, "Memory of Water: Storage of Information and Spontaneous Growth of Knowledge", in A. L. Tota e T. Hagen (eds.), *Routledge International Handbook of Memory Studies*, Routledge, London 2016, pp. 500–511.

Dekel, Irit and Tota, Anna Lisa, Editorial, in *European Journal of Cultural and Political Sociology*, Special Issue in Honour of Vera Sozberg. Co-edited by Irit Dekel and Anna Lisa Tota, vol. 4, 2017, pp. 243–251.

Drott, Eric, "Resistance and Social Movements", in J. Shepherd and K. Devine (eds.), *The Routledge Reader on The Sociology of Music*, Routledge, London 2015, pp. 171–179.

Eco, Umberto, *Lector in fabula*, Bompiani, Milano 1979.

Elster, Jon (ed.), *The Multiple Self*, Cambridge University Press, Cambridge 1985.

Emoto, Masamaru, *The Hidden Messages in Water*, Simon & Schuster, New York 2005.

Epictetus, *The Works of Epictetus: His Discourses, in Four Books, the Enchiridion, and Fragments*, trans. by Thomas Wentworth Higginson, Thomas Nelson and Sons, New York 1890.

Eyerman, Ron, *Cultural Trauma. Slavery and the Formation of African American Identity*, Cambridge University Press, Cambridge 2001.

Eyerman, Ron, Music in Movement: Cultural Politics and Old and New Social Movements, in *Qualitative Sociology*, vol. 25, 2002, pp. 443–458.

Ferdinand, Malcom, La littérature pour penser l'écologie postcoloniale caribéenne, in *Multitudes*, vol. 60, 2015, pp. 65–71.

Fisch, Richard, Weakland, John H. e Segal, Lynn, *The Tactics of Change: Doing Therapy Briefly*, Jossey-Bass, San Francisco 1982.

Fiske, John, *Reading the Popular*, Unwin and Hyman, Boston, MA 1989.

Franck, Georg, "How Time Passes. On Conceiving Time as a Process", in R. Buccheri, M. Saniga and W.M. Stuckey (eds.), *The Nature of Time: Geometry, Physics and Perception*, Kluwer, Dodrecht 2003, pp. 91–103 [On-line at: http://www.iemar.tuwien.ac.at/publications].

Fromm, M. Gerard (ed.), *Lost in Transmission. Studies of Trauma across Generations*, Karnac Books, London 2012.

Gagliano, Monica, *Thus Spoke the Plant: A Remarkable Journey*, North Atlantic Books, Berkeley, CA 2018.

Gandhi, Mohandas Karamchand, *The Collected works of Mahatma Gandhi*, 100 vol., The Publications Division, Ministry of Information and Broadcasting, Government of India, Nuova Delhi 1969–2001.

Gardner, Howard, *Frames of Mind. The Theory of Multiple Intelligences*, Basic Books, New York 1983.

Garfinkel, Harold, "A Conception of, and Experiment with, 'Trust' as a Condition of Stable Concerted Actions", in O. J. Harvey (ed.), *Motivation and Social Interaction: Cognitive Determinants*, Ronald Press, New York 1963, pp. 187–238.

Garfinkel, Harold, "What Is Ethnomethodology", in *Studies in Ethnomethodology*, Prentice-Hall, Englewood Cliffs, NJ 1967, pp. 19–33.

Gili, Guido and Mangone, Emiliana, Is a Sociology of Hope Possible? An Attempt to Recompose a Theoretical Framework and a Research Programme, in *The American Sociologist*, 2022, open access.

Goffman, Erving, *The Presentation of Self in Everyday Life*, Doubleday, Garden City, NY 1959.

Goffman, Erving, *Encounters: Two Studies in the Sociology of Interaction*, The Bobbs-Merrill Company, Indianapolis IN 1961a.

Goffman, Erving, *Asylums: Essays on The Social Situation of Mental Patient and Other Inmates*, Anchor Books, New York, 1961b.

Goffman, Erving, *Stigma. Notes on the Management of the Spoiled Identity*, Penguin, London, 1963.

Goffman, Erving, *Interaction Ritual*, Doubleday, Garden City, NY 1967.

Goodman, Nelson, *Languages of Art. An Approach to a Theory of Symbols*, The Bobbs-Merrill Company, Indianapolis IN 1968.

Goody, Jack, *The Domestication of the Savage Mind*, Cambridge University Press, Cambridge 1977.

Grass, Günter, *Ich zeichne immer, auch wenn ich nicht zeichne*, Katalog zur Ausstellung im Kullturforum Burgkloster, Lübeck 1997.

Griffiths, Tom, The Humanities and the Environmentally Sustainable Australia, in *Australian Humanities Review*, vol. 43, 2007, open access.

Gruzinski, Serge, *Images at War: Mexico from Columbus to Blade Runner*, Duke University Press, Durham, NC 2001.

Gurdjieff, Georges I., *Rencontres avec des hommes remarquables*, René Julliard, Paris 1960.

Gurdjieff, Georges I., *All and Everything. Beelzebub's Tales to His Grandson. An Objectively Impartial Criticism of the Life of Man, Volume 1*, Dutton, New York 1964.

Halbwachs, Maurice, *Les cadres sociaux de la mémoire*, Paris, Mouton 1976 (orig. ed. 1925).

Hall, Stuart, "Encoding/Decoding", in Id. et al. (eds.), *Culture, Media, Language*, Hutchinson, London 1980, pp. 128–38.

184 Bibliography

Han, Byung-Chul, *Saving Beauty*, John Wiley & Sons, Hoboken NJ 2017.
Han, Byung-Chul, *Non-things: Upheaval in the Lifeworld*, trans. by Daniel Steuer, Polity Press, Cambridge 2022.
Haraway, Donna, *Simians, Cyborgs, and Women: The Reinvention of Nature*, Routledge, New York 1991.
Haraway, Donna, *Staying with the Trouble: Making Kin in the Chthulucene*, Duke University, Durham, NC 2016.
Harvey, David, *The Condition of Postmodernity. An Enquiry into the Origins of Cultural Change*, Wiley-Blackwell, Cambridge, 1989.
Hebdige, Dick, *Subculture. The Meaning of Style*, Methuen, London 1979.
Heidegger, Martin, *Building Dwelling Thinking*, in *Poetry, Language, Thought*, trans. by Albert Hofstadter, Harper Colophon Books, New York 1971 (orig. ed. 1954).
Hillman, James, *L'anima dei luoghi: conversazione con Carlo Truppi*, Rizzoli, Milano 2004.
Hölderlin, Johann Christian Friedrich, Hyperion, or the Hermit in Greece, trans. by Howard Gaskill, Open Book Publishers, Cambridge 2019.
hooks, bell, *Ain't I a Woman: Black Women and Feminism*, Long Haul Press, Boston, MA 1981.
hooks, bell, *Reel to Real. Race, Sex and Class at the Movies*, Routledge, New York 1996.
hooks, bell, *Black Looks. Race and Representation*, Taylor and Francis, London 2015.
Hume, David, *A Treatise of Human Nature* (Reprinted from the original edition in three volumes and edited, with an analytical index, by L.A. Selby-Bigge), Clarendon Press, Oxford 1896 (orig. ed. 1738).
Husserl, Edmund, *Zur Phänomenologie des inneren Zeitbewußtseins*, M. Nijhoff., The Hague 1905 [Partial English translation *The Phenomenology of Internal Time Consciousness*, Indiana University Press, Bloomington 1996].
Husserl, Edmund, *Méditations cartésiennes. Introduction à la phénoménologie*, Colin, Paris 1931.
Illich, Ivan, *Limits to Medicine, Medical Nemesis: The Expropriation of Health*, Penguin, London 1974.
Ingold, Tim, "Three in One: On Dissolving the Distinctions Between Body, Mind and Culture published with the title 'Evolving Skills'", in H. Rose and S. Rose (eds.), *Alas Poor Darwin, Arguments against Evolutionary Psychology*, Jonathan Cape, London 2000a, pp. 225–246.
Ingold, Tim, *The Perception of the Environment*, Routledge, London 2000b.
Ingold, Tim, Footprints through the Weather-World: Walking, Breathing, Knowing, in *The Journal of the Royal Anthropological Institute*, vol. 16, 2010, pp.121–139.
Ingram, Mrill, *Orphan Spaces: The Art and Science of Melding Survival and The Sublime*, paper presented to Society and the Sea conference, 6–7 September 2018, University of Greenwich, London 2018, pp. 1–7.
Iser, Wolfgang, *The Implied reader: Patterns of Communication in Prose Fiction from Bunyan to Beckett*, John Hopkins University Press, Baltimore, MA and London 1974 (orig. ed. *Der Implizite Leser: Kommunikationsformen des Romans von Bunyan bis Beckett*, Fink, München 1972).
Jauss, Hans Robert, *Kleine Apologie der ästetischen Erfahrung*, Universitätsverlag GmbH, Konstanz 1972.
Jauss, Hans Robert, "From the History of Reception to Aesthetic Experience", in R. C. Holub (ed.), *Reception Theory*, Methuen, London 1984, pp. 53–81.

Jedlowski, Paolo, *Intanto*, Mesogea, Messina 2020.

Jorgensen, Sven Erik, "The Importance of Memory in Ecology", in A. L. Tota and T. Hagen (eds.), *Routledge International Handbook of Memory Studies*, Routledge, London 2016, pp. 511–518.

Kelman, Ari, Rethinking the Soundscape: A Critical Genealogy of a Key Term in Sound Studies, in *Senses & Society*, vol. 5, 2010, pp. 212–234.

Kohn, Eduardo, *How Forest Think: Toward an Anthropology Beyond the Human*, University of California Press, Berkeley, CA, 2013.

Korzybski, Alfred, *Science and Sanity: An Introduction to Non-Aristotelian Systems and General Semantics*, The International Non-Aristotelian Library Publishing Company, Lakeville, CT 1950 (I ed. 1933).

Kwame Harrison, Anthony, "Hip Hop and Race", in J. Shepherd and K. Devine (eds.), *The Routledge Reader on The Sociology of Music*, Routledge, London 2015, pp. 191–200.

LaBelle, Brandon, *Sonic Agency. Sound and Emergent Forms of Resistance*, Goldsmiths Press, London 2018.

Lacan, Jacques, Écrits: *The First Complete Edition in English*, trans. by Bruce Fink, W. W. Norton & Co Inc., New York 2007.

Lacroix, Michel, *Le culte de l'émotion: Redécouvrir les sensations simples*, J'ai lu, Paris 2002.

Lahman, Mary, *Awareness and Action. A Travel Companion*, Institute of General Semantics, Englewood, New York 2018.

Laing, Ronald David, *The Divided Self: An Existential Study in Sanity and Madness*, Tavistock Publication, London 1959.

Lasch, Christopher, *The Minimal Self: Psychic Survival in Troubled Times*, Norton, New York 1984.

Latouche, Serge, *Essays on frugal abundance*, Simplicity Institute, Melbourne 2014.

Latour, Bruno, On Technical Mediation – Philosophy, Sociology, Genealogy, in *Common Knowledge*, vol. 3, 1994, pp. 29–64.

Latour, Bruno, "Anthropology at the Time of the Anthropocene", in M. Brightman and J. Lewis (eds.), *The Anthropology of Sustainability. Beyond Development and Progress*, Palgrave MacMillan, London 2017, pp. 35–51.

Le Goff, Jacques, *The Medieval Imagination*, trans. by Arthur Goldhammer, University of Chicago Press, Chicago, IL 1988.

Leder, Drew, *The Absent Body*, University of Chicago Press, Chicago, IL and London 1990.

Lewis, Simon and Maslin, Mark Andrew, Defining the Anthropocene, in *Nature*, vol. 519, 2015, pp. 171–180.

Lingiardi, Vittorio, *Mindscapes. Psiche nel paesaggio*, Raffaello Cortina, Milano, 2017.

McCombs, Maxwell and Shaw, Donald, The Agenda-Setting Function of Mass Media, in *The Public Opinion Quarterly*, vol. 36, 1972, pp. 176–187.

McCormick, Lisa, "Music as Social Performance", in R. Eyerman and L. McCormick (eds.), *Myth, Meaning and Performance: Towards a New Cultural Sociology of the Arts*, Paradigm Publisher, Boulder 2006, pp. 121–144.

Magnusson Margareta, *The Gentle Art of Swedish Death Cleaning: How to Free Yourself and Your Family from a Lifetime of Clutter*, Scribner, New York 2017.

Mancuso, Stefano, *Plant revolution. Le piante hanno già inventato il nostro futuro*, Giunti, Firenze 2007.

Mancuso, Stefano, *La nazione delle piante*, Laterza, Roma-Bari 2009.

186 Bibliography

Mancuso, Stefano, *Planting Our World*, trans. by Gregory Conti, Other Press LLC 2023 (orig. ed. *La pianta del mondo*, Laterza, Roma-Bari 2020).

Markova, Dawna and Powell, Anne R., *How Your Child Is Smart: A Life-Changing Approach to Learning*, Red Wheel Weiser, Newburyport, MA 1992.

Marontate, Jan, Robertson, Megan and Clarkson, Nathan, "Soundscapes as Commemoration and Imagination of The Acoustic Past", in A. L. Tota and T. Hagen (eds.), *Routledge International Handbook of Memory Studies*, Routledge, London 2016, pp. 519–532.

Maturana, Humberto R. and Varela, Francisco J., *El àrbol del conocimiento*, Editorial Universitaria, Santiago del Chile 1984.

McCraty, Rollin, "Implicit Memory, Emotional Experience and Self-Regulation: The Heart's Role in Raising our Consciousness Baseline", in A. L. Tota and T. Hagen (eds.), *Routledge International Handbook of Memory Studies*, Routledge, London 2016, pp. 473–488.

Mead, George Herbert, *Mind, Self & Society: From the Standpoint of a Social Behaviorist*, University of Chicago Press, Chicago, IL 1934.

Melucci, Alberto, *Passaggio d'epoca. Il futuro è adesso*, Feltrinelli, Milano, 1994.

Melucci, Alberto, *The Playing Self: Person and Meaning in the Planetary Society*, Cambridge University Press, Cambridge 1996.

Mengerink, Mark. A., "Hitler, the Holocaust, and Heavy Metal Music: Holocaust Memory and Representation in the Heavy Metal Subculture 1980-Present", in S._Towe Horsfall, J.-M. Meij and M. D. Probstfield (eds.), *Music Sociology. Examining the Role of Music in Social Life*, Routledge, London 2013, pp. 177–187.

Merleau-Ponty, Maurice, "Eye and Mind", trans. by Carleton Dallery, in Id., *The Primacy of Perception*, Northwestern University Press, Evanston, IL 1964.

Merleau-Ponty, Maurice, *The Visible and the Invisible*, Nortwestern University, Evanston 1968 (orig. ed. *Le visible et l'invisible*, Gallimard, Paris 1964).

Mitchell, W. J. Thomas, *What Do Pictures Want? The Lives and Loves of Images*, The University of Chicago Press, Chicago & London 2005.

Montale, Eugenio, *Cuttlefish Bones (1920–1927)*, trans. by William Arrowsmith, W. W. Norton & Company, New York 1994 (orig. ed. *Ossi di seppia*, Piero Gobetti editore, Torino 1925).

Naess, Arne, *The Selected Works of Arne Naess*, Kluwer Academic Publisher, Amsterdam 2005.

Narvàez, Rafael F., *Embodied Collective Memories. The Making and Unmaking of Human Nature*, University Press of America, Lanham, MD 2013.

Nhat Hanh, Thich, *The Art of Communicating*, Harper Collins, New York 2013.

Nietzsche, Friedrich, *The Gay Science*, trans. Josefine Nauckhoff, Cambridge University Press, Cambridge 2001 (orig. ed. *Die fröhliche Wissenschaft*, in *Nietzsches Werke, Kritische Gesamtausgabe*, Herausgegeben von Giorgio Colli, Mazzino Montinari, Wolfram Groddeck, und Michael Kohlenbac, Walter de Gruyter, Berlin- New York 1978; I ed. 1882).

Norberg-Schulz, Christian, *Existence, Space & Architecture*, Praeger, London 1971.

Norberg-Schulz, Christian and Anna Maria Norberg-Schulz, *Genius loci: Towards a Phenomenology of Architecture*, Academy Editions, London 1980.

Nussbaum, Martha C., *Justice for Animals. Our Collective Responsibility*, Simon & Schuster, New York 2022.

Olivetti, Adriano, "Ai lavoratori di Pozzuoli". Discorso di Adriano Olivetti per l'inaugurazione dello stabilimento di Pozzuoli, 23 aprile 1955, in Id., *Città dell'uomo*, Edizioni di Comunità, Milano 2012.

Penone, Giuseppe, *Scritti*, Elettra, Milano 2022.

Petersen, Alan, *The Body in Question. A Socio-Cultural Approach*, Routledge, London 2007.

Pietromarchi, Luca, *Zero virgola io. Prose brevi dalla terapia intensiva*, Viella, Roma 2021.

Pinch, Trevor and Bijsterveld, Karin (eds.), *The Oxford Handbook of Sound Studies*, Oxford University Press, Oxford 2012.

Plato, *Phaedrus*, in *Collected Works of Plato*, trans. by Alexander Nehamas and Paul Woodruff, Hackett, London 1997.

Proust, Marcel, *Swann's Way: In Search of Lost Time*, Volume 1, trans. by Lydia Davis, Penguin Classics, London 2003 (orig. ed. *À la recherche du temps perdu*, *Gallimard, Paris 1954*).

Raimo, Veronica, *Niente di Vero*, Einaudi, Torino 2022.

Recalcati, Massimo, *L'ora di lezione. Per un'erotica dell'insegnamento*, Einaudi, Torino 2014.

Recalcati, Massimo, *The Mother's Hands: Desire, Fantasy and the Inheritance of the Maternal*, Polity Press, Cambridge 2019 (orig. ed. *Le mani della madre. Desiderio, fantasmi ed eredità del materno*, Feltrinelli, Milano 2015).

Rendell, Jane, *Art and Architecture: A Place Between*, I. B. Tauris, London 2006.

Rilke, Rainer Maria, *The Notebooks of Malte Laurids Brigge*, trans. by Michael Hulse, Penguin, London 2009.

Rose, Deborah Bird, van Dooren, Thorm, Chrulew, Matthew, Cooke, Stuart, Kearnes, Matthew and O' Gorman, Emily, Thinking Through the Environment. Unsettling the Humanities, in *Environmental Humanities*, vol. 1, 2012, pp. 1–5.

Rose, Deborah Bird and Robin, Libby, The Ecological Humanities in Action: An Invitation, in *Australian Humanities Review*, vol. 31, 2004, pp. 31–32.

Rosenthal, Robert and Jacobson, Lenore, *Pygmalion in the Classroom: Teacher Expectation and Pupils' Intellectual Development*, Holt, Rinehart and Winston, New York 1968.

Rottenberg, Catherine, *The Rise of Neoliberal Feminism*, Oxford University Press, Oxford 2018.

Roy, Arundhati, *The God of Small Things*, Penguin, New Delhi 1997.

Sacks, Oliver, *The Man Who Mistook His Wife for a Hat*, Picador, London 1985.

Sacks, Oliver, *Musicophilia. Tales of Music and the Brain*, Knopf, New York 2007.

Salleh, Ariel (ed.), *Eco-Sufficiency and Global Justice: Women Write Political Ecology*, Pluto Press, London 2009.

Santavirta, Torsten and Mikko Myrskylä, Reproductive Behavior Following Evacuation to Foster Care During World War II, in *Demographic Research*, vol. 33, 2015, pp. 1–30.

Santavirta, Torsten, Santavirta, Nina, Betancourt, Theresa S., Gilman, Stephen E., Long Term Mental Health Outcomes of Finnish Children Evacuated to Swedish Families During the Second World War and Their Non-evacuated Siblings: Cohort Study, in *BMJ. British Medical Journal (International Ed.)*, vol. 350, n. g7753, 2015.

Sapienza, Goliarda, *Ancestrale*, La Vita Felice, Milano 2013.

188 Bibliography

Sartori, Giovanni, *Homo videns. Televisione e post-pensiero*, Laterza, Roma-Bari 2000.

Sartre Jean Paul, *L'Imaginaire. Psychologie phénoménologique de l'imagination*, Gallimard, Paris 1948.

Schafer, Murray R., *The Soundscape: Our Sonic Environment and the Tuning of the World*, Alfred A. Knopf, New York 1977 (II ed., 1994).

Schilthuizen, Menno, *Darwin Comes to Town. How the Urban Jungle Drives Evolution*, Picador, London 2018.

Schulz von Thun, Friedemann, *Miteinander reden 1: Störungen und Klärungen. Allgemeine Psychologie der Kommunikation*, Rowohlt Taschenbuch Verlag, Hamburg 2014 (I ed. 1981).

Schütz, Alfred, *Der sinnhafte Aufbau der sozialen Welt. Eine Einleitung in die verstehende Soziologie*, Springer, Wien 1932.

Shonkoff, Jack, P. and Meisels, Samuels J. (eds.), *Handbook of Early Childhood Intervention*, Cambridge University Press, Cambridge 2000.

Simmel, Georg, *Philosophie des Geldes*, Duncker & Humblot, Leipzig 1900.

Simmel, Georg, "The Metropolis and Mental Life", in K. H. Wolff (ed.), *The Sociology of Georg Simmel*, The Free Press, New York 1950, pp. 409–424 (orig. ed. Simmel, Georg, *Die Großstädte und das Geistesleben*, Suhrkamp Verlag, Berlin 1903).

Slabbekoorn, Hans, Songs of the City. Noise-Dependent Spectral Plasticity in the Acoustic Phenotype of Urban Birds, in *Animal Behaviour*, vol. 85, 2013, pp. 1089–1099.

Slabbekoorn, Hans and Peet, Margriet, Birds Sing at a Higher Pitch in Urban Noise, in *Nature*, vol. 424, 2003, p. 267.

Soerlin, Sverker and Warde, Paul, "Making the Environment Historical. An Introduction", in Id. (eds.), *Nature's End*, Palgrave MacMillan, London 2009, pp. 1–23.

Spillman, Lyn, *What Is Cultural Sociology*, Polity Press, Cambridge 2019.

Steiner, Rudolf, *Die Philosophie der Freiheit: Grundzüge einer modernen Weltanschauung*, Emil Ferber, Berlin 1894.

Sterne, Jonathan (ed.), *The Sound Studies Reader*, Routledge, London 2012.

Sterne, Jonathan, "Soundscape, Landscape, Escape", in K. Bijsterveld (ed.), *Soundscapes of the Urban Past: Staged Sound as Mediated Cultural Heritage*, Columbia University Press, New York 2013, pp. 181–193.

Strate, Lance, Narcissism and Echolalia, Sense and the Struggle for the Self, in *Speech Communication Annual*, vol. 14, 2000, pp. 14–62.

Strate, Lance, *Concerning Communication. Epic Quests and Lyric Excursions within the Human Lifeworld*, Institute of General Semantics, New York 2022.

Taleb, Nassim Nicholas, *The Black Swan. The Impact of the Highly Improbable*, Penguin, London 2007.

Taleb, Nassim Nicholas, *Antifragile: Things That Gain from Disorder*, Random House, New York 2012.

Tatsumi, Nagisa, *The Art of Discarding: How to Get Rid of Clutter and Find Joy*, Hachette, New York 2017.

Terzani, Tiziano, *La fine è il mio inizio*, Longanesi, Milano 2006.

Tevis, Walter, *The Queen's Gambit*, Random House, New York 1983.

Thompson, Emily, *The Soundscape of Modernity: Architectural Acoustics and The Culture of Listening in America, 1900–1933*, The MIT Press, Cambridge, MA 2001.

Bibliography **189**

Thoreau, Henry D., "Walking", in Paul Lauter (ed.), *The Heath Anthology of American Literature: Early Nineteenth Century 1800–1865 (vol. B)*, Houghton Mifflin, Boston, MA, 2006.

Thoreau, Henry D., *The Journal of Henry David Thoreau 1837–1861*, New York Review Books Classics, New York, 2009.

Tillion, Germaine, *Alla ricerca del vero e del giusto, testi scelti e presentati da Tzvedan Todorov*, Medusa, Milano 2006 (orig. ed. *A la recherche du vrai et du juste:* à *propos rompus avec le siècle*, Seuil, Paris 2001).

Toffler, Alvin, *Future Shock*, Random House, New York 1970.

Tolkien, John Ronald Reuel, *The Lord of the Rings*, George Allen & Unwin, London 1954–55.

Tomasi di Lampedusa, Giuseppe, *Il Gattopardo*, Feltrinelli, Milano 1958.

Tompkins, Peter and Bird, Christopher, *The Secret Life of Plants: A Fascinating Account of the Physical, Emotional, and Spiritual Relations Between Plants and Man*, Harper & Row, New York 1973.

Tota, Anna Lisa (ed.), *Gender e media. Verso un immaginario sostenibile*, Meltemi, Roma 2008.

Tota, Anna Lisa, "When Sociology Meets the Work of Art: Analytical Framework to Study Artistic Production and Reception", in Michael Barber and Jochen Dreher (eds.), *The Interrelation of Phenomenology, Social Sciences and the Arts*, Springer, New York, 2014a, pp. 95–116.

Tota, Anna Lisa, "Creative Bodies and 'Creative Leib' in Everyday Life", in Hubert Knoblauch, Mark Jacobs and Ren Tuma (eds.), *Culture, Communication and Creativity; Reframing the Relations of Media, Knowledge, and Innovation in Society*, Peter Lang Verlag, Frankfurt, 2014b, pp. 81–98.

Tota, Anna Lisa, "Dancing the Present. Body Memory and Quantum Field Theory", in A. L. Tota and T. Hagen (eds.), *Routledge International Handbook of Memory Studies*, Routledge, London 2016, pp. 458–472.

Tota, Anna Lisa, *Eco-Words. The Ecology of Conversation*, Routledge, London 2023.

Tota, Anna Lisa and Hagen, Trever (eds.), *Routledge International Handbook of Memory Studies*, Routledge, London 2016.

Tota, Anna Lisa and De Feo, Antonietta, "Arts as Agency: The Potential of the Arts in Educational Settings", in *Arting Education: Reinventing Citizens of the Future*, special guest editors Anna Lisa Tota and Antonietta De Feo, Non-Traditional and Traditional, Inequalities in Italian Education, Scuola Democratica, n. 2, May/August, 2022, pp. 225–238.

Ungaretti, Giuseppe, *Selected Poems*, trans. by Patrick Creagh, Penguin, London 1971 (orig. ed. "Silenzio in Liguria", in Id., *Sentimento del tempo*, Mondadori, Milano 1933).

Vallortigara, Giorgio, *Altre menti. Lo studio comparato della cognizione animale*, Il Mulino, Bologna 2000.

Vallortigara, Giorgio, *Pensieri della mosca con la testa storta*, Adelphi, Milano 2021.

Van Dijk, Teun A., "New(s) Racism: A Discourse Analytical Approach", in S. Cottle (ed.), *Ethnic Minorities and the Media*, Open University Press, Philadelphia, PA 2000, pp. 211–226.

Van Zoonen, Lisbet, *Feminist Media Studies*, Sage, London 1994.

Velasco-Pufleau, Luis, No sound is innocent: Réflexions sur l'appropriation et la transformation de l'expérience sonore de la violence extrême, *Filigrane. Musique, esthétique, sciences, société*, vol. 23, 2018, online.

190 Bibliography

Velasco-Pufleau, Luis, When Only War Can Kill the Silence: Listening to No One Is Innocent after 13 November 2015, *Volume!*, vol. 15, 2019, online, pp. 1–10.

Velasco-Pufleau, Luis, Listening to Terror Soundscapes. Sounds, Echoes, and Silences in Listening Experiences of Survivors of the Bataclan Terrorist Attack in Paris, *Conflict and Society: Advances in Research*, vol. 7, 2021, pp. 60–77.

Von Glasersfeld, Ernst, *Die erfundene Wirklichkeit: wie wissen wir, was wir zu wissen glauben? Beitrage zum Konstruktivismus*, Piper & Co. Verlag, München 1981.

Wagner-Pacifici, Robin, Theorizing the Restlessness of Events, in *American Journal of Sociology*, vol. 115, 2010, pp. 1351–1386.

Wagner-Pacifici, Robin, "Reconceptualizing Memory as Event. From 'Difficult Pasts' to 'Restless Events'", in A. L. Tota and T. Hagen (eds.), *Routledge International Handbook of Memory Studies*, Routledge, London 2016, pp. 22–27.

Watzlawick, Paul, *How Real Is Real: Confusion, Disinformation, Communication*, Random House, New York 1976.

Watzlawick, Paul (ed.), *The Invented Reality: How Do We Know What We Believe We Know? (Contributions to Constructivism)*, Norton & Company, New York; London 1984 (orig. ed. *Die erfundene Wirklichkeit: wie wissen wir, was wir zu wissen glauben? Beitrage zum Konstruktivismus*, Piper & Co. Verlag, München 1981).

Watzlawick, Paul, Beavin, Janet H. and Jackson, Don D., *Pragmatics of Human Communication: A Study of Interactional Patterns, Pathologies, and Paradoxes*, Norton & Company, New York-London 1967.

Watzlawick, Paul, Weakland, John H. and Fisch, Richard, *Change: Principles of Problem Formation and Problem Resolution*, Norton, New York 1974.

Weber, Max, *Science as a Vocation* (edited by Peter Lassman, Irving Velody, Herminio Martins), Routledge, London and New York 2015 (orig. ed. *Wissenschaft als Beruf: erster Vortrag*, Duncker & Humblot, München-Leipzig 1919).

Werner, Emmy E. and Smith, Ruth S., *Vulnerable But Invincible: a Longitudinal Study of Resilient Children and Youth*, Adams Bannister Cox, New York 1982.

Werner, Emmy E. and Smith, Ruth S., *Journeys from Childhood to Midlife: Risk, Resilience, and Recovery*, Cornell University Press, Ithaca, NY 2001.

Wing Sue, Derald and Spanierman, Lisa Beth, *Microaggressions in Everyday Life*, John Wiley, New York 2020.

Wittgenstein, Ludwig, *Philosophical Investigations*, trans. by G.E.M. Anscombre, Basil Blackwell, Oxford 1953 (orig. ed. *Philosophische Untersuchungen*, Basil Blackwell, Oxford 1953).

Wittmann, Marc, *Gefühlte Zeit. Kleine Psychologie der Zeitempfindens*, Verlag C. H. Beck, München 2013.

Wolf, Christa, *Kassandra/Voraussetzungen einer Erzählung: Kassandra*, Aufbau Verlag, Berlin und Weimar 1983.

Wohlleben, Peter, *Das geheime Leben der Bäume. Was sie fühlen, wie sie kommunizieren – die Entdeckung einer verborgenen Welt*, Ludwig Verlag, München 2015.

Zeldin, Theodore, *Conversation: How Talk Can Change Our Lives*, Hidden Spring, New York 1998.

Zohar, Danah, Marshall, I. N., *The Quantum Self: Human Nature and Consciousness Defined by the New Physics*, William Morrow & Co., New York, NY 1990.

INDEX

Note: *Italic* page numbers refer to figures and page numbers followed by "n" denote endnotes.

acoustic past 109–114
adaptation 124, 153
adversity 4, 54, 119
Adatto, K. 66
aesthetics: cognitive organization 13, 14; human intervention 6; of money 82–84; quality 63, 139
aesthetic-symbolic extension of the self 13
agency 98, 107, 111, 114
agenda-setting theory 128
Alzheimer's disease 113
Angelico, B. 20
animal bodies 158–159
Ansdell, G. 114
The Ant and the Grasshopper 161
anterograde amnesia 47
Anthropocene 136, 145–147
anthropology 77–78, 151–152
antifragile 54, 56, 119
anti-vaxxers 129
Anzieu, D. 61
artificial intelligence 21, 22
art-media workshop 81
Asperger's syndrome 88–90
Augé, M. 10, 70, 75, 77, 78
authoritativeness 172
autism spectrum disorder 89

auto-ethnographic approach 4, 105, 140
autopilot syndrome 24, 48, 49

Baggins, F. 92
Baranski, C. 86
Barba, E. 173
Barrow, T. 91
Bateson, G. 118
Battiston, G. 76
Bauman, Z. 24, 59, 66, 82
Beckett, S. 112
biographical identity 11
biological diversity 138
black swans 50–55, 119
Braidotti, R. 78
breadth of vision 122
Brown, W. 84
Brundtland, Gro Harlem: *Our Common Future* 142

Cáceres Flores, B.I. 144, 145
Cage, J. 99
Canzone Segreta (2020-2021) 108
capitalism 60, 103, 146, 177
capitalist economic system 154
Capitalocene 146
Capps, L. 49
Cassirer, E. 76

192 Index

Cassano, F. 44, 117, 119; *Pensare a piedi* 117
Cerulo, M. 37
chain of thought 12, 170
Chao, M. 107
chickenification 157
cicadas 105, 159–162
citizenship skills 19, 20
Clément, G.: *Manifesto for a Third Landscape* 140
Clinton, H. 85
Coccia, E. 62, 124, 125, 136, 148, 149, 151; *The Life of Plants: A Metaphysics of Mixture* 148
Colombo, F. 33, 34
commodification 11, 158, 159
communication studies 149, 155
compulsive decluttering 59–60
consciousness 39, 48, 66, 153, 154, 156–158
Consejo Cívico de Organizaciones Populares e Indígenas de Honduras (COPINH) 144
conservationism 60
consonant words 173
constructing unreality 39–41
COVID-19 pandemic 50, 80, 113, 128, 131
cultural contact 78
cultural hegemony 76, 77, 79, 153
cultural nomadism 78
Cyborg Manifesto (Haraway) 162
cyborgs 21, 44, 162–165

Darwin Comes to Town (Schilthuizen) 141
Davis, A. 95
De Matteis, S. 26
dementia 113, 114
DeNora, T. 57, 111, 112, 114, 120
De Saussure, F. 76
Díaz, A.: *Happiness is expensive* 24, 65, 65
die Anmut 172
die Gnade 172
discrimination 76, 77, 81, 95, 164
disposophobia 24, 58–60
domestication 67n1
domestic space organization 24, 58–60
döstädning 15, 16
Downton Abbey (2010–15) 14, 81, 90–92

Downton Abbey: A New Era (2022) 90
dwelling of the self 14, 15, 17, 62–63

earthing 132
eco-/environmental terrorism 144–145
ecofeminism 145
ecohistory 145
ecological mind: corporeality of thoughts 126; elastic 119–120; external environment 124–126; fluid and flexible 126–127; hopeful 120–121; impermanence 130–133; infinite horizon 122; lingering 118; public discourse 128–130; rhythm 121–122; sustainability 122–124; symbolic/environmental pollution 127–128; thinking on foot 118–119
ecological mission 20
ecological thinking 44, 56–57, 66, 116, 140, 158, 171
ecology: acoustic 102; animal bodies 158–159; political 145; practising 46; public discourse 128–130; of sounds *see* soundscapes; stressing 148; words and thoughts 170, 172
economic growth 142
ecoshutter 139–140
ecoterrorists 144–145
eco-thoughts: anxious 60, 81; chain of 12; collective intelligence 170; corporeality 126, 173; crowding 41–42; free flow 34; immensity 122; mindscapes 38; predisposition 57; school of 17–22; sustainability 143; temporality 43, 174
Eco, U. 73
eco-words 126; aggressive 31; drawing 75; errors 57; eternal love 133; face of 35; physical sound 30; spatialisation of the self 11–12; toxic and poisonous 26; *see also* eco-thoughts
Eco-Words: The Ecology of Conversation (Tota) 11, 12, 33, 52, 57, 61, 126
egg/chick-making machine 157
elasticity 53, 119
elastic mind 119–120
Elgar, E. 99
embodied debt 146
Emoto, M. 153
enemy within, polluting mind 41–42

Index **193**

Engler, M. 90
environing 170
environment/environmental: disasters 144; harmony, index of 177; humanities 145–147; philosophy 145
Epictetus pill 3, 4
eroticism 74
Essam, R. 107
ethnographic qualitative research methods 106
Eun-bin, P. 88
everyday scripts 7–10
Extraordinary Attorney Woo 88–90, 154
The Eye and the Mind (Merleau-Ponty) 143

face 34, 35, 40, 67n11
Feher, M. 84
Fellowes, J. 90
Ferdinand, M. 146
fetishes 77
Fiorucci, M. 121
Fleming, I. 92
Florrick, A. 85, 86, 88
Florrick, P. 85
Fonda, J. 87
Francis, P. 130
Frank, S. 86
Future Shock (Toffler) 42

Gagliano, M. 136, 151, 152
Gallagher, P. 87
Gandhi, M. 143
Gardner, W. 86
generalised anaesthesia 37
Genesis (2013) 144
genius 9, 88–90
Genovesi, P. 76
gentle kindling 172
gestures 17, 121, 173
Giallini, M. 76
Gill, R. 85
Giudice, E. del 153
Goffman, E. 33, 34, 35, 67n11
Goodman, N. 100
The Good Wife (2009–16) 81, 85, 86
Grace and Frankie (2015–22) 81, 87
Grass, G. 75
gratuitousness 172
grazia 172
Griffiths, T. 145
Guadagnino, L. 34

Halbwachs, M. 18
Hall, S. 74, 76, 77, 79, 81
Han, B.-C. 19, 118, 136, 148; *Saving Beauty* 148
Happiness is expensive (Díaz) 24, 65, 65
Haraway, D. 44, 79, 136, 162, 164; *Cyborg Manifesto* 162
harmonic rhythm 121
Harry Potter's fantasy world 92–94
Harvey, D. 42
hegemonic thinking 150
Heidegger, M. 63
Herbert, J.M. 90
Hill, J.B. 145
Hölderlin, F. 178
Hollway, W. 80
homologation 78
homophobia 76, 94
homo videns 71
Hood, R. 82, 83
hope 57, 59, 111–113, 119–121
Hume, D. 12, 71
humiliation 25
hypercommunication 102–103
hyper-modernity 78, 97n16
hypertrophic beings 18

identity badges 24, 59, 64
identity formation 33
Illich, I. 64, 130
impermanence 16, 55, 130–133
The Importance of Memory in Ecology (Jørgensen) 153
ingenious mental mechanism 7
Ingold, T. 63, 118
instrumental turn function 56–57
intellectuality 37
intersectionality 70, 94–97, 162

Jedlowski, P. 12, 13
Jonze, S. 162
Jørgensen, Sven Erik 152–153; *The Importance of Memory in Ecology* 153

Kauffman, M. 87
keyboard warrior 35
Kohn, E. 136, 151, 152, 173, 174, 175
Kruger, B. 37, 38, *38*

La Casa de Papel 82–84
La Chanson Secrète 108

194 Index

Lacroix, M. 37
La Fontaine, Jean de 161
la force tranquille 171–172
Latouche, S. 66
Latour, B. 146
Leeson, L.H. 164
Leopardi, G. 122, 134n11
Lerner, W. 84
The Life of Plants: A Metaphysics of Mixture (Coccia) 148
Lingiardi, V. 5, 15, 169
literary ecocriticism 145
living future 174, 175
Lockhart, D. 86
Logic Paralyzes the Heart (Leeson) 164
Loose Cannons (Özpetek) 30
Lord of the Rings 92

Magdalene, M. 34
Magnusson, M. 15
Malfoy, D.L. 93
Malfoy, N. 93
Mancuso, S. 55–57, 136, 137, 151; *Planting Our World* 55, 137
Manifesto for a Third Landscape (Clément) 140
Mannino, T. 31, 140, 157, 165
Margulies, J. 85
Markova, D. 22
Mastandrea, V. 76
Materia Prima 162
May, T. 85
McRobbie, A. 85
Melucci, A. 12, 52, 153
memorisation 109, 110
Mengerink, M. 111
mental processes 6
mental scripts 2, 7–10, 47–49
Merleau-Ponty, M. 136, 143, 168
Messiaen, O. 114
metropolitan phenomena 37
The Milk of Dreams (2022) 37, *38*, 164
mind–body dualism 44
mindfulness 66
mindscapes 2, 4–7
mirror of reality 96
Mitterrand, F. 171, 172
Money Heist (2017–21) 82
mongoose strategy 27–28
Montagnier, L. 153
Moore, J. 146
morality 9, 36, 124, 158
Morris, H.J. 87
motor/speech disorders 113

Mubarak, H. 107
musical ethnography 106
musicalisation 111–113
musical mediation of social experience 106
musical self 98, 99, 106–109, 111
music-in-action 106–107
music into agency 106
music therapy 113, 114
mutual recognition 34

Naess, A. 148, 158
National Plan for Recovery and Resilience 53
natural landscapes 2, 5–6
nature and culture home 136–142
neoliberal feminism 84–88
neuroscience 155–156
news industry 130
Nhat Hanh, T. 66
Nietzsche, F. 46, 47
noise pollution 98, 99, 101–106, 141
nostalgia 44, 90–92, 94, 120

Ochs, E. 49
Olivetti, A. 11, 177, 178
organising principle 138, 142
orphan spaces 11
Our Common Future (Brundtland) 142
Özpetek, F.: *Loose Cannons* 30

Penone, G. 100, 115n13, 169; *Voglio scrivere sui muri* 169
Pensare a piedi (Cassano) 117
personal experience 50–51
phantom limb syndrome 62
Piano Nazionale di Ripresa e Resilienza (PNRR) 53
Pina, Á. 82
place-lessness of the spaces 10
plagiarism 20
plantations 150
Planting Our World (Mancuso) 55, 137
plantlike writing 152
plant neurobiology 151–152
pluralism 129
politeness 29
political correctness 88
political ecology 145
political system 130
pollution: air traffic 143; domestic space organisation 58–60; marketing solution 64–66; noise 99, 101–106, 141; skin-ego to Self-Home 61–63;

speech *see* speech pollution; sustainability 70, 74–75; symbolic domain 73, 127; time perception, pathological forms of *see* time perception; visual *see* visual pollution
popular wisdom 15
pornography 74
postmodernist perspective 96
power of images 75–77
primitive men, thoughts and beliefs of 147
probability theory 50–51
protest movements 107
Proust, M. 6, 8–10, 16, 17, 32
psychic experience 5
psychological defence mechanism 39
psychological trap 28
public discourse 53, 71, 111, 128–130, 153
public ethics 72, 130
public memory 84, 111

quantum theory 46
The Queen's Gambit (Tevis) 81, 86

racism 72, 73, 81, 94–97, 111, 164
Raimo, V. 123
Recalcati, M. 19, 177
reception theory 72
recognition process 33, 34
relative tranquillity 7
Rendell, J. 118
resilience 53–54, 56–57, 119
Resilience: A Journal of the Environmental Studies 145
responsible sustainability 143–144
restlessness of events 46, 54, 122–123
Rhode Island School of Design (RISD) 65
Rilke, R.M. 173, 177
The Rise of Neoliberal Feminism (Rottenberg) 84
Robin, L. 145
Rodari, G. 161
romanticism 176
Rose, D.B. 27, 28, 145
Rossi, S. 108
Rottenberg, C. 84, 85, 86; *The Rise of Neoliberal Feminism* 84
Rowling, J.K. 92, 94

Sacks, O. 62, 113, 126
sacred manifestation 176–178
Salgado, Juliano Ribeiro: *The Salt of the Earth* 144

Salleh, A. 146
The Salt of the Earth (Wenders and Salgado) 144
Sartori, G. 71
saudade 120
Saving Beauty (Han) 148
Schafer, M.R. 98, 99, 101, 110, 122, 159
Schilthuizen, M. 141, 155; *Darwin Comes to Town* 141
schizophrenia 71
Schmid, W. 114
school violence 17–22
Schütz, A.: *The Stranger* 81
Scott, A. 86
screen-saver landscapes 5
secularism 178
Séguéla, J. 171
self-esteem 21, 40, 45, 64
self-fulfilling prophecies 72–73
Self-Home 24, 58, 60, 61–63, 90, 124
self-perception 35
self-sabotage techniques 41
semiotic power of subjects 96
sexism 72, 73, 81, 94–97, 164
sexual discrimination 40
Simmel, G. 37, 56
Simpson, F. 114
skin-ego 61–63
Smith, R.S. 53
social: acceptability 74; conflicts 73, 77–80; discourse 46, 157; inequality 2, 76, 79, 95; legitimisation 75, 76; vulnerability 88, 89
socialisation 17, 61, 95
sociological paradigm 107
sociology of music 104, 106, 113
soundscapes: acoustic past 109–114; cognitive modality 99; definition 99–100; macrocosmic musical composition 99; musical self and wax candle 106–109; noise pollution 101–106; perceptual-sensory dimensions 100; physical environment 100; researcher 160
sounds/music and memory: biographies, soundtracks of 111; mental alchemy 113–114; musicalisation 111–113; public memory 111; sounds of world 110; traumatic acoustic body 109–110
soundtracks 99, 101–106, 111, 114, 144
spatialisation of the self 11, 12, 58
speciesism 164

196 Index

speech pollution: childhood 25; constructing unreality and verbal microaggressions 39–41; emotions and empathy 37–39; humiliation/abuse 25; improbable and hilarious situations 26; limitation 26; masks and nicknames 33–36; mongoose strategy 27–28; monologue 28–29; pathological invitations 36–37; polluting mind 41–42; real question 30–32; small external boycotts and manipulations 32–33; trauma 26; unstoppable 28–29; voice tone 29–30
The Stranger (Schütz) 81
Suárez-Rodríguez, M. 141
subjectivity: dwellings of 13, 80; environment 177; masking 34; musical self 99, 108; notion of 68n59; parallel stories and events 13; physicality and materiality 61; reality and 96; self ceases 16; space of free 174–175
sustainability: concept 142; ecological mind 117, 122–123; environmental and symbolic 75; pollution and 74–75; responsible 143–144; trauma 46; visions 142
sustainable: dissemination 76; dominant classes 76; imaginary 72, 77, 79; nostalgia 120; thinking and responsible action 136, 142–147
The Swing of the Stars 49

Taleb, N.N. 50, 51, 54, 55, 119
technologies of gender 95
Tedeschi, A. 153
teleological fallacy 55
television series: advertising 79; art-media workshop 81; *Downton Abbey* 90–92; dwellings of subjectivity 80; encoding/decoding model 81; *Extraordinary Attorney Woo* 88–90; *The Good Wife* 84–88; *La Casa de Papel* 82–84; *Money Heist* 82; *The Queen's Gambit* 84–88
Tevis, W. 86; *The Queen's Gambit* 81, 86
thinking on foot 117–119
Thompson, E. 100
Thoreau, H. 137
Tillion, G. 175
time machine 47–49

time perception: black swans and unresolved issues 50–55; bodily memory 46; computer's temporality 43; design to growth 55–57; ecological thinking 44; emotional and cognitive capabilities 45; mediated/direct experience 43; pathological form 45; restlessness of events 46; slow thinking 44; speed 43; temporal acceleration 42; temporality of trauma 46–47; time machine 47–49; traumatic time 47
Toffler, A.: *Future Shock* 42
Tolkien, J.R.R. 92
Tomlin, L. 87
toxic conversation 9, 26, 29, 66
toxic cultures: democratic society 94; inequalities and discrimination 77; intersectionality 94–97; negative imagery 70, 94
trauma 26, 40, 45, 46, 63, 110, 126, 131–132
traumatic events 110, 122
Trump, I. 85

Ungaretti, G. 6, 172
United Nations Environment Programme (UNEP) 142
urban model 102
urban planning 55, 140

Vallortigara, G. 136, 155
Van Dijk, T.A. 73
Velasco-Pufleau, L. 109
verbal microaggressions 24, 39–41
victim blaming 40, 61
vigilant stillness 6
virtual space 12
Visconti, L. 90
visual pollution: audience theories 70, 74; discontinuous perceptions 71; hero's journey 92–94; images, racist/sexist 72–75; public discourse 71; reasons 71–72; sexism, racism and mental pathologies 94–97; social conflicts 77–80; television series, thoughts and images *see* television series; war of dreams/power of images 75–77
Voeikov, V. 153
Voglio scrivere sui muri (Penone) 169
vulnerability 26, 148, 170–173, 178

Wagner-Pacifici, R. 46, 54, 122
war of dreams 70, 73, 75–77
war of images 75–76
Watzlawick, P. 39
wax candle, metaphor of 106–109
Wenders, Wim: *The Salt of the Earth* 144
Werner, E.E. 53

Wittgenstein, L. 154
Wohlleben, P. 150
woods and seas memories 152–154
World Soundscape Project 110

Zanzotto, A. 176
Zúñiga Cáceres, B.I. 144

Printed and bound by CPI Group (UK) Ltd, Croydon, CR0 4YY
01/12/2024
01797774-0006